fondue cooking

300 creative ideas for any occasion

Rhonda Lauret Parkinson

BORDERS®

EASY cuisine

fondue cooking

300 creative ideas for any occasion

To Anthony and Robert,
for their unending patience and understanding

Published by Adams Media, an F+W Publications Company
57 Littlefield Street, Avon, MA 02322 U.S.A.
www.adamsmedia.com

ISBN 10: 1-59869-220-8
ISBN 13: 978-1-59869-220-4

Printed in China.

J   I   H   G   F   E   D   C   B   A

This publication is designed to provide accurate and authoritative information with regard to
the subject matter covered. It is sold with the understanding that the publisher is not engaged
in rendering legal, accounting, or other professional advice. If legal advice or other expert
assistance is required, the services of a competent professional person should be sought.
—From a *Declaration of Principles* jointly adopted by a Committee of the
American Bar Association and a Committee of Publishers and Associations

Many of the designations used by manufacturers and sellers to distinguish their products are
claimed as trademarks. Where those designations appear in this book and Adams Media was
aware of a trademark claim, the designations have been printed with initial capital letters.

Previously published as *The Everything® Fondue Cookbook.*

Contents

Introduction

WHY IS FONDUE MAKING A COMEBACK? Fondue's transformation from a Swiss specialty to an international favorite began in the late 1950s, at European ski resorts. Tired skiers found that a meal of crusty bread dipped in good Swiss cheese—along with a glass of wine or port—made the perfect finish to a hard day on the slopes.

Of course, the origins of fondue date back further than the après-ski crowd. It's believed that cheese fondue was invented sometime during the sixteenth century. Swiss farm families needed to find a way to make cheese and bread that had been prepared in the summer last throughout the cold winter months. Melting the hardened cheese in warmed wine made it edible. Aged, crusty bread was the perfect dipper. Thus, the classic Swiss cheese fondue was born.

But the Swiss weren't the only ones to discover the delights of cooking food communally in a large pot. Many Asians celebrate Chinese New Year—China's largest traditional holiday—with hot pot parties. Everyone gathers around the hot pot—traditionally a large copper pot with a chimney in the middle—and cooks an assortment of meat or seafood and vegetables in a simmering broth. At the end of the meal, the hostess ladles out the broth, which by now is richly flavored from all the dipped foods.

And then, of course, there is the French take on fondue, fondue bourguignonne. Cubes of tender beef are cooked in heated oil and dipped in a number of spicy seasonings and sauces. Pickles, relishes, and other garnishes complete the dish. Meanwhile, Italian bagna cauda consists of anchovies bathed in cream and flavored with aromatic garlic. Fresh garden vegetables make up the dippers.

Still, in North America, people are most familiar with the melting varieties of fondue. Fondue's popularity reached its peak in the 1960s and 1970s, when it became a staple at house parties. In the late sixties, cheese fondue was joined by chocolate dessert fondues, made by melting rich chocolate with cream and serving it with fresh fruit or cake for dipping. However, by the 1980s, fondue had fallen out of favor. Along with disco pants and Donna Summer albums, fondue pots were gradually relegated to the closet.

So, why is fondue becoming trendy again? People are rediscovering fondue's basic appeal. There is something infinitely satisfying about gathering together around a communal dish to enjoy a meal. Not to mention the fact that everyone can cook the food according to his or her own preference.

Of course, fondues have become more sophisticated since the 1960s. Fondues made with melted cheese and chocolate are still popular. However, the cheese is as likely to be French Brie or Italian Parmigiano-Reggiano as the two standard fondue cheeses, Swiss Gruyère and Emmenthal. Similarly, chocolate fondues have come a long way since the mid-1960s, when a chef at New York's Chalet Swiss restaurant treated journalists to a bar of Toblerone chocolate melted with cream, accompanied by strawberries for dipping.

At the same time that tastes have become more sophisticated, our definition of what can be classified as a fondue has expanded. In its broadest sense, a fondue is any meal that is served in a communal pot. Fondues can be hot or cold, an appetizer, dessert, or main dish. With a little imagination, soups, casseroles, stews, and even punch can be transformed into a fondue.

Furthermore, while hosts are rediscovering its value as a conversational icebreaker, fondue has evolved into more than just a party food. Serving food fondue-style is a great way to liven up the weekday family meal. And nothing beats a chocolate fondue for two served over an open flame to enhance the romantic atmosphere for Valentine's Day or a special anniversary.

Chapter 1
Fondue Fundamentals

After fading out of fashion for a brief period, fondue is making a comeback. Why not? Fondues are the perfect answer for any food-oriented gathering, from a house party to an informal family dinner. Better still, fondue is easy to make. All it takes is the right equipment and ingredients, plus a few basic cooking tips.

The Fondue Family

The word "fondue" comes from the French verb *fondre,* meaning "to melt." Strictly speaking, that would limit fondues to the cheese and chocolate variety, since both involve melting food in warmed liquid. A broader definition separates fondues into four basic categories: cheese, broth-based, oil-based, and dessert.

Cheese fondues consist of high-fat cheese that has been slowly melted in a liquid. Usually the liquid is wine, but beer, ale, or even milk can be used. Traditionally, garlic is rubbed around the inside of the saucepan to give the mixture extra flavor. Adding lemon juice and cornstarch or flour helps keep the cheese from curdling.

> Ideally, fondue cheese should have a fat content of at least 45 percent. Low-fat cheeses are harder to melt and may curdle. If using cheese with a fat content below 45 percent, try combining it with a high-fat cheese and adding extra cornstarch to compensate.

In broth-based fondues, food is cooked in a simmering broth. Reputed to have been invented by Mongol warriors, Mongolian hot pot was probably the original broth-based fondue. Today, many Asian countries have their own version of a hot pot dish, such as Korean bulgogi and Japanese shabu-shabu. Sukiyaki, Japan's most popular one-pot meal, technically doesn't qualify as a hot pot dish, since the food isn't cooked in broth. However, it can still be considered a type of fondue.

In oil-based fondues, the fondue pot becomes a type of deep-fat fryer. Bite-sized morsels of meat, seafood, or vegetables are cooked by submerging them in a pot of simmering oil or shortening. The first and most famous oil-based fondue, fondue bourguignonne, consists of tender cubes of beef that are skewered, cooked in hot oil, and served with an assortment of sauces and spices for dipping. Often, although not always, seafood and vegetables are coated with batter before deep-frying, both to protect them from the hot oil and to seal in their natural juices.

Last, but definitely not least, are the dessert fondues. The standard dessert fondue consists of chocolate that is melted with cream over low heat. Spices and a liqueur may be added for extra flavor. Fresh fruit and slices of pound cake or sponge cake traditionally make up the dippers. However, quick and easy dessert fondues can also be made by replacing the melted chocolate and cream with yogurt, sour cream, or even ice cream.

Some experts consider Bacchus fondues to be a fifth type of fondue. Named after the Roman god of wine, Bacchus fondues are cooked in red or white wine instead of oil. Vegetable or chicken broth may be added to the wine for extra flavor.

Fondue Etiquette

Fondue's transformation from yesterday's fad to the latest craze has been relatively recent. As a result, many of your guests may be first-time fonduers. There are a few steps you can take to make the process more relaxed and enjoyable for everyone.

Set the table so that everything is within easy reach. Ideally, the fondue pot and burner, dippers, condiments, sauces, and side dishes should be set up in the middle of a large table. Fondue can be a bit messy, so be sure to lay out a large tablecloth and provide plenty of napkins. Provide each guest with an individual place setting, including plates, cutlery, and soup bowls if required.

Set two dipping forks at each place at the table. Providing guests with one fork for dipping and another for eating accomplishes two goals. First, it subtly discourages the practice of double dipping, whereby a guest dips his food into the fondue, takes a bite, and then places the fork back into the fondue (this is a common problem with cheese and chocolate fondues). Second, it ensures guests don't accidentally burn their lips on hot prongs when eating food cooked in oil.

Always let guests know if you will be serving batter-fried foods. While fun, cooking with batter can be a messy experience, as everyone uses their fingers to spread the batter on the food before dipping it into the hot oil. Guests will appreciate it if you warn them in advance to dress casually. (Providing bibs also helps!)

Most fondue pots come equipped with six dipping forks, which means you may not have enough to provide each guest with two. Another option is simply to provide each guest with one dipping fork and a regular table fork for eating.

Finally, plan on having one fondue pot accommodate four people. More than four, and problems can arise with dipping forks clashing and food falling into the fondue. Furthermore, in the case of oil-based fondues, adding too much food can lower the oil temperature to the point where the oil needs to be reheated on the stove. While many fondue books suggest six as the optimum number, this should be reserved for larger pots such as electric fondue pots and Asian hot pots.

The Star of the Show—the Fondue Pot

Fondue pots have come a long way since Swiss farm families melted cheese in an earthenware cooking pot called a caquelon. Fondue pots come in a number of shapes, sizes, and materials. Still, there are a few general things to look for when shopping for a fondue pot:

- Does it come with a complete set of instructions on how to use the pot, including the heat source?
- Does it come with instructions on cleaning, including information about whether it is safe to place the pot in the dishwasher or oven?
- Does it come with a number of recipes designed specifically for use with that type of pot?
- Does the set include a rack to keep the pot stable when it is set on the heated burner?
- Does it come with a set of dipping forks?

- If the pot is meant to be used with oil-based fondues, does it have a set of metal inserts at the top for holding the fondue forks?
- Is it designed with features such as a long handle that make lifting easier?

Fondue Pot Material

The most common types of fondue pot are made of stainless steel, aluminum, or cast iron. Designed to handle the high temperatures needed for oil fondues, these can also be used to cook broth-based fondues. However, they are not the best option for cheese and dessert fondues, which can curdle or scorch at high temperatures.

An adaptation of the original Swiss earthenware pot, ceramic pots are specifically designed for cooking cheese fondues. The heat is distributed slowly and evenly, preventing the cheese from curdling. This makes them perfect for chocolate fondues as well, since chocolate has a tendency to seize when overheated. However, ceramic pots can't handle the high temperatures needed for cooking food in oil.

Dessert fondue pots are small ceramic pots that use a candle for the heat source. Inexpensive and designed to comfortably hold between one and two cups of melted chocolate, they are the ideal for serving a romantic chocolate fondue dessert for two. However, the open flame doesn't provide enough heat for cheese fondues.

As the name implies, an electric fondue pot replaces the burner with electricity as the heat source. An electric fondue pot is ideal for cooking oil-based fondues: the thermostatically controlled temperature setting frees you from having to worry about reaching and maintaining the proper temperature for cooking food in oil. However, like stainless steel, aluminum, and cast-iron pots, it can be difficult to set the temperature low enough to prevent chocolate from scorching or cheese from curdling.

Finally, the Asian hot pot is a large communal cooking pot specifically designed for cooking food in a simmering broth. Traditionally, the hot pot—also known as a firepot—was heated by charcoal, which came up through a chimney in the middle of the pot. A "moat" circling the chimney held the heated broth. Today, modern hot pots are frequently made of aluminum or stainless steel. Electricity, gas, or alcohol has replaced charcoal as the heat source.

A special type of hot pot, designed for fiery Szechwan cuisine, splits the broth into two compartments. This allows cooks to prepare two types of broth. Noted for its spiciness, the first broth is seasoned with garlic, chilies, and Szechwan peppercorns. The second is a traditional hot pot broth, which is similar to a consommé. Guests are free to choose which broth to cook their food in.

Which Fondue Pot Should You Buy?

For cooks wanting to hone their skills by preparing several types of fondue, it's tempting to splurge on at least three fondue pots: a stainless steel pot for cooking broth- and oil-based fondues, a regular-sized ceramic pot for preparing cheese and chocolate fondues, and a smaller-sized dessert fondue pot for romantic evenings. Those who cook frequently with hot oil could even add an electric fondue pot to the list. And there is always the option of cooking broth-based fondues in an authentic Asian hot pot.

However, for cooks with limited budgets, another option is to purchase a stainless steel or aluminum pot with a ceramic insert. The metal pot can take the heat needed for oil- and broth-based fondues. As for cheese and chocolate fondues, the melted cheese or chocolate is poured into the ceramic bowl, which fits snugly inside the metal bowl. To prevent the ceramic dish from cracking, it may be necessary to first add boiling water to the metal pot.

While it may not be the best choice for a first fondue pot, an electric hot pot has two major advantages over other types of fondue pots. First, it means that all the cooking can be done at the table. Second, electric pots are frequently larger than other models. This makes it easier to prepare fondue for a crowd. Definitely consider purchasing an electric model as a secondary fondue pot if you plan to cook oil- and broth-based fondues on a regular basis.

Fondue Fuel

With the exception of electric fondue pots and certain types of Asian hot pots, most fondue pots use alcohol-fueled burners to keep the food warm. Small and shaped like a skillet, the burner sits directly underneath the fondue pot. Heat regulation is controlled through its long handle: rotating the handle opens or closes holes at the top of the burner. Opening the holes provides a hotter flame, while closing them has the opposite effect. The two most common types of fondue fuel are liquid alcohol and fuel gel or paste. More expensive than liquid alcohol, fuel gel has the advantage of lasting longer and being safer since it can't splash. Leftover gel can be sealed in foil and reused.

Fondue fuel gels come in bottles or foil-covered containers. To use the bottled gel, it's necessary to line the bottom of the burner with tinfoil. With the foil containers, just insert the container and tear off the cover. Liquid fuel is poured into the burner. Depending on the type of fuel, the retention compartment in the middle of the burner may or may not be removed. Always follow the manufacturer's instructions on how to use the burner in that specific model of fondue pot.

While the fondue burner is fairly simple to use, there are a few safety tips you should keep in mind. First, never attempt to ignite a fondue burner using a cigarette lighter. Always light it with a match. Second, don't attempt to refuel the burner while it is still hot. Extinguish the flame by setting the cover on the burner, and allow the burner to cool before replacing the fuel.

Cooking Fondue—from Stovetop to Table

A common misconception is that all the cooking for fondue takes place at the table. In reality, fondue burners can't compete with the kitchen stove. Fondue sets aren't designed to melt cheese or bring oil to the high temperatures needed for deep-frying food. With a few exceptions—such as electric fondue pots and traditional Asian hot pots—preparing fondue is a two-part process. The first stage takes place in the kitchen, over the stovetop element.

Whether more than one pot must be used depends on the type of fondue being prepared. For example, oil is normally heated right in the fondue pot on the stove element. By contrast, cheese is melted in a saucepan and then transferred to the fondue pot.

As for broth, it all depends on how much is needed. Twelve cups of broth—meant to keep the broth boiling away while feeding Mongolian hot pot to a crowd—obviously won't fit in a standard-sized fondue pot. It only makes sense to heat the broth in a large saucepan and refill the fondue pot throughout the meal as needed. However, for smaller amounts, it's okay to heat the broth right in the fondue pot (provided the pot is designed to handle broth fondues) and transfer the pot containing the heated broth from the stove element to the table.

In the Kitchen

There is no question that the fondue pot is the centerpiece of any fondue party. However, it's also important to use the proper equipment while preparing food for the fondue. Curdled cheese, scorched chocolate, or improperly heated oil can ruin a fondue. It can be very frustrating to spend a large amount of money on quality chocolate or first-rate cheese from a cheese shop, only to have the food rendered inedible before it ever gets near the fondue pot. Here are a few tips on what equipment to use when preparing food for a fondue.

First and foremost, never melt chocolate directly in a saucepan. If you have one, a double boiler is ideal for melting chocolate. Fill the bottom section up to the halfway point with boiling water, place the chocolate and melting liquid in the top half, and melt over low heat. If you don't have a double boiler, a metal bowl placed over a pot half-filled with barely simmering water works just as well.

Like chocolate, cheese scorches easily. In addition, overcooked cheese can develop a rubbery texture. Always use a heavy-bottomed metal saucepan when melting cheese, and cook slowly over low heat.

Finally, a candy or deep-fry thermometer is ideal for ensuring that the oil has reached the high temperatures needed for cooking. Ideally, the thermometer should have a clamp so you can clamp it on the side of the fondue pot. That way, you'll know when the oil is hot enough to serve the fondue, and you can gauge the temperature during cooking. Be prepared to take a break during the meal to reheat the oil on the stove if necessary.

Table Accessories

The most important utensil is the fondue dipping fork. Longer than regular table forks, dipping forks are designed to spear food and hold it while immersing it in the fondue. Many are color coded, which helps prevent mix-ups at the table. Most have two prongs at the end, but there are special forks with three prongs designed for picking up bread and cheese at the same time. Dipping forks can be made of wood or metal: when purchasing metal forks, make sure they come with a heatproof handle to prevent heat from traveling up the fork and burning the user's hand.

Made of mesh with a long handle, fondue dipping baskets are essentially small strainers. Used primarily in broth fondues, they add variety by allowing you to cook soft foods such as lettuce, spinach, and dumplings that are difficult to spear with a fork. In oil fondues, they are often used when it's more convenient to cook a side dish all at once. For example, in Breaded Red Snapper (page 135), the chopped onion is cooked in the dipping basket, leaving guests free to dip the pieces of breaded fish. Another handy accessory for broth- and oil-based fondues is a party tray with a large number of compartments for holding dipping sauces.

Are Individual Dipping Bowls (Ramekins) Necessary?

For hygienic reasons, people frequently prefer to have individual bowls of dipping sauces for oil- and broth-based fondues. Individual dipping bowls remove any concerns about double dipping, since a communal dipping bowl isn't used. Furthermore, it's a good idea for dishes where fondued food can mix in with the dipping sauces. One example is Harvest Apple Fondue (page 193), where the apple slices and melted chocolate may form a gooey mess when rolled in the crushed peanuts. But it's really a matter of personal preference. When providing ramekins, be sure to adjust the quantity of dipping sauce called for in the recipe, to ensure that everyone has at least ¼ cup of every type of dip.

Staple Ingredients

There are certain staple ingredients that you'll want to keep on hand to make your favorite fondue recipes:

- Lemon juice to add to cheese fondues
- Cornstarch or potato flour for thickening cheese fondues
- A good dry white wine for melting the fondue cheese
- Vegetable oil or peanut oil for cooking oil-based fondues
- Extra-virgin olive oil to use when preparing bread dippers for cheese fondues
- Garlic cloves to use with cheese fondues
- Frozen homemade broth to use in broth-based fondues

When choosing ingredients for oil- and broth-based fondues, there are three basic rules to follow: aged beef, fresh fish, and firm vegetables. Aged cuts of beef such as round are more tender and flavorful than less mature cuts are. Firm vegetables such as broccoli and cauliflower will hold their shape better when cooked in oil or broth than softer vegetables will. Finally, fresh fish is generally more flavorful than frozen. Like vegetables, firm-fleshed fish such as snapper and cod will hold their shape better in a fondue.

Basic Ingredients for Melting Fondues

Melting fondues focus on one main ingredient such as cheese or chocolate. The liquid used to melt the primary ingredient also plays a key role. It's important to choose both with care.

Cheese

The best type of cheese for fondue is a hard cheese that has been aged for several months. Hard cheeses have a sharp flavor, are easy to dice or shred, and melt easily due to their high fat content. The two standard Swiss fondue cheeses, Gruyère and Emmenthal, both fall into this category.

There are a number of ways to classify cheese, from the region of origin to the type of milk used. For fondue purposes, it's best to look at the fat and moisture content of the cheese. A good fondue cheese has a high-fat content and a medium-to-low moisture content.

Semisoft cheeses contain more moisture than hard cheeses but still melt fairly easily. They can be used alone or combined with other cheeses in a fondue. Examples of semisoft cheeses include Dutch Gouda, Danish Havarti, and Italian provolone and Fontina. While valued for their sharp flavor, fresh cheeses such as Brie, feta, and Gorgonzola usually play a secondary role in a fondue. A small amount of the crumbled cheese is paired with a larger amount of hard or semisoft cheese. Finally, soft cheeses such as cottage or ricotta are normally used only in dessert fondues.

Cheese-Melting Liquid

Alcohol plays a role in both the beginning and the final stages of preparing cheese fondue. Traditionally, white wine is used to melt the fondue cheese. When it's time to add the cornstarch thickener, a small amount of alcohol helps dissolve the cornstarch while providing extra flavor.

For best results, use a dry white wine or flat beer with cheese fondue. Both have a high acidity level, which helps the cheese melt more easily. In addition, unlike more robust red wines, their flavor will not interfere with the taste of the cheese.

Kirsch is traditionally added in the final stages of preparing cheese fondue. A type of cherry brandy, the high alcohol content of kirsch means that only a small amount is required. However, choosing which alcohol to finish off the fondue is really a matter of personal taste. Feel free to experiment with other types of brandy, or to dissolve the cornstarch in the same type of wine used to melt the cheese. Another option is to forego extra alcohol altogether and dissolve the cornstarch in water.

Cheese fondues can also be made by melting cheese with milk. This is a good choice when you're serving fondue for the whole family or melting softer cheeses such as ricotta. Expect to use less liquid when replacing wine with milk in a fondue recipe.

Decadent Chocolate

When entertaining, always use the highest-quality chocolate possible for the fondue. Couverture, the best type of chocolate, must contain at least 32 percent cocoa butter. At the other end of the spectrum, compound chocolate contains no cocoa butter at all. Instead, cocoa powder and vegetable oil are used in its composition.

Chocolate is also classified based on the amount of chocolate liquor (chocolate solids made by grinding the cocoa bean) it contains, and what other ingredients have been added. Semisweet chocolate, also known as dark and bittersweet chocolate, must contain at least 35 percent chocolate liquor. Milk chocolate replaces a portion of the chocolate liquor used in semisweet chocolate with milk solids. This gives it a smoother texture.

As the name implies, sweet chocolate contains a higher amount of sweeteners than semisweet chocolate does. It must contain at least 15 percent chocolate liquor. Finally, unsweetened chocolate is basically chocolate liquor without any added sweeteners.

Designed to hold their shape when baked in cookies, chocolate chips contain less cocoa butter and are harder to melt than other chocolate types. (Some brands remove the cocoa butter altogether and replace it with vegetable fat). Normally, this makes them a poor choice for dessert fondues. However, they come in a variety of intriguing flavors, from peppermint to butterscotch. Feel free to use chocolate chips when entertaining family and friends, but stick with other types of chocolate for more formal occasions.

There are no hard and fast rules about what type of chocolate to use in dessert fondues. However, most people prefer the taste of semisweet chocolate. Milk chocolate can also be used and has the advantage of being less expensive. Avoid using unsweetened chocolate unless the recipe calls for it, or be prepared to add a large quantity of sugar to compensate.

Cream—the Fresher the Better!

Cream is the second most important ingredient in a dessert fondue. Formed when whole milk is allowed to stand to the point where the fatty part rises to the top, cream is classified based on the amount of fat it contains. The longer the milk stands, the greater the fat content of the cream that is produced.

How long does it take to make cream?
It all depends on the type of cream you want to produce. Light cream comes from milk that has been left standing for at least twelve hours, while it takes over twenty-four hours to produce whipping cream.

The lightest type of cream is half-and-half, which combines equal parts light cream and milk. The fat content of half-and-half falls between 10 and 18 percent. Light cream—also known as coffee cream—has a fat content of between 18 and 30 percent.

Whipping cream is separated into two categories. The fat content of light whipping cream is between 30 and 36 percent. Heavy whipping cream—also known as heavy cream or double cream—has a fat content of over 36 percent.

The texture and cooking properties of heavy cream mean that it is frequently partnered with chocolate in fondue recipes. Besides having a rich texture, heavy cream is less likely to curdle than creams with a lower fat content. However, it can be hard to find, as many supermarkets stock only light whipping cream. Half-and-half, light cream, and light whipping cream can all be used in fondue recipes. Devonshire cream, which has an even higher fat content than heavy cream, is too thick to work well in chocolate fondues.

In addition to real cream, canned evaporated milk and sweetened condensed milk are also used in chocolate fondues. As its name implies, evaporated milk is milk with moisture (approximately 60 percent) removed through evaporation. Sweetened condensed milk goes through a similar process, but sugar is added to replace the evaporated milk.

CHAPTER 2
Classic Cheese Fondues

Classic Swiss Cheese Fondue

Serves 4–6

Be patient
while
stirring the
cheese!
The results
will be
worth the
wait.

1½ pounds Gruyère cheese
1 loaf French bread
1 garlic clove
1½ cups dry white wine
1 tablespoon lemon juice

2 tablespoons cornstarch
3 tablespoons kirsch
⅛ teaspoon cayenne pepper
1 tablespoon caraway seeds

1. Finely dice the Gruyère cheese and set aside. Cut the French bread into cubes and set aside.
2. Smash the garlic, peel, and cut in half. Rub the garlic around the inside of a medium saucepan. Discard. Add the wine to the saucepan and warm on medium-low heat. Don't allow the wine to boil.
3. When the wine is warm, stir in the lemon juice. Add the cheese, a handful at a time. Stir the cheese continually in a sideways figure eight pattern. Wait until the cheese is completely melted before adding more. Don't allow the fondue mixture to boil.
4. When the cheese is melted, dissolve the cornstarch in the kirsch and add to the cheese, stirring. Turn up the heat until it is just bubbling and starting to thicken. Stir in the cayenne pepper and caraway seeds. Transfer to a fondue pot and set on the burner. Serve with the French bread for dipping.

Swiss Fondue Origins

Fondue originated hundreds of years ago in Swiss mountain villages, created by farm families looking for a way to use cheese and bread that had hardened during the cold winter months. Someone discovered that hardened cheese becomes perfectly edible when melted, and that crusty bread makes the perfect accompaniment. Swiss fondue is sometimes called Neuchâtel Fondue due to the fact that it was originally made with Neuchâtel wine.

Neuchâtel Two Cheese Fondue

½ pound Emmenthal cheese
½ pound Gruyère cheese
1 garlic clove
1 cup dry white wine
2 teaspoons lemon juice
1½ tablespoons cornstarch

2 tablespoons kirsch
¼ teaspoon nutmeg
A pinch of black pepper
1 large parsley sprig, minced
Toasted Bread Cubes
   (page 245)

Serves 4–6

The classic Swiss cheese with holes, Emmenthal has a light color and a delicate nutty flavor.

1. Finely dice the cheeses and set aside. Smash the garlic and cut in half.
2. Rub the garlic around the inside of a medium saucepan. Discard. Add the wine to the pan and cook on low heat. Don't allow the wine to boil.
3. When the wine is warm, stir in the lemon juice. Add the cheese, a handful at a time. Stir the cheese continually in a sideways figure eight pattern. Wait until the cheese is completely melted before adding more. Don't allow the fondue mixture to boil.
4. When the cheese is melted, dissolve the cornstarch in the kirsch and stir into the cheese. Turn up the heat until it is just bubbling and starting to thicken. Stir in the nutmeg, black pepper, and parsley. Transfer to a fondue pot and set on the burner. Serve with the bread cubes for dipping.

Measuring Wine for Fondue

The age of the cheese can affect the amount of wine needed for a cheese fondue. Aged Emmenthal from a specialty cheese shop will absorb wine at a different rate than a less ripe block purchased at a local supermarket. Different types of cheeses also have varying absorption rates. A general rule of thumb is to use 1 cup of wine, beer, or juice for every pound of cheese, but this is a guideline only. If you're uncertain how much liquid is needed, try adding only half the amount called for in the recipe. Keep the remaining half warm in a separate saucepan, and add as needed while melting the cheese.

Marinated Cheese Fondue

Serves 4–6

For extra flavor, reserve one or two tablespoons of the cheese marinade and stir into the fondue mix during the final stages of cooking.

2 cups apple juice
4 teaspoons lemon juice
2 servings Marinated Cheese Cubes (page 73)

¼ cup cornstarch
6 tablespoons kirsch
1 loaf French bread, cut into cubes

1. Warm the apple juice in a saucepan on medium-low heat. When the juice is warm, add the lemon juice. Add the cheese cubes a handful at a time, and stir continuously in a sideways figure eight pattern. Do not add more cheese until it is completely melted.
2. When all the cheese is melted, dissolve the cornstarch in the kirsch and stir into the cheese mixture. Turn up the heat until it just begins to bubble and thicken. Transfer to a fondue pot and set on the burner. Serve with the French bread for dipping.

Swiss Cheese and Apple Fondue

Serves 2–4

Tart apple takes center stage in this variation on Classic Swiss Cheese Fondue (page 16).

½ pound Emmenthal cheese
1 baguette
1 garlic clove
1 cup dry white wine

1 cup Spicy Apple Chutney (page 52)
2 teaspoons cornstarch
3 teaspoons water

1. Cut the cheese into thin slices and the baguette into cubes.
2. Smash the garlic, peel, and cut in half. Rub the inside of a medium saucepan with the garlic. Discard. Add the wine to the pan and cook on low heat. Don't allow the wine to boil.
3. When the wine is warm, stir in the chutney and heat through.
4. Dissolve the cornstarch in the water and stir into the fondue to thicken. As soon as the mixture thickens, transfer to a fondue pot and set on the burner. Serve with the sliced cheese for dipping. Eat the bread with the dipped cheese. If you run out of cheese, dip the bread into the fondue.

Plowman's Lunch Fondue

1 pound Gruyère cheese
1 garlic clove
2 tablespoons butter
  or margarine
1 cup dry white wine
2 teaspoons lemon juice
1 tablespoon cornstarch

1½ tablespoons water
¼ teaspoon ground white
  pepper, or to taste
1 teaspoon turmeric
1 loaf sun-dried tomato bread
1 jar pickles

Serves 3–4

Find the sharp flavor of Gruyère cheese a little over-powering? Feel free to reduce the amount and add a milder cheese such as Emmenthal.

1. Finely dice the Gruyère cheese and set aside. Smash the garlic, peel, and cut in half. Rub the garlic around the inside of a medium saucepan and discard. Add the butter and stir over low heat until it melts.
2. Add the wine. When the wine is warm, stir in the lemon juice. Add the cheese, a handful at a time. Stir the cheese continually in a sideways figure eight pattern. Wait until the cheese is completely melted before adding more. Don't allow the fondue mixture to boil.
3. When the cheese is completed melted, dissolve the cornstarch in the water and stir into the cheese. Turn up the heat until it is just bubbling and starting to thicken. Stir in the white pepper and turmeric. Transfer the fondue to a fondue pot and set on the burner. Slice the bread into cubes. Use dipping forks to dip the bread cubes into the cheese. Eat with the pickles.

Colorful Turmeric

Known for its dramatic golden color, turmeric enhances the appearance of fondues without overpowering the cheesy flavor. Stir a tiny amount into the fondue just before serving. If you don't have turmeric, another option is to add saffron, which also has a lovely golden color. However, saffron is more pungent than turmeric, so use sparingly.

Curry Fondue

Serves 3–4

Havarti's delicate flavor is quite subtle in this recipe. To bring it out further, use a mild Cheddar cheese.

2 fresh green jalapeño peppers
¼ pound aged Cheddar cheese
¼ pound Havarti with dill
½ pound Gruyère cheese
1 garlic clove
1¼ cups white wine
2 teaspoons lemon juice

1 tablespoon cornstarch
1½ tablespoons kirsch
1¼ teaspoons mild curry powder
12–15 grape tomatoes, sliced
Basic Bruschetta (page 246), cut into cubes

1. Slice the jalapeño peppers lengthwise, remove the seeds, and chop coarsely. Dice the Cheddar and Havarti cheeses, and finely dice the Gruyère cheese. Smash the garlic, peel, and cut in half. Rub the garlic around the inside of a medium saucepan. Discard.

2. Add the wine to the pot and cook on low heat. Don't allow the wine to boil. When the wine is warm, stir in the lemon juice. Add the cheese, a handful at a time. Stir the cheese continually in a bowtie or sideways figure eight pattern. Wait until the cheese is completely melted before adding more. Don't allow the cheese to boil.

3. When the cheese is melted, dissolve the cornstarch in the kirsch and add to the cheese, stirring. Turn up the heat until it is just bubbling and starting to thicken. Add the chili peppers. Stir in the curry powder.

4. Transfer to a fondue pot and set on the burner. Serve with the bruschetta cubes and the grape tomatoes for dipping. (Use dipping forks to dip the grape tomatoes into the fondue).

Sweet Herb Fondue

Sweet Herb Mix (page 47)
1½ cups dry white wine
½ pound Emmenthal cheese
½ pound Havarti cheese
    with dill
¼ pound medium Cheddar
    cheese

1 garlic clove, smashed and
    cut in half
1 teaspoon lemon juice
3 teaspoons cornstarch
4 teaspoons water
1 sourdough baguette,
    cut into cubes

Serves 4–6

Can't find
Havarti
with dill?
Feel free to
use regular
Havarti and
add fresh
dill to the
herb mix-
ture.

1. Add the Sweet Herb Mix to the wine and leave for 2 hours.
2. Finely dice the Emmenthal, and dice the Havarti and Cheddar cheeses. Smash the garlic clove, peel, and cut in half. Rub the garlic around the inside of a medium saucepan. Discard. Warm the wine-and-herb mixture on medium-low heat. Do not bring the wine to a boil.
3. When the wine is warm, add the lemon juice. Remove the bay leaf (which was contained in the Sweet Herb Mix) from the wine. Add the cheese, a handful at a time. Stir the cheese continually in a sideways figure eight pattern. Wait until the cheese is completely melted before adding more.
4. When the cheese is melted, dissolve the cornstarch in the water and add to the cheese, stirring. Turn up the heat until it is just bubbling and starting to thicken. Transfer to a fondue pot and set on the burner. Serve with the baguette cubes for dipping.

Delicious Dill

Even though it is a member of the parsley family, dill has a delicate but slightly pungent flavor that sets it apart. Fresh dill weed is used to flavor sauces, marinades, and salads. When cooking with dill weed, be sure to add it in the final stages of preparation, as heating can weaken its distinct flavor.

Blue Cheese Fondue

Serves 4

To vary the texture and flavor, replace ½ pound of the soft blue cheese with a hard cheese such as Cheddar or Gruyère.

1 pound blue cheese
1 loaf French bread
6 ounces cooked ham
2 tablespoons butter or margarine

2 tablespoons flour
1 cup milk
¼ teaspoon nutmeg
¼ teaspoon paprika
1 tablespoon sour cream

1. Crumble the blue cheese and set aside. Cut the French bread into cubes and thinly slice the ham.
2. Melt the butter in a saucepan over medium-low heat and stir in the flour. Slowly add the milk, stirring.
3. Add the crumbled blue cheese, a handful at a time. Stir the cheese continually in a bowtie or sideways figure eight pattern. Wait until the cheese is completely melted before adding more. Don't allow the cheese to boil.
4. When the cheese is melted, turn the heat up until it is just bubbling and starting to thicken. Stir in the nutmeg and paprika. Transfer to a fondue pot and set on the burner. Just before serving, swirl in the sour cream. Serve with the French bread cubes for dipping and eat with the ham slices.

Cutting Cheese

The harder the cheese, the more finely it needs to be cut. Be sure to finely dice hard cheeses like Emmenthal and Gruyère. Semisoft cheeses like Havarti can be diced less finely or cubed, while soft cheeses will crumble easily. Fondue cheese can also be coarsely grated or shredded. However, don't grate too thinly or the cheese will form clumps in the fondue. Be sure to use the coarse edge of a cheese grater.

Sweet Goat Cheese with Roasted Red Peppers

1½ pounds goat cheese
1 garlic clove
1½ cups dry white wine
1 tablespoon lemon juice
1 tablespoon cornstarch
3 tablespoons kirsch

2 tablespoons chopped fresh
  tarragon
1 loaf stale bread
¼ cup olive oil
Roasted Red Peppers (page 150)

Serves 4–6

Did you know? The first mention of grated goat's cheese melted in wine can be traced back to Homer's Iliad.

1. Crumble the goat cheese. Smash the garlic, peel, and cut in half. Rub the garlic around the inside of a medium saucepan. Discard. Add the wine to the pan and warm on medium-low heat. Don't allow the wine to boil.
2. When the wine is warm, stir in the lemon juice. Add the cheese, a handful at a time, and stir continuously in a sideways figure eight pattern. Wait until the cheese is completely melted before adding more. Don't allow the fondue mixture to boil.
3. When the cheese is melted, dissolve the cornstarch in the kirsch and add to the cheese, stirring. Turn the heat up until it is just bubbling and starting to thicken. Stir in the fresh tarragon leaves. Transfer to a fondue pot and set on the burner. Toast the bread and drizzle a small amount of olive oil around the edges. Cut into cubes. Serve the fondue with the peppers as a side dish and the stale bread for dipping.

Choosing Peppers for Roasting

Not all bell peppers are meant for the grill. A lengthy period ripening on the vine gives red bell peppers a sweet flavor and thin skin that makes them ideal for roasting. The skin can be pulled off in one piece and the seeds are easy to remove. Young green bell peppers have a thick skin that makes roasting more difficult. Yellow and orange bell peppers fall somewhere in between.

Fondue Provolone

Serves 4–6

Emmenthal balances the sharp flavor of provolone in this recipe. Serve with a robust Italian red wine.

½ pound provolone cheese
1 pound Emmenthal cheese
2 tablespoons flour
½ teaspoon dried basil, or to taste
⅛ teaspoon dried oregano, or to taste

1 garlic clove
1½ cups dry white wine
2 tablespoons lemon juice
2 tablespoons tomato paste
1 loaf French or Italian bread, cut into cubes

1. Finely dice the provolone and Emmenthal cheeses. Mix the flour with the basil and oregano. Toss the two cheeses with the flour and spices.
2. Smash the garlic, peel, and cut in half. Rub the garlic around the inside of a medium saucepan. Discard. Add the wine to the saucepan and warm on medium-low heat. Don't allow the wine to boil.
3. When the wine is warm, stir in the lemon juice. Add the cheese, a handful at a time. Stir the cheese continually in a sideways figure eight pattern. Wait until the cheese is completely melted before adding more. Don't allow the fondue mixture to boil.
4. When the cheese is melted, stir in the tomato paste. Heat through, and then turn up the heat until the mixture bubbles and starts thickening. Transfer to a fondue pot and set on the burner. Serve with the bread cubes for dipping.

Doubling Up

Need more fondue to feed a crowd? Take a basic cheese fondue recipe and double the amount of cheese but not the liquid. Instead, increase the liquid by only 1½ times. The different ratio is related to how liquid evaporates and the surface area of the saucepan. If the liquid is doubled, the fondue may develop a soupy texture.

Four Spice Cheese Fondue

1 pound spiced Gouda cheese
1 tablespoon flour
⅛ teaspoon garlic salt
⅛ teaspoon black pepper
¼ cup red onion, finely chopped
1½ tablespoons butter or
   margarine

1 small bay leaf
1 cup Heineken beer
2 teaspoons lemon juice
1½ teaspoons cornstarch
1 teaspoon cognac
Toasted Bread Cubes (page 245)
3 apples, sliced

Serves 3–4

Bay leaf's sharp taste nicely complements sweet red onion. For extra flavor, add a few teaspoons of chopped pearl onion.

1. Remove the rind from the Gouda cheese and shred.
2. Mix together the flour, garlic salt, and black pepper. Toss with the cheese.
3. Sauté the onion in the butter or margarine. Add the bay leaf and cook until the onion is soft and translucent. Remove the bay leaf.
4. Warm the beer in a medium saucepan but do not boil. When the beer is warm, add the lemon juice. Add the cheese gradually, stirring constantly in a sideways figure eight pattern. Wait until the cheese is completely melted before adding more. Don't allow the fondue mixture to boil.
5. When the cheese is nearly melted, add the onion. Stir for another minute; then dissolve the cornstarch in the cognac and stir into the fondue. Turn up the heat until the fondue is just bubbling and starting to thicken. Transfer to a fondue pot and set on the burner. Serve with the bread cubes and apples for dipping. (Broccoli, cauliflower, and mushrooms also make good dippers for this recipe.)

Using Bay Leaves

Bay leaf's strong aroma makes it a popular addition to soups, stews, and numerous other dishes, but the pointed leaves can be a choking hazard. Be sure to remove bay leaves before serving a dish.

Pub Fondue

Serves 4–6

Cooked shallots have a delicate flavor that sets them apart from larger onions. Feel free to use them in beer- or wine-based fondues.

1¼ pounds medium Cheddar cheese
1 tablespoon flour
1 sprig parsley, chopped
A pinch (no more than ⅛ teaspoon) garlic powder
1 teaspoon paprika
1 tablespoon butter or margarine
½ cup onion, chopped

1 small shallot, chopped
1 cup beer, preferably flat
2 teaspoons lemon juice
2 teaspoons Worcestershire sauce
4 apples, cored and cut into thin slices
1 sourdough baguette, cut into cubes

1. Cut the Cheddar cheese into cubes. Combine the flour, parsley, garlic powder, and paprika. Toss the cubed cheese with the flour mixture and set aside.
2. Melt the butter or margarine in a pan. Add the onion and shallot and sauté until the onion is translucent but not browned. Turn off the heat and let sit in the pan.
3. Warm the beer in a medium saucepan, without bringing to a boil. Add the lemon juice. Add the cheese gradually, a handful at a time, stirring constantly. Make sure the cheese doesn't come to a boil. Don't add more until the cheese is fully melted.
4. When the cheese is nearly melted, add the onion and shallot. Stir for another minute, and then turn up the heat until it is just bubbling and starting to thicken. Stir in the Worcestershire sauce. Transfer to a fondue pot and set on the burner. Serve with the sliced apples and baguette cubes for dipping. Add other dippers such as pickles and tomatoes as desired.

Dieter's Fondue

2 ounces of any reduced-fat
  hard cheese
½ cup skim milk
2 cups cottage cheese
2 tablespoons chopped fresh
  basil
2 parsley sprigs, chopped

⅓ cup cranberry juice
1 garlic clove
4 tablespoons margarine
4 tablespoons flour
Black pepper to taste
¼ teaspoon cayenne pepper
1 package breadsticks

Serves 4–6

This recipe
allows you
to enjoy
fondue and
keep down
the fat and
calories at
the same
time.

1. Dice the hard cheese. In a metal bowl, combine the skim milk, cottage cheese, basil, parsley, and cranberry juice.
2. Smash the garlic clove, peel, and cut in half. Rub garlic around the inside of a medium saucepan; discard. Add the margarine and melt on low heat. Stir in the flour.
3. Add the cottage cheese mixture and the hard cheese. Stir slowly over low heat until the cheese is melted and the mixture thickens. Stir in the black pepper and cayenne pepper. Whisk to remove any lumps in the flour if necessary.
4. Transfer the mixture to a fondue pot and set on the burner. Serve with the breadsticks for dipping.

Chilled Cheese

Don't worry about bringing refrigerated cheese to room temperature before using it in a fondue. Chilled cheese is easier to cut, and proper cutting speeds up the melting time. If you don't have time to cool the cheese in the refrigerator, try putting it in the freezer 30 minutes prior to making the fondue.

Ham and Cheese Fondue

Serves 4–5

Worcester-shire sauce adds spice to a basic ham-and-cheese dish. You could also use Tabasco or another hot sauce.

1¼ pounds medium Cheddar cheese
1 baguette
1 cup mushrooms
1½ cups cooked ham
1 green onion
2 tablespoons butter or margarine
1 cup beer

2 teaspoons lemon juice
1 tablespoon cornstarch
1½ tablespoons water
1 teaspoon kirsch
2 teaspoons Worcestershire sauce
⅛ teaspoon black pepper, or to taste

1. Cut the Cheddar cheese into cubes and set aside. Slice the baguette into cubes and set aside. Wipe the mushrooms with a damp cloth and slice. Cut the cooked ham into cubes. Dice the green onion.
2. Heat the butter in a medium saucepan. Add the mushrooms and sauté until tender. Add the beer and warm on low heat. When the beer is warm, add the lemon juice. Add the cheese gradually, stirring continually in a sideways figure eight pattern until it is completely melted.
3. When the cheese is melted, dissolve the cornstarch in the water and add to the cheese, stirring. Turn up the heat until it is just bubbling and starting to thicken. Add the kirsch, the Worcestershire sauce, and the black pepper. Taste and adjust the seasonings if desired.
4. Transfer the cheese to a fondue pot and set on the burner. Invite guests to place a baguette cube and a piece of ham on their fork before dipping into the fondue.

Using Lemon Juice

In addition to adding flavor, tart lemon juice boosts the acidity level of the liquid base, making it easier to melt the cheese. Feel free to add a few teaspoons of lemon juice whenever you're uncertain about the acidity level of a wine, beer, or fruit juice.

Tropical Fondue

2 mangoes
½ pound Emmenthal cheese
½ pound Gruyère cheese
1 garlic clove
1¾ cups dry white wine
2 teaspoons lemon juice
½ tablespoon cornstarch

2 tablespoons kirsch
¼ teaspoon nutmeg
Black pepper to taste
1 cup Mint and Cilantro
   Chutney (page 48)
Toasted Bread Cubes (page 245)

Serves 4

Can't find
Emmenthal
in the deli
section? This
popular Swiss
cheese has
several dif-
ferent
spellings—try
looking for
Emmental or
Emmenthaler
cheese.

1. Cut the two mangoes in half, remove the pits, and cut into slices. Finely dice the cheeses.
2. Smash the garlic, peel, and cut in half. Rub the garlic around the inside of a medium saucepan. Discard. Add the wine to the pan and cook on low heat. Don't allow the wine to boil.
3. When the wine is warm, stir in the lemon juice. Add the cheese, a handful at a time. Stir the cheese continually in a sideways figure eight pattern. Wait until the cheese is completely melted before adding more. Don't allow the fondue mixture to boil.
4. When the cheese is melted, dissolve the cornstarch in the kirsch and stir into the cheese. Turn up the heat until it just bubbles and starts to thicken. Stir in the nutmeg and black pepper. Add the chutney. Thin the mixture by adding another ¼ cup of warmed wine if desired.
5. Transfer to a fondue pot and set on the burner. Serve with the bread cubes and sliced mangoes for dipping.

Swiss Classics—Emmenthal and Gruyère Cheese

Switzerland's most famous cheese, Emmenthal is the Swiss cheese with holes featured in cartoons with mice and rats. Its mild, nutty flavor combines well with stronger cheeses. Considered to be the classic fondue cheese, Gruyère has an intriguing spicy flavor that strengthens considerably upon heating. When combining Emmenthal and Gruyère in a fondue, use equal amounts of each or increase the ratio of Emmenthal to compensate for Gruyère's stronger flavor.

Breakfast Fondue

Serves 4–6

For extra flavor, garnish with grated Cheddar cheese and 2 tablespoons of chopped bacon or bacon bits.

1 loaf bread
¾ pound Gruyère cheese
¾ pound Emmenthal cheese
2 green onions
1 garlic clove
1½ cups dry white wine
1 tablespoon lemon juice

2 tablespoons Worcestershire sauce
Salt and pepper to taste
12 eggs
1 teaspoon cornstarch
2 teaspoons water

1. Toast the bread, cut into squares, and set aside. Finely dice the cheeses. Mince the green onions.
2. Smash the garlic, peel, and cut in half. Rub the garlic around the inside of a medium saucepan. Discard. Add the wine to the pan and warm on medium-low heat. Don't allow the wine to boil.
3. When the wine is warm, stir in the lemon juice. Add the cheese, a handful at a time. Stir the cheese continually in a sideways figure eight pattern. Wait until the cheese is completely melted before adding more. Don't allow the fondue mixture to boil.
4. When the cheese is melted, turn up the heat until it is just bubbling and starting to thicken. Stir in the Worcestershire sauce, salt and pepper, and green onion. Whisk in the eggs and scramble. Dissolve the cornstarch in the water and add to the mixture to thicken. Transfer to a fondue pot and set on the burner. Serve with the toasted bread for dipping.

Fondue Fit for a Philosopher

Famed gourmand Brillat-Savarin introduced Americans to his own version of fondue in the early 1800s. By whisking in several eggs in the final stages of cooking, he transformed a traditional Swiss fondue into a cheese-loaded version of scrambled eggs. The Swiss immediately denounced the dish as not being true fondue. Nonetheless, today eggs make a frequent appearance in fondue cookbooks. For extra protein, try adding eggs to Welsh Rarebit (page 178) or Plowman's Lunch Fondue (page 19).

Chèvre Fondue

1½ pounds chèvre goat cheese
2 tablespoons fresh basil,
   chopped
1 tomato
¼ cup margarine
1 garlic clove
1½ cups dry white wine, divided

1 tablespoon cornstarch
3 tablespoons kirsch
¼ teaspoon paprika
1 loaf sourdough bread, cut
   into cubes
Marinated Tomatoes (page 147)

Serves 4–6

For best
results, use
soft,
unripened
goat cheese.
Its light,
mild taste
combines
nicely with
the stronger
flavors in
the mari-
nated veg-
etables.

1. Crumble the goat cheese and toss with the chopped basil. Wash the tomato, pat dry, and slice.
2. Heat the margarine in a frying pan and sauté the sliced tomato. Turn down the heat and keep warm while preparing the fondue.
3. Smash the garlic, peel, and cut in half. Rub the garlic around the inside of a saucepan. Leave the garlic in the pan and add 1¼ cups of wine. Warm the wine over medium-low heat but do not allow to boil.
4. When the wine is warm, add the goat cheese, a handful at a time. Stir the cheese continually in a sideways figure eight pattern. Wait until the cheese is completely melted before adding more. (Goat cheese melts quite quickly.) Don't allow the fondue mixture to come to a boil.
5. When the cheese is melted, dissolve the cornstarch in the kirsch and stir into the cheese mixture. Turn up the heat until it is just bubbling and starting to thicken. Stir in the paprika. Add the remaining ¼ cup of wine if necessary. Stir in the sliced tomato. Transfer to a fondue pot and set on the burner. Serve with the sourdough bread cubes for dipping. Eat with the Marinated Tomatoes.

Dutch Fondue

Serves 4–6

To give this dish a more authentic Dutch flavor, replace the kirsch with Dutch gin. For a stronger cheesy taste, leave the rind on the Gouda cheese and add to the fondue.

1 pound Gouda cheese
½ pound Edam cheese
1½ tablespoons flour
3 teaspoons caraway seeds
½ teaspoon ground cumin

1½ cups Heineken Beer
4 bay leaves
1½ tablespoons kirsch
½ teaspoon nutmeg
1 baguette, cut into cubes

1. Remove the rind from the Gouda cheese. Finely dice the Edam and the Gouda. Combine the flour, caraway seeds, and cumin. Toss the cheese with the flour mixture.
2. Place the beer in a medium saucepan and add the bay leaves. Warm the beer on low heat, being sure not to boil. When the beer is warm, remove the bay leaves.
3. Add the cheese gradually, stirring continually in a bowtie or sideways figure eight motion. Wait until the cheese has completely melted before adding more. Don't allow the fondue mixture to boil.
4. When the cheese is completely melted, turn up the heat until it just bubbles and starts to thicken. Stir in the kirsch and the nutmeg.
5. Transfer to a fondue pot and set on the burner. Serve with the baguette cubes for dipping.

Thinning a Cheese Fondue

To make a fondue thinner, add more wine, beer, or whatever liquid forms the base. Warm the liquid and add 1 teaspoon at a time, stirring, until the fondue reaches the desired level of thickness.

Three Cheese Fondue

1 loaf stale bread
½ pound Gruyère cheese
½ pound Emmenthal cheese
½ pound Tilsit cheese
1 garlic clove
1½ cups dry white wine

1 tablespoon lemon juice
1 teaspoon cornstarch
2 tablespoons kirsch
Freshly ground white pepper
   to taste
1 sprig parsley, chopped

Serves 4–6

Don't be put off by Tilsit's pungent odor. The Danish cheese has an intriguing spicy taste that makes a nice complement to Gruyère.

1. Toast the bread and cut into cubes. Finely dice the Gruyère and Emmenthal cheeses. Dice the Tilsit cheese.
2. Smash the garlic, peel, and cut in half. Rub the garlic around the inside of a medium saucepan. Discard. Add the wine to the pan and warm on medium-low heat. Don't allow the wine to boil.
3. When the wine is warm, stir in the lemon juice. Add the cheese, a handful at a time. Stir the cheese continually in a sideways figure eight pattern. Wait until the cheese is completely melted before adding more. Don't allow the fondue mixture to boil.
4. When the cheese is completely melted, dissolve the cornstarch in the kirsch and stir into the fondue. Turn up the heat until it is just bubbling and starting to thicken. Stir in the white pepper and parsley. Transfer to a fondue pot and set on the burner. Serve with the toast cubes for dipping.

Thickening a Cheese Fondue

Having trouble getting the fondue to thicken? Turn up the heat, add a bit of cornstarch mixed with water, and stir quickly with a whisk. Another option is simply to add more cheese.

"Crab Rangoon" Fondue

Serves 4–6

Dry white wine can be substituted for the milk, but don't use beer— its strong taste will overpower the delicate flavors of crabmeat and cream cheese.

2 pounds broccoli and cauliflower
1 tablespoon butter or margarine
¼ cup onion, chopped
1 green onion
6 ounces canned crabmeat, drained

8 ounces cream cheese
1 teaspoon Worcestershire sauce
½ teaspoon soy sauce
¼ cup milk
2 teaspoons lemon juice
Crackers

1. Wash the broccoli and cauliflower and pat dry. Remove the stems and cut the flowerets into 1-inch pieces that can be speared with a dipping fork. Set aside.
2. Melt the butter or margarine in a frying pan. Sauté the onion until it is tender. Mince the green onion.
3. Combine the crabmeat, cream cheese, Worcestershire sauce, soy sauce, sautéed onion, and minced green onion. Mix thoroughly.
4. Rub the inside of a saucepan with a piece of onion. Warm the milk in the saucepan on medium-low heat. Add the lemon juice. Gradually add the crabmeat mixture, stirring.
5. Transfer to a fondue pot and set on the burner. Serve with the broccoli and cauliflower for dipping. Eat with the crackers.

Crab Rangoon History

Despite being named after the capital city of Burma, this popular appetizer is an American creation. To prepare Crab Rangoon as an appetizer, the crabmeat-and-cream-cheese filling is stuffed into wonton wrappers and deep-fried. But it also makes a great fondue!

Raspberry Swirl

1 pound Havarti cheese

1½ cups fresh raspberries

4 teaspoons lime juice

4 teaspoons sugar

¾ cup dry white wine, divided

2 teaspoons lemon juice

4 teaspoons cornstarch

5 teaspoons water

1 baguette, cut into cubes

Serves 3–4

The juicy texture and delicate flavor of raspberries nicely complements sweet and creamy Havarti cheese.

1. Dice the Havarti cheese. Wash and drain the raspberries. Process the berries, lime juice, and sugar in a blender or food processor until smooth.
2. Warm ½ cup of the wine in a medium saucepan on medium-low heat. Don't allow the wine to boil. Keep the remaining ¼ cup of wine warming in a separate saucepan.
3. When the wine is warm, stir in the lemon juice. Add the cheese, a handful at a time. Stir the cheese continually in a sideways figure eight pattern. Wait until the cheese is completely melted before adding more. Don't allow the fondue mixture to boil.
4. When the cheese is melted, stir in the raspberry purée and heat through. Dissolve the cornstarch in the water and add to the cheese, stirring. Turn up the heat until it is just bubbling and starting to thicken. Add the remaining ¼ cup of wine if necessary. Transfer to a fondue pot and set on the burner. Serve with the baguette cubes for dipping.

Garlic Fondue

Serves 3–4

Garlic nicely balances the sharp flavor of Gruyère in this recipe. For extra color, add a few parsley sprigs.

1½ pounds Gruyère cheese
5 garlic cloves
1½ cups dry white wine
2 teaspoons lemon juice
1½ tablespoons cornstarch

2 tablespoons kirsch
1 tablespoon dry mustard
1 sun-dried tomato baguette, cut into cubes

1. Remove the rind from the Gruyère cheese and finely dice.
2. Smash and peel the garlic cloves. Cut one of the cloves in half. Take one half and rub around the inside of a medium saucepan.
3. Add the wine and the garlic cloves and cook on low heat. Don't allow the wine to boil.
4. When the wine is warm, stir in the lemon juice. Add the cheese, a handful at a time. Stir the cheese continually in a sideways figure eight pattern. Wait until the cheese is completely melted before adding more. Don't allow the fondue mixture to boil.
5. When the cheese is melted, dissolve the cornstarch in the kirsch and stir into the cheese. Turn up the heat until it just bubbles and starts to thicken. Stir in the dry mustard. Transfer to a fondue pot and set on the burner. Remove the garlic cloves if desired. Serve with the baguette cubes for dipping.

Choosing Cheese for Fondue

Unfortunately for dieters, the best fondue cheeses are high in fat. Cheeses with a fat content of at least 40 percent melt more easily and produce a creamier fondue. A few examples of good fondue cheeses include Swiss hard cheeses such as Emmenthal, Gruyère, and raclette; semisoft cheeses such as Gouda, Gorgonzola, and Havarti; and soft Brie.

Italian Cheese Fiesta

12 ounces provolone cheese
7 ounces Gorgonzola cheese
1 tablespoon plus 2 teaspoons
flour
½ teaspoon dried oregano
⅛ teaspoon garlic powder

7 ounces Asiago cheese
1 garlic clove
1 cup dry white wine
1 tablespoon plus 1 teaspoon
lemon juice
Italian breadsticks, for dipping

Serves 4–6

Cilantro and Mint Dressing (page 62) can hold its own against these strong and spicy Italian cheeses.

1. Finely dice the provolone and Gorgonzola cheeses. Mix the flour with the oregano and garlic powder. Toss the two cheeses with the flour and spices. Crumble the Asiago cheese into the mixture.
2. Smash the garlic, peel, and cut in half. Rub the garlic around the inside of a medium saucepan. Discard. Add the wine to the saucepan and warm on medium-low heat. Don't allow the wine to boil.
3. When the wine is warm, stir in the lemon juice. Add the cheese, a handful at a time. Stir the cheese continually in a sideways figure eight pattern. Wait until the cheese is completely melted before adding more. Don't allow the fondue mixture to boil.
4. When the cheese is melted, turn up the heat until it is just bubbling and starting to thicken. Transfer to a fondue pot and set on the burner. Serve with the Italian breadsticks for dipping.

Curdled Cheese Cure

Adding starch helps keep the cheese from curdling when cooked. Cornstarch and potato starch are normally added in the final stage of cooking, just before the fondue is transferred to a fondue pot. Flour is another option, but it can impart a powdery taste if not cooked long enough. For best results, combine the flour with the cheese or cook it in butter in the saucepan before adding the wine.

Four Cheese Fondue

Serves 4–6

For a different flavor, try substituting Cheddar cheese for the Gruyère and topping with 2 ounces of grated Parmesan instead of Cheddar.

½ pound Emmenthal cheese
½ pound Gruyère cheese
½ pound Havarti cheese
½ green or red bell pepper
1 garlic clove
2 cups white wine
1 tablespoon lemon juice
2 tablespoons cornstarch
3 tablespoons brandy
Black pepper to taste
¼ teaspoon nutmeg, or to taste
2 ounces Cheddar cheese, grated
1 French baguette, cut into cubes

1. Finely dice the Emmenthal and Gruyère cheeses, and dice the Havarti. Wash the bell pepper, pat dry, and cut into cubes.
2. Smash the garlic, peel, and cut in half. Rub the garlic around the inside of a saucepan. Add the wine and heat over medium-low heat until warm. Do not allow the wine to boil.
3. Stir in the lemon juice. Add the cheese, a handful at a time, and stir continually in a sideways figure eight pattern. Do not add more cheese until it is melted.
4. When all the cheese is nearly melted, stir in the bell pepper cubes. Dissolve the cornstarch in the brandy and stir into the cheese. Turn up the heat until it just bubbles and starts to thicken. Add the black pepper and nutmeg. Sprinkle the grated Cheddar cheese on top. Transfer to a fondue pot and set on the burner. Serve with the baguette cubes for dipping.

What to Drink with Cheese Fondue?

When it comes to combining alcoholic beverages and cheese fondue, the safest option is to stick with the wine, beer, or cider used to cook the fondue. However, kirsch brandy, often added in the final stages of cooking, also works well with many cheese fondues. For those who prefer a nonalcoholic beverage, possible choices include tea or a nonalcoholic punch.

Autumn Harvest Fondue

¾ pound Emmenthal cheese
¾ pound Gruyère cheese
2 cinnamon sticks
1 tablespoon coriander seeds
1 whole star anise (optional)
1¾ cups apple juice

1 tablespoon lemon juice
2 tablespoons cornstarch
3 tablespoons apple schnapps
¼ teaspoon nutmeg
3 cups sliced apples
Toasted Flatbread (page 245)

Serves 4–6

A spice bag is a quick and easy way to lend flavor to a simple cheese fondue.
It can be used with wine- and beer-based fondues.

1. Finely dice the cheeses. Break the cinnamon sticks into several pieces. Place the cinnamon, the coriander seeds, and the star anise (if using) on a piece of cheesecloth about 6 inches by 6 inches. Use a piece of string to tie the cheesecloth and attach a cork to the other end of the string.
2. Heat the apple juice in a saucepan over medium-low heat. When the apple juice is warm, stir in the lemon juice. Add the spice bag, keeping the cork over the side of the saucepan so the bag can be pulled out.
3. When the apple juice is warm, remove the spice bag. Add the cheese, a handful at a time, stirring continually in a sideways figure eight pattern. Do not add more cheese until it is melted.
4. When all the cheese is melted, dissolve the cornstarch in the apple schnapps and stir into the fondue. Turn up the heat until it just bubbles and starts to thicken. Stir in the nutmeg. Transfer to a fondue pot and set on the burner. Serve with the sliced apples and flatbread for dipping.

Create Your Own Cheese Fondue

Want to experiment with adding your favorite spicy cheese to a fondue? For best results, try combining a small amount with a good melting cheese that isn't too strong in flavor, such as Emmenthal. If that works, try increasing the amount the next time you make the fondue. Be sure to add only as much wine as is needed. If you want to move completely away from the Swiss cheeses, try using the cheese alone at first to see how it works in the fondue before attempting to combine it with another cheese.

Swiss Appenzeller Fondue

Serves 4–6

Appenzeller's strong flavor is used in small amounts to enhance the flavor in a fondue. Feel free to experiment by substituting Dijon mustard for the dry mustard.

½ pound Appenzeller cheese
½ pound Gruyère cheese
½ pound Emmenthal cheese
1 garlic clove
1½ cups apple cider, divided
2 teaspoons lemon juice
1 tablespoon cornstarch
2 tablespoons cognac
1 teaspoon dry mustard
Freshly ground black pepper
   to taste
1 loaf stale bread, cut into
   cubes

1. Finely dice the cheeses and set aside.
2. Smash the garlic, peel, and cut in half. Rub the garlic around the inside of a medium saucepan. Discard. Add 1¼ cups apple cider to the saucepan and warm on medium-low heat, without allowing to boil.
3. When the cider is warm, stir in the lemon juice. Add the cheese, a handful at a time. Stir the cheese continually in a sideways figure eight pattern. Wait until the cheese is completely melted before adding more. Don't allow the fondue mixture to boil.
4. When the cheese is melted, dissolve the cornstarch in the cognac and add to the cheese, stirring. Turn up the heat until it is just bubbling and starting to thicken. If necessary, add the remaining ¼ cup of cider. Stir in the dry mustard and freshly ground pepper. Transfer to a fondue pot and set on the burner. Serve with the bread cubes for dipping.

Swiss Fondue Cheeses

Don't feel you need to limit yourself to Gruyère and Emmenthal cheeses when making Swiss fondue. Different regions of Switzerland have developed their own special fondue recipes featuring locally produced cheeses. Appenzeller and Vacherin à Fondue are frequently found in eastern Swiss fondues, while raclette and Gruyère is a popular combination in fondues from the Fribourg region.

Italian Cheese Fondue
with Béchamel Sauce

¾ pound Gorgonzola cheese
¾ pound mozzarella cheese
1 clove garlic
1¼ cups milk, divided
2 tablespoons butter
2 tablespoons flour

1 tablespoon cornstarch
2 tablespoons cream
1 teaspoon nutmeg
2 tablespoons brandy
1 loaf Italian bread, cut into
   cubes

Serves 4–6

Serve with Roasted Red Peppers (page 150) or Marinated Tomatoes (page 147) for a complete meal. For extra flavor, add ¼ cup of mozzarella and increase the amount of milk as needed.

1. Finely dice the Gorgonzola and mozzarella. Smash the garlic, peel, and cut in half.
2. Warm the milk in a small saucepan. In a separate medium saucepan, rub the garlic around the inside and then discard the garlic. Melt the butter in the saucepan with the garlic and stir in the flour. Add 1 cup of the warmed milk. Cook over low heat for about 10 minutes, whisking to form a creamy sauce.
3. Add the cheese, a handful at a time. Stir the cheese continually in a sideways figure eight pattern. Wait until the cheese is completely melted before adding more. Don't allow the fondue mixture to boil. Add the remaining ¼ cup of milk as needed.
4. When the cheese is melted, dissolve the cornstarch in the cream and add to the fondue, stirring. Turn up the heat until it is just bubbling and starting to thicken. Stir in the nutmeg and the brandy. Transfer to a fondue pot and set on the burner. Serve with the Italian bread cubes for dipping.

Ricotta Cheese in Apple Cider

Serves 4-6

Apple cider's tart flavor makes an interesting contrast with sweet ricotta cheese. Be sure to use only as much cider as needed.

½ loaf whole wheat bread, sliced
1 garlic clove
1 cup apple cider
2 teaspoons lemon juice
1 pound ricotta cheese
2 teaspoons caraway seeds

1. Toast the bread slices and cut into cubes approximately 1 inch thick.
2. Smash the garlic, peel, and cut in half. Rub the garlic around the inside of a medium saucepan. Discard. Add the apple cider to the saucepan and warm on medium-low heat.
3. When the cider is warmed, stir in the lemon juice. Gradually stir in the cheese. Stir the cheese continually in a sideways figure eight pattern to soften. When the cheese has melted, turn up the heat until it is just bubbling and starting to thicken. Stir in the caraway seeds. Transfer to a fondue pot and set on the burner.

Deep-Fried Cheese

Serves 4

Feel free to experiment with different types of cheese, such as Danish Fontina and Gouda.

½ pound Cheddar cheese
½ pound Monterey Jack cheese
2 eggs
1 tablespoon milk
¼ teaspoon paprika
½ teaspoon sugar
3 cups oil, or as needed
½ cup flour
Quick and Easy Batter
   (page 80)

1. Cut the cheeses into cubes, about ¾ inch thick. Beat the eggs with the milk, paprika, and sugar. Make sure the eggs are beaten thoroughly.
2. Add the oil to the fondue pot, making sure it is not more than half full. Heat the pot on a stove element over medium-high heat.
3. When the oil is hot, move the fondue pot to the table and set up the burner. Coat the cheese cubes with the flour. Dip the cheese into the egg wash and then cover with the batter. Spear the cheese with a dipping fork and cook in the hot oil until the batter browns (about 30 to 40 seconds). Drain on paper towels if desired. Cool and eat.

Parmigiano-Reggiano Classic

1 fresh truffle
4 ounces Parmigiano-Reggiano
  cheese
6 ounces Gorgonzola cheese
1 tablespoon flour
1 tablespoon dried oregano
4 ounces Asiago cheese

1 garlic clove
1 cup dry white wine
1 tablespoon lemon juice
2 tablespoons cooked ham,
  chopped
Bruschetta Fondue Cubes with
  Vegetables (page 247)

Serves 4–6

To enhance the Italian flavors, use plum tomatoes when preparing the Bruschetta Fondue Cubes with Vegetables.

1. Pat the truffle dry with a damp cloth and slice thinly. Remove the rinds from the Parmigiano-Reggiano and Gorgonzola cheeses and finely dice. Mix the flour with the oregano. Toss the two cheeses with the seasoned flour. Crumble the Asiago cheese into the mixture.

2. Smash the garlic, peel, and cut in half. Rub the garlic around the inside of a medium saucepan. Discard. Add the wine to the saucepan and warm on medium-low heat. Don't allow the wine to boil.

3. When the wine is warm, stir in the lemon juice. Add the cheese, a handful at a time. Stir the cheese continually in a sideways figure eight pattern. Wait until the cheese is completely melted before adding more. Don't allow the fondue mixture to boil.

4. When the cheese is melted, turn up the heat until it is just bubbling and starting to thicken. Transfer to a fondue pot and set on the burner. Just before serving, sprinkle with the chopped ham and sliced truffle. Serve with the bruschetta cubes for dipping.

Brie and Pesto

This fondue tastes excellent served with a French baguette or Italian breadsticks.

1 pound Brie cheese
2 tablespoons flour
1 garlic clove
1 cup dry white wine

2 teaspoons lemon juice
Roasted Red Pepper Pesto
(page 61)

1. Cut the Brie into cubes. Toss the cheese cubes with the flour and set aside.
2. Smash the garlic, peel, and cut in half. Rub the garlic around the inside of a medium saucepan. Discard. Add the wine to the saucepan and warm on medium-low heat. Don't allow the wine to boil.
3. When the wine is warm, stir in the lemon juice. Add the cheese, a handful at a time. Stir the cheese continually in a sideways figure eight pattern. Wait until the cheese is completely melted before adding more. Don't allow the fondue mixture to boil.
4. When the cheese is melted, turn up the heat until it is just bubbling and starting to thicken. Stir in the Roasted Red Pepper Pesto. Heat through, transfer to a fondue pot, and set on the burner.

Perfect Pesto

For a more authentic touch when preparing pesto, use a mortar and pestle to pound the basil leaves, garlic, and pine nuts. Keep pounding while adding the cheese, and then slowly stir in the olive oil.

CHAPTER 3

Spices and Sauces for Dipping

Curried Yogurt

Yields 1 cup

The smooth texture and unusual flavors in this dip make it a nice accompaniment to Classic Beef Bourguignonne (page 88).

1 cup plain yogurt
1 teaspoon lemon juice
1 teaspoon lime juice
¾ teaspoon curry powder
1 tablespoon water
1½ teaspoons garlic, chopped

Combine all the ingredients and process in a food processor or blender. Cover and refrigerate until ready to serve.

Seafood Cocktail Sauce

Yields 1 cup

Increase or decrease the heat by adjusting the amount of chili sauce. Serve with Breaded Red Snapper (page 135).

½ celery stalk
3 teaspoons prepared horse-radish
1 cup ketchup
2 teaspoons lemon juice
½ teaspoon Worcestershire sauce
½ teaspoon hot chili sauce, or to taste
¼ teaspoon black pepper

1. Finely dice the celery until you have 4 tablespoons. Stir the horse-radish into the ketchup. Add the diced celery. Combine the lemon juice with the Worcestershire sauce and add to the ketchup mixture. Stir in the chili sauce and black pepper.
2. For best results, cover and refrigerate for several hours before serving.

Sweet Herb Mix

1 sprig parsley, stem removed
1 sprig thyme
1 mint leaf

⅓ bay leaf
A pinch (under ⅛ teaspoon) sage

Chop the parsley and thyme sprigs and shred the mint leaf. Combine all the ingredients together. Use immediately.

Yields about 3 tablespoons

This interesting mix gives Sweet Herb Fondue (page 21) its distinct flavor.

Sweet Banana Chutney

2 large bananas
⅓ cup balsamic vinegar
1 teaspoon brown sugar

¼ teaspoon allspice
1 teaspoon water

1. Peel and thinly slice the bananas. In a medium saucepan, bring the balsamic vinegar and sliced bananas to a boil. Continue to cook the mixture, stirring frequently, until the bananas and vinegar are fully blended. If using smaller bananas, add more slices as required.
2. Stir in the brown sugar and allspice. Add the water if needed. Heat through. Store in the refrigerator until ready to serve with the fondue.

Yields ⅔ cup

Balsamic vinegar helps bring out bananas' natural sweetness. This fruit chutney makes a nice accompaniment to savory pork.

Mint and Cilantro Chutney

Yields ¼ cup

The fresh flavor of mint provides an interesting contrast to cilantro's musky aroma. Use with less-highly seasoned meat fondues.

⅓ cup cilantro leaves, chopped
½ cup mint leaves, chopped
3 tablespoons plain yogurt
1½ teaspoons lemon juice
1 tablespoon red onion, chopped

1 teaspoon sugar
1 tablespoon dark raisins
⅛ teaspoon cayenne pepper, or to taste

Combine all the ingredients and process in a blender or food processor until smooth.

Aioli

Yields ¾ cup

Aioli's pungent flavor nicely complements seafood dishes and beef fondues. Refrigerated in a sealed container, it will last for a few days.

4 large garlic cloves
2 teaspoons lemon juice, or to taste
2 egg yolks

¾ cup extra-virgin olive oil
Salt and freshly ground black pepper to taste
Cayenne pepper to taste

1. Smash the garlic cloves, peel, and mash thoroughly with a mortar and pestle. Stir in the lemon juice. Stir in the egg yolks.
2. Add the olive oil, a few drops at a time, whisking constantly. After adding 2 to 3 teaspoons, the sauce should begin to take on the consistency of mayonnaise. Then you can begin adding the rest of the olive oil in a slow, steady stream, still whisking constantly.
3. Add the salt, pepper, and cayenne. Taste and adjust the seasonings if desired. Cover and refrigerate until ready to serve.

Quick and Easy Blender Hollandaise Sauce

2 tablespoons white wine vinegar
2 tablespoons lemon juice
2 tablespoons fresh dill, chopped
1/2 cup butter

3 large egg yolks
1/8 teaspoon cayenne pepper

Yields 3/4 cup

Serve this rich sauce with Classic Beef Bourguignonne (page 88) or whenever you want a flavorful accompaniment to beef, chicken, or seafood oil-based fondues.

1. Warm the white wine vinegar, lemon juice, and chopped dill. In a separate small saucepan, melt the butter and keep it hot without burning.
2. Place the white wine vinegar mixture in a blender and process for about 10 seconds. Add the egg yolks and the cayenne pepper.
3. Pour the butter into the blender and process on high speed for at least 40 seconds or until the sauce has thickened. (*Note:* If the sauce is not thick enough, place it in the top of a double boiler over hot, but not boiling, water, and whisk until thickened. Remove from the heat as soon as it's thickened.) Refrigerate until ready to serve.

Light Horseradish Dressing

2 sprigs parsley
2/3 cup plain yogurt

2 tablespoons horseradish
2 teaspoons lemon juice

Yields 2/3 cup

This tasty dressing gives dieters a low-calorie alternative to traditional horseradish dressings made with sour or whipping cream.

Chop the parsley. Combine all the ingredients and serve the dressing immediately.

Marvelous Mango Chutney

Yields 1 cup

Did you know? Mangoes are an excellent source of vitamin A. Use in cooking, or enjoy them fresh with a bit of lemon.

1¼ cups mango flesh from 2 medium ripe mangoes
¼ cup balsamic vinegar
3 tablespoons seedless raisins
1 teaspoon ginger, minced

1 tablespoon sugar
¼ teaspoon salt
A pinch (up to ⅛ teaspoon) chili powder, optional

1. To cut the mango flesh, cut a small slice off the stem end of the mango. Cut the mango in half, going around the pit in the middle. This will give you three sections: the section of flesh around the pit, and the two halves on either side. Cut the fruit around the section with the pit into small pieces. For the other two sections, lightly score the flesh without cutting through the skin, then gently push on the skin so it is almost turned inside out. The pieces of scored fruit will come out easily.
2. Combine the mango, balsamic vinegar, raisins, ginger, sugar, and salt in a saucepan and bring to a boil, stirring continually. Turn down the heat to low and let the chutney simmer, uncovered, for another 35–45 minutes.
3. If using the chili powder, add it at this point and simmer for another couple of minutes. Taste and adjust the seasonings as desired. Cool and refrigerate in a sealed container.

Selecting Mangoes

When choosing mangoes, don't be fooled by appearances. Like many other types of fruit, mangoes come in a variety of colors. A green mango may be fully matured, while a mango with a bright orange skin may need to ripen for a few more days. Look for mangoes that have a pleasant aroma and are firm to the touch. Unripe mangoes can impart a sour flavor to a dish during cooking. If this happens, compensate by adding more sugar.

Honey Mustard Sauce

⅔ cup beef broth
3 tablespoons butter or
    margarine
3 tablespoons flour
3 tablespoons Dijon mustard

3 tablespoons honey
1 teaspoon water
¼ teaspoon chili powder, or
    to taste

Yields 1 cup

Provide guests with an alternative to richer sauces such as Quick and Easy Blender Hollandaise Sauce (page 49) or spicy dips.

1. If using homemade or packaged beef broth, warm the broth in a small saucepan. If using an instant bouillon cube, prepare according to the directions on the package.
2. Combine the butter and flour in a saucepan over low heat, stirring. Slowly stir in ⅓ cup of the beef broth. Mix in the mustard and honey.
3. Add the remaining ⅓ cup of the beef broth. Turn up the heat to thicken. Add the water and the chili powder. Serve warm.

"Horseradish"

½ cup mayonnaise
2 teaspoons garlic powder
2 teaspoons lemon juice
1 teaspoon chili powder

4 teaspoons sugar
1 teaspoon cayenne pepper,
    or to taste

Yields ½ cup

This recipe comes in handy whenever you don't have any prepared horseradish or fresh horseradish root on hand.

Combine all the ingredients. Serve immediately or store in a sealed container in the refrigerator.

Spicy Apple Chutney

Yields 1 cup

If you have one, a mortar and pestle is ideal for blending together the chutney ingredients.

2 apples, peeled, cored, and
   sliced
½ cup rice vinegar
¼ teaspoon nutmeg
¼ teaspoon cumin
1 teaspoon lemon juice

3 tablespoons sultana raisins
1 tablespoon plus 1 teaspoon
   sugar
¼ teaspoon curry paste
2 tablespoons water

1. Combine the apples, rice vinegar, nutmeg, cumin, lemon juice, raisins, sugar, and curry paste in a medium-sized saucepan. Bring to a boil, stirring continuously. Simmer for about 50 minutes, stirring occasionally, until the raisins are soft and the chutney has a texture similar to porridge. Add the 2 tablespoons of water if necessary.
2. Remove the chutney and process in a blender or food processor for just a few seconds so that it is well combined but chunky, not smooth. Refrigerate until ready to use.

Versatile Chutney

A staple of Indian cuisine, chutney's intriguing mix of spices can be used to enhance many different types of dishes. Fruit-based chutney adds flavor and texture to a standard Swiss cheese fondue. To try, simply follow the recipe for Classic Swiss Cheese Fondue (page 16) and substitute ½ cup of chutney for the seasonings. Add more warmed wine if necessary.

Mild Curry Sauce

½ cup red onion, finely chopped

2 tablespoons plus 2 tea-
spoons garlic, finely
chopped

2 tablespoons plus 2 tea-
spoons fresh ginger, finely
chopped

½ cup plus 4 teaspoons butter
or margarine

4 tablespoons flour

½ cup plus 4 teaspoons
unsweetened coconut flakes

1 teaspoon mild curry powder

1 cup chicken broth

Cayenne pepper to taste

Salt to taste

Yields ²/₃ cup

This recipe
lets you enjoy
the flavor of
curry without
the burning
heat found in
hotter sauces.

1. Slowly cook the red onion, garlic, and ginger with the butter until the onion is tender. Stir in the flour. Add the coconut and the curry powder.

2. Add the chicken broth and turn up the heat to medium, stirring all the while to thicken. Add the cayenne pepper and salt. Mix well and serve warm.

How Much Dip Should You Serve?

A general rule of thumb is to serve at least ½ cup of dipping sauce for every ½ pound of meat cooked. In addition, you'll want to serve at least two or three dips for variety.

Béarnaise Sauce

Yields 1 cup

Having trouble getting the sauce to thicken? Try removing it from the heat and adding cold water, 1 tablespoon at a time.

⅓ cup white wine vinegar
5 tablespoons white wine
1 tablespoon shallot, chopped
2½ tablespoons fresh tarragon, chopped
⅔ cup butter
4 large egg yolks

1¼ tablespoons parsley, chopped
¼ teaspoon cayenne, or to taste
Salt to taste
½ teaspoon sugar

1. Combine the white wine vinegar, wine, shallot, and tarragon in a saucepan. Heat until the sauce is reduced to ⅓ cup. Cool and strain by lining a funnel with cheesecloth, and then straining the sauce through the funnel.
2. While the white wine vinegar mixture is heating, melt the butter in a small saucepan. Keep the butter warm on low heat without burning.
3. Place the white wine vinegar mixture in the top of a double boiler, over water that is hot but not boiling. (If you don't have a double boiler, use a metal bowl placed over a saucepan half-filled with simmering water.) Make sure the bottom of the top boiler does not touch the heated water. Slowly add the egg yolks and butter, whisking constantly. When the mixture has thickened, whisk in the parsley, cayenne, salt, and sugar. Whisk until the sauce has thickened.
4. Serve the sauce immediately or cover and refrigerate until ready to serve. If preparing ahead of time, the refrigerated sauce can be served warm or cold. If serving warm, reheat by placing the bowl containing the sauce inside another bowl filled with hot water. Stir briefly. This prevents the sauce from curdling.

Rich Béarnaise Sauce

Cayenne adds bite to this creamy yellow sauce that goes nicely with beef and shellfish. For extra flavor, try adding 1 tablespoon of minced fresh mushrooms or truffles to the white wine vinegar mixture.

Homemade Tartar Sauce

2 egg yolks
½ cup salad oil, divided
¼ teaspoon salt
1 tablespoon white wine
    vinegar
1 teaspoon lemon juice
1 teaspoon prepared mustard
    (such as Dijon)

A pinch of cayenne
1 teaspoon capers (about 8),
    finely chopped
2 tablespoons onion, finely
    chopped
1 pickle, chopped

Yields about ½ cup

The trick to
making tartar
sauce is to
make sure the
eggs are at
room temper-
ature and to
add only a
few drops of
oil at a time.

1. Put the egg yolks into a metal bowl and whisk vigorously. Add 1 table-spoon salad oil and continue whisking. Repeat with a second table-spoon of salad oil. Whisk in the salt.
2. Add the white wine vinegar. Add 2 more tablespoons salad oil, a few drops at a time, whisking vigorously. The mixture should emulsify and thicken.
3. Once the mixture has emulsified, add the lemon juice, mustard, cayenne, capers, onion, and pickle. Add the remaining ¼ cup of salad oil and process in a blender or food processor. For best results, chill for an hour to give the flavors a chance to blend.

Make Your Own Mayonnaise

Tartar sauce is simply mayonnaise enhanced with capers, pickle, onion, and sea-sonings. Follow the first two steps of this recipe whenever you want to prepare a rich mayonnaise with more flavor than manufactured brands have.

Thai Peanut Sauce

Yields ¾ cup

Made with anchovy extract, nuoc mam fish sauce plays the same role in Vietnamese cuisine that salt and pepper do in American cooking.

½ cup peanut butter
4 tablespoons sugar
4 teaspoons red curry paste
3 tablespoons plus 1 teaspoon lime juice

½ cup plus 2 tablespoons coconut milk
1 teaspoon nuoc mam fish sauce

Combine all the ingredients except for the fish sauce in a blender or food processor. Process until smooth. Remove and add to a saucepan. Cook on low heat, stirring continuously, for at least 5 minutes. Stir in the fish sauce. Serve warm or at room temperature.

Basic Chinese Hot Mustard

Yields ½ cup

Hot mustard's sharp bite goes well with Asian hot pot or oil-based meat fondues.

½ cup dry mustard
½ cup water

Combine the dry mustard with the cold water to form a paste. The mustard will be at its hottest in 10–15 minutes, and will slowly weaken after that. For best results, use immediately.

Lemony Horseradish

½ cup mayonnaise
4 teaspoons prepared horseradish
1 teaspoon garlic powder

2 teaspoons shallot, finely
 chopped
4 teaspoons lemon juice

Combine the mayonnaise, horseradish, garlic powder, and shallot. For a stronger flavor, squeeze the excess vinegar out of the prepared horseradish. Stir in the lemon juice. Prepare just before serving and use immediately.

Yields ½ cup

Shallots add a delicate sweetness to this sauce, which nicely balances the tart lemon and fiery horseradish. Serve with beef or seafood fondues.

Quick and Easy Tartar Sauce

2 teaspoons capers (about 16),
 finely chopped
½ cup mayonnaise
2 teaspoons onion, finely chopped

1 teaspoon parsley, chopped
2 tablespoons pickle, chopped
2 teaspoons lemon juice

Rinse the capers. Combine all the ingredients except for the lemon juice and blend well. Stir in the lemon juice. For best results, refrigerate for at least 1 hour before serving to allow the flavors to blend.

Confusing Capers

Despite their frequent pairing with anchovies, capers are not a type of seafood. Instead, the green, bullet-shaped buds come from the caper bush. The distinctive bitter and salty taste of capers comes from pickling them in vinegar and salt.

Yields ½ cup

Feel free to increase the flavor by adding more capers. Serve with seafood fondues such as Cod in Herbed Batter (page 140).

Guacamole

Yields 1½ cups

Serve gua-
camole with
corn chips or
tortilla chips.
For extra fire,
substitute hot
salsa for the
mild salsa.

2 avocados
½ tomato
1½ green onions
4 teaspoons lemon juice

½ teaspoon chili powder,
or to taste
¼ teaspoon ground cumin
1 tablespoon mild salsa

1. Peel the avocados and slice lengthwise. Remove the pit and mash the
   flesh (a mortar and pestle is ideal for this). Chop the tomato into
   small pieces. Finely dice the green onions.
2. Mix the tomato and green onion with the mashed avocado. Stir in the
   lemon juice, chili powder, cumin, and salsa. For best results, refrigerate for 30 minutes to allow the flavors to blend, then serve.

Teriyaki-Style Dipping Sauce

Yields ½ cup

This recipe
takes a stan-
dard teriyaki
sauce and
replaces the
Japanese rice
wine with
pineapple
juice and
adds aromatic
garlic.

1 green onion
⅓ cup lite soy sauce
¼ cup pineapple juice

1½ teaspoons brown sugar
⅛ teaspoon garlic powder
A few drops Asian sesame oil

Dice the green onion. Combine the green onion with the soy sauce,
pineapple juice, brown sugar, and garlic powder. Drizzle the sesame
oil over and blend well. For best results, refrigerate the sauce until
ready to use. Serve cold.

Soy and Wasabi Sauce

1 shallot
1 green onion
1 tablespoon wasabi paste
6 tablespoons soy sauce,
   divided

2 tablespoons butter
2 tablespoons lemon juice
1 teaspoon Dijon mustard,
   optional

Yields ½ cup

This pungent sauce lends flavor to seafood dishes. Feel free to increase the amount of wasabi if desired.

1. Peel and chop the shallot. Mince the green onion. Mix the wasabi paste with 2 tablespoons of soy sauce and set aside.
2. In a small saucepan, melt the butter. Add the shallot and green onion and cook on low heat until the shallot is tender. Add the remaining 4 tablespoons of the soy sauce and the lemon juice.
3. Add the wasabi and soy sauce mixture. Stir in the Dijon mustard, if using. Keep stirring until the ingredients are blended together. Serve warm, immediately.

Horseradish with Sour Cream

½ cup sour cream
2 teaspoons shallots, minced

2 tablespoons prepared horseradish
½ teaspoon ginger, minced

Yields ½ cup

Ginger's clean bite takes the edge off the sharp taste of horseradish. Use with seafood fon-dues.

Combine all the ingredients. Cover and refrigerate until ready to use.

Horseradish Cream

Yields ½ cup

For best results, squeeze out any excess water or vinegar when measuring the prepared horseradish. This will heighten the flavor.

½ cup whipping cream
2 tablespoons prepared
  horseradish

½ teaspoon lemon juice
1 teaspoon Worcestershire
  sauce

In a metal bowl, beat the whipping cream until it stiffens. Stir in the horseradish, lemon juice, and Worcestershire sauce. Cover and refrigerate until ready to serve.

Quick Honey Mustard

Yields ½ cup

Honey mustard makes a nice complement to ham, beef, or chicken dishes.

½ cup Dijon mustard
2½ teaspoons honey

Freshly ground white pepper
  to taste

Blend all the ingredients together until smooth. Refrigerate for a few hours before serving to give the flavors time to blend.

Italian Pesto with Basil and Pine Nuts

1 cup packed fresh basil
  leaves
4 garlic cloves
4 tablespoons pine nuts

6 tablespoons extra-virgin
  olive oil
4 tablespoons Parmesan
  cheese, grated

Chop the basil leaves. Smash, peel, and chop the garlic. Process the basil, garlic, and pine nuts in a food processor or blender. Slowly add the olive oil and keep processing until the pesto is creamy. Add the grated Parmesan cheese. Serve immediately.

Yields 1 cup

Feel free to experiment by substituting porcini sheep's milk cheese for the Parmesan, or replacing the basil with licorice-flavored fennel leaves.

Roasted Red Pepper Pesto

2 Roasted Red Peppers
  (page 150)
4 garlic cloves
1½ cups packed parsley leaves
4 tablespoons pine nuts

4 tablespoons Parmesan
  cheese, grated
5 tablespoons olive oil
Fresh cracked black pepper
  to taste

1. Remove the skin from the roasted red peppers. Remove the seeds and chop the pepper finely. Smash and peel the garlic cloves.
2. Purée the roasted red peppers in a blender or food processor. Remove. Combine the parsley leaves, garlic cloves, and pine nuts in the food processor and chop. Mix the parsley mixture with the puréed red peppers, and stir in the grated Parmesan cheese and olive oil. Add the fresh cracked black pepper. Serve immediately.

Yields 1 cup

Roasted red peppers take center stage in this variation on traditional Italian pesto flavored with basil and pine nuts.

Cilantro and Mint Dressing

Yields ⅔ cup

This light dressing would make a good accompaniment to most meat and seafood fondues.

4 garlic cloves
1 fresh green jalapeño pepper
⅓ cup packed cilantro leaves, chopped
⅓ cup packed mint leaves, chopped
2 tablespoons pine nuts

2 tablespoons walnut pieces, chopped
2 teaspoons lemon juice
2 tablespoons Parmesan cheese, grated
3 tablespoons olive oil

1. Smash, peel, and mince the garlic cloves. Cut the jalapeño pepper lengthwise, remove the seeds, and chop coarsely.
2. Process the cilantro leaves, mint leaves, garlic, jalapeño pepper, pine nuts, walnut pieces, and lemon juice in a blender or food processor. Add the grated cheese and process again. Remove, place in a bowl, and slowly stir in the olive oil. Cover and refrigerate until ready to serve.

Pesto Mayonnaise

Yields about 1 cup

Serve Pesto Mayonnaise with Beef Carpaccio fondue (page 95) or Italian Pesto Fondue with Ham (page 180).

Italian Pesto with Basil and Pine Nuts (page 61)
1 tablespoon plus 2 teaspoons mayonnaise

½ teaspoon lemon juice

Place the pesto in a mixing bowl and stir in the mayonnaise and lemon juice. For best results, cover and refrigerate for 1 hour to give the flavors a chance to blend. Keep refrigerated until ready to use.

Golden Hot Mustard

2 teaspoons cold water
1/4 cup dry mustard
2 tablespoons vinegar

1 teaspoon sugar
1 teaspoon turmeric

Yields 1/3 cup

Add the water slowly to the dry mustard, a few drops at a time, until the mustard is moistened. Wait 15 minutes. Add the vinegar, mixing in thoroughly to form a smooth paste. Stir in the sugar and turmeric. Cover and store in the refrigerator until ready to use.

Adding vinegar keeps this mustard hot. Refrigerated in a sealed container, it will last for several days.

Yogurt and Dill Dressing

1 cup yogurt
1 tablespoon plus 1 teaspoon
   lemon juice
1 tablespoon fresh baby dill,
   chopped

1 sprig fresh thyme leaves,
   stem removed
1 1/2 teaspoons Dijon mustard,
   or to taste

Yields 1 cup

Combine all the ingredients. Refrigerate, covered, until ready to serve.

This simple dressing nicely complements the sweet, spicy flavor of Teriyaki Marinated Salmon (page 129).

White Sauce for Seafood

Yields ²/₃ cup

Finely chop the capers and sprinkle over the sauce during the final stages of cooking.

2½ tablespoons butter
2 tablespoons flour
2 tablespoons cream
1 cup milk

2 teaspoons lemon juice
1 parsley sprig, chopped
Salt and pepper to taste
4 capers, optional

1. Melt the butter in a saucepan on low heat. Blend in the flour thoroughly and cook for another 2 to 3 minutes, taking care not to burn the flour. Turn up the heat to medium-low and mix in the cream. Slowly add the milk, whisking constantly until the sauce thickens.
2. Stir in the lemon juice, parsley, and salt and pepper. Add capers, if using. Use immediately or keep warm on low heat, stirring occasionally, until ready to serve with the fondue.

White Sauce for Vegetables

Yields ²/₃ cup

This flavorful sauce makes an excellent topping for vegetables cooked in broth. It will comfortably serve 4 to 6 people.

2½ tablespoons butter, unsalted
2 tablespoons flour
2 tablespoons cream

1 cup milk
⅛ teaspoon celery salt
⅛ teaspoon paprika

1. Melt the butter in a saucepan on low heat. Blend in the flour thoroughly and cook for another 2 to 3 minutes, taking care not to burn the flour. Turn up the heat to medium-low and mix in the cream.
2. Slowly add the milk, whisking constantly until the sauce thickens and bubbles. Stir in the celery salt and paprika. Use immediately or keep warm on low heat, stirring occasionally, until ready to serve.

Speedy Garlic Mayonnaise

4 large garlic cloves
¾ cup mayonnaise

2 teaspoons Dijon mustard

Yields ¾ cup

Smash and peel the garlic. Using a mortar and pestle, mash the garlic thoroughly. In a bowl, mix the mashed garlic with the mayonnaise and Dijon mustard. Refrigerate until ready to serve.

This quick and easy version of aioli eliminates the work of preparing the mayonnaise. Serve with Teriyaki Marinated Salmon (page 129).

Hot or Cold?

Sauces that are heated during the cooking process, such as White Sauce for Vegetables (page 64), should be served warm. On the other hand, dips made with perishable ingredients such as mayonnaise should be chilled until ready to serve.

Sour Cream and Mustard Dip

½ green onion
1 cup sour cream
2½ tablespoons Dijon mustard

1 teaspoon lemon juice
1 teaspoon fresh parsley, chopped

Yields 1¼ cups

Mince the green onion. Combine all the ingredients. Refrigerate, covered, until ready to serve.

This recipe can be used as a dip with seafood fondues, ham, raw vegetables, or crackers and breadsticks.

French Pistou with Cheese

Yields ²/₃ cup

The French version of pesto, pistou is used to flavor vegetable, seafood, and chicken dishes. It is the main ingredient in Soup au Pisto.

1½ cups packed fresh basil leaves, chopped
3 or 4 large garlic cloves
2 tablespoons Gruyère cheese, grated

4 tablespoons extra-virgin olive oil
Freshly ground black pepper to taste

Chop the basil leaves. Smash, peel, and chop the garlic cloves. Process the chopped basil, garlic, and grated Gruyère cheese in a food processor or blender. Slowly add the olive oil while continuing to process, until the pesto is a creamy paste. Season with the pepper.

Sukiyaki Sauce

Yields 1¼ cups

Sake is available in Asian markets and in the international cuisine section of many supermarkets. Use with Sukiyaki dishes such as Japanese Sukiyaki (page 170).

½ cup soy sauce
½ cup Vegetable Broth (page 83)

2 tablespoons sugar
¼ cup Japanese sake

Combine all the ingredients. Bring to a boil and let simmer for a few minutes before using.

Cooking with Sake

Besides being a popular alcoholic beverage, sake is frequently used in cooking. It lends a sweet taste to Sukiyaki Sauce. Made with glutinous rice, mirin is a sweeter version of sake, with a lower alcohol content.

Fondue Béchamel Sauce

¾ cup milk
2 tablespoons butter
2 tablespoons flour
2 tablespoons cream

½ cup total of Cheddar and
  Monterey Jack cheese,
  shredded
1 teaspoon caraway seeds

Yields 1 cup

Looking for a
change? Try
combining
this fondue
sauce with
your favorite
vegetables.

1. Warm the milk in a small saucepan. In a separate saucepan, melt the
   butter on low heat and stir in the flour. Be careful not to let the flour burn.
2. Add the cream to the butter-and-flour mixture. Blend well, and then
   slowly pour into the warmed milk. Cook over low heat for about 10
   minutes, whisking continuously to form a creamy sauce.
3. Add the cheese, a handful at a time. Stir the cheese continually in a
   sideways figure eight pattern. Wait until the cheese is completely
   melted before adding more. Don't allow the fondue mixture to boil.
   Stir in the caraway seeds. Use immediately.

Extra Hot Pot Dipping Sauce

2 teaspoons coriander seeds
½ cup soy sauce
½ cup peanut butter
2 tablespoons plus 2 teaspoons
  sugar

½ cup water
2 teaspoons hot chili sauce

Yields 1¼ cups

Hot chili
sauce gives
this dipping
sauce extra
bite. Serve
with Classic
Mongolian
Hot Pot (page
167) or Mixed
Meat Hot Pot
(page 168).

Grind the coriander seeds in a coffee grinder or with a mortar and
pestle. Combine with the soy sauce, peanut butter, sugar, and water in
a food processor or blender and process until smooth. Stir in the chili
sauce. Store in a sealed container in the refrigerator until ready to use.

Hot Pot Dip for Beef

Yields 1¼ cups

Dark soy sauce and sesame seed oil can be purchased in the ethnic cuisine section of many supermarkets or at an Asian grocery store.

1 garlic clove
¾ cup peanut butter
¼ cup chicken broth
½ cup dark soy sauce
4 teaspoons sugar

¼ cup water
1 teaspoon hot chili sauce, or to taste
1 teaspoon sesame seed oil, or to taste

Smash, peel, and chop the garlic clove. Combine the chopped garlic, peanut butter, chicken broth, dark soy sauce, sugar, and water in a blender or food processor and process until smooth. Stir in the hot chili sauce and sesame seed oil and mix well. Store in a sealed container in the refrigerator until ready to use.

Lemon-Soy Dressing (Ponzu)

Yields 1 cup

Tart lemon nicely balances the flavor of soy sauce in this simple dip. Serve with Shabu-Shabu (page 173) or Shabu-Shabu with Noodles (page 174).

1 Chinese dried mushroom, optional
⅔ cup soy sauce

⅓ cup lemon juice
½ teaspoon rice vinegar

1. If using the dried mushroom, soak in warm water for 20 minutes to soften. Squeeze out the excess water and slice.
2. Combine all the ingredients. For best results, prepare a few hours ahead of time to give the flavors a chance to blend. Remove the dried mushroom slices before serving. The sauce will last for several days if stored in a sealed container in the refrigerator.

Sesame Dipping Paste

4 tablespoons plus 2 tea-
   spoons soybean paste
4 tablespoons chicken broth
2 teaspoons soy sauce

1 teaspoon rice vinegar
2 teaspoons sesame seeds
½ teaspoon lemon juice

Combine all the ingredients. For best results, make this strong flavored dip a few hours ahead of time to give the flavors a chance to blend.

Yields about ⅔ cup

Soybean paste
is the main
ingredient in
Japanese
miso soup. It
has a spongy
texture and a
salty taste.

Nut-Free Hot Pot Dipping Sauce

¼ cup soy sauce
¼ cup Chinese rice wine or
   dry sherry

2 tablespoons Worcestershire
   sauce
1 tablespoon plus 1 teaspoon
   sugar

Combine the soy sauce, rice wine, and Worcestershire sauce in a small saucepan. Stir in the sugar. Bring to a boil, then cool. For best results, do not serve for 2 hours, to give the flavors time to blend.

Yields about ⅔ cup

Use this
simple dip
with any type
of hot pot
dish or meat
cooked in
broth.

Sweet and Sour Sauce with Tomato Paste

Yields 1 cup

This sauce makes a flavorful addition to chicken and pork fondues cooked in oil.

⅔ cup pineapple juice
⅓ cup red wine vinegar

¼ cup sugar
¼ cup tomato paste

Warm the pineapple juice and red wine vinegar in a small saucepan on low heat. Add the sugar, stirring to dissolve. Add the tomato paste and bring to a boil, stirring to make a smooth sauce. Keep warm on low heat until ready to serve.

Sweet and Sour Sauce

Yields 1⅓ cups

Serve alone with an Oriental fondue, or halve the recipe and serve with other dipping sauces.

2 tablespoons cornstarch
4 tablespoons water
1 cup pineapple juice
4 tablespoons cider vinegar
3 teaspoons soy sauce

6 teaspoons Worcestershire sauce
½ cup brown sugar
⅛ teaspoon ground ginger
⅛ teaspoon ground coriander

1. Dissolve the cornstarch in the water and set aside. Combine the pineapple juice, cider vinegar, soy sauce, and Worcestershire sauce and set aside.
2. In a small saucepan, melt the brown sugar over low heat, stirring continuously. Add the pineapple juice mixture. Turn up the heat and bring to a boil.
3. Give the cornstarch and water mixture a quick stir and add to the sauce, stirring to thicken. Stir in the ground ginger and the coriander. Remove from the heat. Serve immediately, or prepare several hours ahead of time to give the flavors a chance to blend.

CHAPTER 4

Marinades, Batters, and Broths

Teriyaki Marinade

1 garlic clove
½ cup soy sauce
3 tablespoons mirin (Japanese rice wine)

2 teaspoons sugar
1 teaspoon ginger, chopped

Smash and peel the garlic clove. Combine all the ingredients. For best results, make ahead of time to give the flavors a chance to blend.

Balsamic Vinegar Marinade

2 garlic cloves
3 tablespoons balsamic vinegar

1 teaspoon liquid honey
½ teaspoon prepared mustard

Smash, peel, and chop the garlic cloves. Combine all the ingredients. Marinate the meat for at least 1 hour before using in the fondue.

Terrific Teriyaki

Used to refer to the Japanese method of grilling meat, the word teriyaki comes from the Japanese words teri, meaning "luster," and yaki, meaning "roast." The secret behind teriyaki lies in the marinade, which consists of sugar, ginger, and Japanese rice wine or mirin. Combined, these three ingredients impart a luster to the roasted meat and provide a tangy sweet-and-sour flavor.

Marinated Cheese Cubes

2 garlic cloves
4 sprigs parsley
½ cup vegetable oil
½ cup balsamic vinegar

2 sprigs thyme, chopped
1 teaspoon sugar
Pinch of cayenne, optional
1 pound sharp Cheddar cheese

Serves 4

Use to make Marinated Cheese Fondue (page 18) or as dippers in a broth fondue.

1. Smash, peel, and chop the garlic cloves. Chop the parsley sprigs until you have 4 tablespoons.
2. Combine the vegetable oil, balsamic vinegar, garlic, chopped parsley, thyme, sugar, and cayenne in a bowl. Pour into a jar and shake well.
3. Cut the cheese into cubes. Lay out the cubes flat in a shallow glass dish and pour the marinade over. Cover and refrigerate overnight. Use as called for in the recipe.

Lemony Ginger Marinade

½ cup white wine
2 tablespoons plus 2 tea-
 spoons lemon juice

1 teaspoon ground ginger
1 teaspoon dried dill seeds
2 teaspoons brown sugar

Yields ½ cup

Feel free to substitute 2 teaspoons of minced ginger for the ground ginger and 2 teaspoons of fresh chopped dill for the dried dill seeds.

Combine all the ingredients. Let the marinade sit, covered and refrigerated, at least 1 hour before using.

How Much Marinade Should You Use?

Less is more when it comes to fondue marinades, since it's important to drain the meat before cooking in hot oil. It's possible to use as little as ⅓ cup of marinade for 1 pound of meat. Go sparingly, and save the extra marinade for tougher cuts of meat that need extra tenderizing.

Quick and Easy Teriyaki Marinade

Yields ½ cup

This marinade is particularly good with salmon or chicken.

2 large slices ginger
½ cup soy sauce

2 tablespoons brown sugar

Grate the ginger finely until you have 2 teaspoons. Combine all the ingredients. Toss with the meat or seafood in a shallow glass dish and refrigerate.

Mediterranean Chicken Marinade

Yields about ½ cup

This recipe works very well with 1½ pounds of chicken that is going to be cooked in an oil-based fondue.

2 medium garlic cloves
½ cup olive oil
2 tablespoons plus 1 teaspoon
   lemon juice

1½ teaspoons fresh tarragon
   leaves

Smash and peel the garlic cloves. Combine all the ingredients. Use a pastry brush to baste the chicken with the marinade. For best results, marinate the chicken for at least 1 hour before cooking in the fondue.

Marinating Times

Beef and chicken should be marinated for 1 hour. By contrast, it takes only 15–30 minutes for the marinade to penetrate most types of seafood. Take care not to marinate too long, or the meat or fish may turn soft and mushy.

Spunky Red Wine Vinegar Marinade

¾ cup red wine vinegar
1 tablespoon Dijon mustard
½ teaspoon freshly squeezed
    ginger juice

3 teaspoons brown sugar
¼ cup vegetable oil

Combine all the ingredients. Place the meat in a shallow glass dish or
zipper-lock plastic bag and pour the marinade over.

Yields 1 cup

Use this spicy
marinade to
lend flavor to
less-highly
seasoned cuts
of beef,
chicken, or
ham.

Sweet and Sour Marinade

2 tablespoons vegetable oil
4 tablespoons rice vinegar
1½ teaspoons light soy sauce

4 teaspoons brown sugar
1 teaspoon ginger, chopped

Combine all the ingredients. Place the meat in a shallow glass dish,
toss with the marinade, and refrigerate for at least 1 hour.

Draining Marinated Meat

*Be sure to drain marinated meat thoroughly before adding to an oil-based
fondue. If any leftover marinade liquid comes into contact with the hot oil,
splattering may occur. For best results, drain the meat ½ hour before cooking
the fondue, and use paper towels to pat dry.*

Yields ½ cup

This is an
excellent
marinade to
use with 1–1½
pounds of
cubed pork or
chicken.

Basic Red Wine Marinade

Yields about ½ cup

Thyme's minty flavor makes an interesting contrast with tart lemon juice. Together, they coax out beef's natural flavors.

⅓ cup red wine
2 teaspoons lemon juice
2 tablespoons olive oil

½ teaspoon fresh thyme leaves, chopped

Combine all the ingredients. Toss the beef in the marinade and refrigerate for at least 1 hour before cooking in the fondue.

Spicy Seafood Marinade

Yields ⅓ cup

Use this simple but spicy marinade to lend flavor to seafood dishes.

1½ teaspoons fresh ground white pepper
1½ teaspoons fresh ground black pepper

1½ teaspoons white sugar
4 tablespoons lemon juice

Combine all the ingredients. Brush on 1¼–1½ pounds of fresh or frozen fish or shellfish.

Dry Mustard and Chili Rub

½ cup dry mustard

2 tablespoons garlic powder

1 tablespoon chili powder

1 tablespoon cumin

Combine all the ingredients. Store in a sealed container until ready to use.

Yields ⅔ cup

Use this spicy rub on chicken wings before cooking them in hot fondue oil, or whenever you're grilling chicken or pork.

Instant Tandoori Rub

2 tablespoons ground coriander

2 tablespoons ground cumin

2 tablespoons ground cayenne pepper

2 teaspoons ground ginger

1 teaspoon sugar

¼ teaspoon garlic powder, or to taste

Combine all the ingredients. Store in a sealed container until ready to use.

Yields about ⅓ cup

Garlic's strong taste can overpower the more delicate aromas of coriander and cumin. Use sparingly at first.

Simple Chicken Rub

Yields 2⅓ table-spoons

Use this spicy rub to lend flavor whenever you are deep-frying chicken. This amount will nicely coat 16 chicken wings or 12 thighs.

2 tablespoons paprika   ½ teaspoon salt
½ teaspoon pepper

Combine all the ingredients. Store in a sealed container until ready to use.

Tempura Batter

Yields 1¼ cups

The trick to making tempura batter is to use very cold water and not to overmix the batter. Use to make deep-fried vegetables and seafood.

1 egg, refrigerated   1 cup flour
1 cup ice-cold water, divided Black pepper, as desired

Combine the egg with ¾ cup cold water. Slowly stir in the flour, adding as much of the remaining ¼ cup of water as is necessary, until the batter has the thin, runny consistency of pancake batter. Add the black pepper if desired. Do not worry about lumps of flour in the batter. For best results, use immediately.

Japanese Beer Batter

1 teaspoon baking soda
1 cup flour
3 teaspoons lemon juice

2 teaspoons Worcestershire sauce
Black pepper to taste
1 cup cold Japanese beer

Yields 1½ cups

1. Sift the baking soda into the flour. Stir in the lemon juice and Worcestershire sauce. Add the fresh ground black pepper.
2. Slowly pour in the beer and mix until the batter has the consistency of heavy cream. Do not add the entire cup if it's not needed. Allow the batter to rest in the refrigerator for 30 minutes before using.

Looking for an alternative to tempura batter? Try this recipe the next time you're deep-frying cod, haddock, or any fish traditionally used to make fish and chips.

Basic Batter

1 teaspoon baking soda
1 cup flour
2 tablespoons vegetable oil
Freshly ground black pepper
   to taste

½ teaspoon cayenne pepper
1 cup soda water

Yields 1¼ cups

1. Sift the baking soda into the flour. Stir in the vegetable oil, black pepper, and cayenne pepper.
2. Slowly add the soda water until you have a batter similar in texture to pancake batter. Feel free to adjust the amount of water or flour to obtain the right consistency. Allow the batter to rest in the refrigerator for 30 minutes before using.

This all-purpose batter can be used with meat, seafood, and vegetables.

Quick and Easy Batter

**Yields about
1¼ cups**

Use this
simple recipe
whenever you
want to deep-
fry meat or
vegetables.

1 teaspoon baking soda
1 cup flour

1 tablespoon vegetable oil
¾ cup beer, preferably flat

Sift the baking soda into the flour, and stir in the vegetable oil. Slowly add ½ cup of the beer, stirring. Add as much of the remaining ¼ cup of beer as is necessary to form a thick batter that is not too runny.

Herbed Seafood Batter

Yields 2 cups

To make fresh
herbs last
longer, wrap
them in a
damp towel
and place in a
plastic bag in
the refriger-
ator. They
should last
for up to a
week.

2 teaspoons baking soda
2 cups flour
2 tablespoons vegetable oil
*2 sprigs baby dill leaves, torn
    into small pieces*

2 sprigs fresh thyme
*⅛ teaspoon each of salt and
    pepper*
4 teaspoons lemon juice
1½ cups beer, preferably flat

1. Sift the baking soda into the flour. Stir in the vegetable oil. Add the dill and thyme leaves and the salt and pepper. Stir in the lemon juice.
2. Slowly add 1¼ cups beer, stirring to form a batter that is thick and drops off the spoon but is not runny. Add the remaining ¼ cup of beer if needed. Use as called for in the recipe.

Homemade Chicken Broth

1 3-pound stewing chicken
1 parsnip
1 carrot
1 celery stalk

16 cups water
3 parsley sprigs
Salt and pepper to taste

Yields about 10 cups

Storebought chicken broth just doesn't have the flavor and nutrition of homemade broth. Feel free to enhance the basic recipe by adding other seasonings and vegetables.

1. Rinse the chicken thoroughly and pat dry. Wash and coarsely chop the parsnip, carrot, and celery.
2. Bring the water to a boil. Add the chicken, vegetables, and parsley to the water and bring to a boil. Skim off the foam that rises to the top. Stir in the salt and pepper. Reduce the heat and simmer, uncovered, for another 1½ hours, occasionally skimming off the foam that rises to the top. Taste and add more seasonings if desired. Remove the solid ingredients and strain.

Fat-Free Broths

One reason behind the popularity of broth-based fondues is that they are lower in fat than oil-based fondues. Nonetheless, meat such as chicken contains a certain amount of fat, which will wind up in the broth if it is not removed. To reduce the fat in basic chicken and meat broths, cool the broth after cooking and refrigerate it. When the broth is chilled, remove the hardened fat from the top.

Vietnamese Beef Broth

Yields 6 cups

Use with Vietnamese Beef Hot Pot (page 177) or to add flavor to beef or vegetable fondues. Nonalcoholic red wine can be used in place of the red wine.

2 garlic cloves
2 green onions
5 cups beef broth
1 cup red wine

3 slices ginger
3 teaspoons hot chili sauce
4½ teaspoons fish sauce

1. Smash and peel the garlic and roughly chop the green onions.
2. Combine all the ingredients in large saucepan and bring to a boil. Transfer enough broth to fill the fondue pot about ⅔ full. Set the fondue pot on the burner, with enough heat to keep the broth simmering throughout the meal. Keep the remaining broth warm on the stove to use as needed.

Asian Chicken Broth

Yields about 10 cups

Use this basic broth as an alternative to Homemade Chicken Broth (page 81) when you are preparing broth-based fondues.

4 pounds chicken wings, backs, and necks
1 garlic clove
2 green onions

4 slices ginger
16 cups water
1 tablespoon rice vinegar

1. Rinse the chicken thoroughly and dry. Smash and peel the garlic.
2. Add the chicken, green onions, ginger, and garlic to the water and bring to a boil. Skim off the foam. Turn down the heat and simmer the broth, covered, for another 1½ hours, skimming off any foam. Stir in the rice vinegar. Remove the solid ingredients and strain the soup through a sieve to remove much of the extra fat.

Chinese Beef Broth

6 cups beef broth
½ cup soy sauce
1 green onion, chopped

4 small slices ginger
2 tablespoons sherry
½ teaspoon five-spice powder

Combine all the ingredients in a large saucepan and bring to a boil. Transfer enough broth to fill the fondue pot about ⅔ full. Set the fondue pot on the burner, with enough heat to keep the broth simmering throughout the meal. Keep the remaining broth warm on the stove to use as needed.

Serves 6

Five-spice powder lends character to this simple broth. Use with Fondue Chinoise (page 166), or whenever you want to add Asian flavor to a standard broth.

Vegetable Broth

4 garlic cloves
1 large yellow onion
2 celery stalks
2 large carrots
1 green bell pepper

2 tablespoons vegetable oil
12 cups water
2 bay leaves
2 sprigs thyme
¼ cup fresh parsley

Yields 12 cups

This flavorful broth makes an excellent base for cooking a vegetable fondue, or it can be used in any recipe calling for vegetable broth.

1. Smash, peel, and chop the garlic. Chop the onion without removing the peel. Chop the celery and carrots into chunks. Cut the green pepper in half, remove the seeds, and chop into chunks.
2. Heat the oil in a large saucepan. Add the chopped onion, garlic, and pepper and cook until the onion is tender and the garlic is aromatic.
3. Add the water, carrots, celery, bay leaves, thyme, and parsley. Bring to a boil, and then simmer on low heat, covered, for at least 1 hour. Remove the ingredients and strain the broth.

Simple Beef Broth

Yields 7 cups

For extra flavor, add a few dashes of freshly ground black pepper or white pepper.

1 green onion
1 garlic clove

5 cups water
2 cups beef broth

Chop the green onion into thirds. Smash and peel the garlic. Combine the green onion and garlic with the water and beef broth. Bring all the ingredients to a boil. Simmer for 5 minutes before using in the fondue.

Basic Mongolian Hot Pot Broth

Yields 6 cups

Use in Classic Mongolian Hot Pot (page 167), in Mixed Meat Hot Pot (page 168), or whenever you want a broth with Asian flavors.

1 green onion
2½ cups Asian Chicken Broth (page 82) or storebought chicken broth
3½ cups water

1 tablespoon rice wine or dry sherry
2 slices ginger (about ½ teaspoon)

Chop the green onion into thirds. Combine all the ingredients and bring to a boil. Simmer for 5 minutes before using in the fondue.

Bland Broth

Traditionally, Mongolian hot pot broth is meant to be similar to consommé, with most of the flavor coming from the meat and vegetables cooked in it. If you find the broth too bland, feel free to change the ratio of chicken broth to water.

Instant Dashi

6 cups water

2¼ teaspoons instant dashi
soup stock

Bring the water to a boil and stir in the instant soup stock. Use immediately as called for in the recipe.

Dashi—Basic Japanese Soup Stock

Dashi is as indispensable to Japanese cooking as chicken broth is to other cuisines. Different varieties of dashi are made with everything from konbu seaweed to dried shiitake mushrooms.

Fish Broth

2 carrots
2 parsnips
2 celery stalks
½ small yellow onion
12 cups water

3 pounds fish heads and
bones
2 bay leaves
¼ teaspoon celery salt
Salt and pepper to taste

1. Chop the carrots, parsnips, and celery into chunks. Peel and coarsely chop the onion.
2. Bring the water to a boil. Combine the vegetables with the fish heads and bones, bay leaves, celery salt, and salt and pepper. Simmer for 1 hour. Cool and strain.

Yields 6 cups

Packages of dashi powder are available in many Western supermarkets. Use with Shabu-Shabu (page 173) and Shabu-Shabu with Noodles (page 174).

Yields 12 cups

Be sure not to use bones from a fatty fish such as salmon or trout. This will affect the flavor.

CHAPTER 5
Beef and Poultry Fondues

Classic Beef Bourguignonne

Serves 4–6

The term bour-guignonne refers to a style of cooking that originated in the Burgundy region in eastern France.

1¾ pounds beef sirloin
5 cups oil, or as needed
Béarnaise Sauce (page 54)

Quick and Easy Blender
  Hollandaise Sauce (page 49)
¼ cup hot chili powder

1. Cut the meat into bite-sized cubes, approximately ¾ inch thick.
2. Add the oil to the fondue pot, making sure it is not more than half full. Heat the pot on a stove element over medium-high heat.
3. When the oil is hot, move the fondue pot to the table and set up the burner. Set out the béarnaise sauce, hollandaise sauce, and ground hot chili powder in small bowls. Use dipping forks to spear the beef cubes. Cook briefly in the hot oil and then dip into the sauces or seasoning. Add other condiments as desired.

Spicy Beef Bourguignonne

Serves 4

Encourage guests to season their meat in the ground white pepper before dipping it into the Curried Yogurt.

1¾ pounds flank sirloin steak
1 sprig tarragon, finely minced
5 cups oil, or as needed

¾ cup freshly ground white
  pepper
Curried Yogurt (page 46)

1. Cut the meat into cubes approximately ¾ inch thick. Mix with the minced tarragon and set aside.
2. Add the oil to the fondue pot, making sure it is not more than half full. Heat the pot on a stove element over medium-high heat.
3. When the oil is hot, move the fondue pot to the table and set up the burner. Set out the ground white pepper and Curried Yogurt in small bowls for dipping. Add other condiments such as horseradish, pickles, and onions as desired.
4. Use dipping forks to spear the beef cubes. Cook briefly in the hot oil and then dip into the seasoning and/or sauce.

Beef Kebabs

1½ pounds beef tenderloin
5 cups oil, or as needed
Mint and Cilantro Chutney
  (page 48)

Speedy Garlic Mayonnaise
  (page 65)
Fried Mushrooms (page 148)

1. Cut the meat into bite-sized cubes, approximately ¾ inch thick.
2. Add the oil to the fondue pot, making sure it is not more than half full. Heat the pot on a stove element over medium-high heat.
3. When the oil is hot, move the fondue pot to the table and set up the burner. Set out the chutney and the garlic mayonnaise in serving bowls. Set out metal skewers with wooden handles instead of dipping forks. Invite guests to place 2 beef cubes and 2 mushroom slices on each skewer. Cook the food briefly and eat with the chutney and mayonnaise.

Serves 4–6

If you want to increase the quantity of vegetables, serve with Roasted Red Peppers (page 150) or French Green Beans with Fondue Béchamel Sauce (page 156).

Fondue au Boeuf

2 pounds beef sirloin
Spunky Red Wine Vinegar
  Marinade (page 75)
2 shallots

5 cups oil, or as needed
¼ cup fresh cracked black
  pepper, or as needed

1. Cut the meat into bite-sized cubes, approximately ¾ inch thick. Place the meat in a glass dish and pour the marinade over. Peel the shallots, chop, and add to the meat. Marinate the meat in the refrigerator for at least 2 hours. Remove excess marinade.
2. Add the oil to the fondue pot, making sure it is not more than half full. Heat the pot on a stove element over medium-high heat.
3. When the oil is hot, move the fondue pot to the table and set up the burner. Set out the fresh cracked black pepper in a serving bowl. Use dipping forks to spear the beef cubes and cook briefly in the hot oil, then dip into the cracked black pepper.

Serves 6

Be sure to dry the marinated meat thoroughly before cooking. Otherwise, there may be splattering when the marinade meets the hot oil.

Meatballs with Basil

Serves 2–4

Serve this simple appetizer with oil-based fondues such as Fondue Tandoori Chicken (page 105).

4 fresh basil leaves
8 ounces ground beef
$\frac{1}{4}$ teaspoon celery salt
1 tablespoon onion, chopped
1 cup cooked rice
2 tablespoons ground cardamom

2 teaspoons ground coriander
1 teaspoon ground cumin
2 teaspoons ground cinnamon
$\frac{1}{4}$ cup plain yogurt
$\frac{1}{4}$ cup sour cream
$4\frac{1}{2}$ cups oil, or as necessary

1. Chop the fresh basil leaves. With your hands, mix together the ground beef, basil leaves, celery salt, onion, and 2 tablespoons of the cooked rice. Shape the ground beef mixture into 9 meatballs the size of golf balls. Roll the ground beef balls into the remainder of the cooked rice so that each ball is well covered.

2. Blend together the ground cardamom, ground coriander, ground cumin, and ground cinnamon. Combine the yogurt and sour cream. Add 2 teaspoons of the blended spices to the yogurt mixture. Store the remainder of the spice mixture in a sealed container to use another time.

3. Add the oil to the fondue pot, making sure it is not more than half full. Heat the pot on a stove element over medium-high heat.

4. When the oil is hot, move the fondue pot to the table and set up the burner. Using metal skewers with wooden handles, skewer the meatballs so that the skewer comes out the other side of the meatball. Cook the meatball in the hot oil for 4 to 5 minutes, until the rice is browned and the meat is cooked through. Serve with the spiced yogurt mixture for dipping.

How to Cut Meat for Oil and Broth Fondues

For oil-based fondues, cutting meat into cubes is the best way to make sure the meat cooks quickly and evenly. For broth-based fondues, the meat should be cut into thin slices.

Beef and Peppers with Clarified Butter

1½ pounds beef tenderloin
2 red bell peppers
1 green bell pepper
10 fresh small mushrooms
1 red onion
2 tablespoons butter
   or margarine

10 ounces clarified butter
1 cup vegetable oil
Horseradish Cream (page 60)
Mint and Cilantro Chutney
   (page 48)

Serves 4

This tastes delicious served with rice. For more variety, add 1 pound of large shrimp and serve with Seafood Cocktail Sauce (page 46) for dipping.

1. Cut the beef into cubes. Wash the red and green peppers and dry thoroughly. Cut in half, remove the seeds, and cut into cubes. Wipe the mushrooms clean with a damp cloth. Dry and cut in half. Peel and chop the onion.

2. Heat the 2 tablespoons of butter in a pan. Add the chopped onion, and sauté until it is soft and translucent. Set aside.

3. Add the clarified butter and the oil to the fondue pot. Heat the pot on a stove element over medium-high heat.

4. When the oil is hot, move the fondue pot to the table, set on the burner, and maintain the heat. Use dipping forks to spear the beef and vegetables. Cook the mushroom slices briefly in the hot oil until golden, and the beef until it is cooked through. Cook the peppers very briefly. Drain on paper towels or a tempura rack if desired. Serve with the horseradish cream for dipping. Eat with the sautéed onion and chutney.

How to Clarify Butter

Clarified butter makes a flavorful alternative to oil for frying. To clarify butter, simply melt the butter over low heat. Let stand for several minutes, until the milk solids and butter fat have separated. Skim the butter fat off the top and use as called for in the recipe.

Rib-Sticking Meat and Potatoes Hot Pot

Serves 4–6

French sauces lend flavor to this simple home-cooked dish. Feel free to add or substitute other vegetables.

Honey Mustard Sauce
  (page 51)
2 pounds beef sirloin steak
4 small potatoes
2 carrots

6 ounces spinach leaves
4 garlic cloves
Simple Beef Broth (page 84)
Béarnaise Sauce (page 54)
Aioli (page 48)

1. Warm the honey mustard sauce over low heat. Cut the meat into thin strips.
2. Wash the potatoes and cook in boiling salted water until tender but not soft. Wash the carrots, peel, and cut lengthwise into thin slices. Blanch briefly in boiling water and drain thoroughly. Wash the spinach leaves and drain thoroughly. Smash and peel the garlic cloves.
3. Heat the broth with the garlic cloves on the stove and bring to a boil. Add the spinach and bring to a boil again. Transfer enough broth to fill the fondue pot about ⅔ full. Set the fondue pot on the burner, with enough heat to keep the broth simmering throughout the meal. (Keep the remaining broth warm on the stove to use as needed.)
4. Ladle a small portion of the broth with spinach into the soup bowls. Invite guests to use chopsticks or dipping forks to cook the beef and remaining vegetables in the hot pot. Dip the cooked beef in the dipping sauces, or enjoy with the bowls of broth.

Oil Safety

For safer cooking, never fill a fondue pot to the top with oil. Instead, fill the pot roughly halfway. At the table, make sure the fondue pot is securely attached to the stand. If the pot has a metal collar, be sure to use it—the collar catches splattering oil. Moreover, most collars have metal inserts to hold the dipping forks. This prevents guests from having to lean over the fondue pot while cooking their food.

Sesame Beef Appetizer

1 cup sesame seeds
10 ounces beef round
¼ cup Quick and Easy Teriyaki
    Marinade (page 74)

4½ cups oil, or as needed
5 tablespoons sesame seed oil

Serves 4

Be sure to wait until the beef slices are cooked to coat them with sesame seeds. Otherwise, the seeds will fall off in the hot oil.

1. Toast the sesame seeds by spreading out on a frying pan and cooking at low heat until they brown. Cool.
2. Cut the beef into thin slices approximately 3 inches long and ½ inch wide. Place in a shallow glass dish. Toss the meat with the marinade. Refrigerate and marinate the meat for 1 hour. Remove any excess marinade and place the meat on a serving platter.
3. Add the oil to the fondue pot, making sure it is not more than half full. Heat the pot on a stove element over medium-high heat.
4. When the oil is hot, move the fondue pot to the table and set up the burner. Invite guests to roll up the beef slices and spear them with a dipping fork or a metal skewer with a wooden handle. Cook in the hot oil briefly until the meat is cooked. Dip into the sesame oil and the toasted sesame seeds.

Open Sesame!

One of the oldest condiments known to man, sesame is mentioned in the classic book of tales, The Thousand and One Arabian Nights. *Various forms of sesame, including seeds, oil, and a type of paste, feature prominently in Asian, Middle Eastern, and African cuisine.*

Classic Bacchus Fondue

Serves 4

The choice
is yours
with
Bacchus
fondues—
either heat
the wine on
the stove or
add directly
to the
fondue pot
and heat at
the table
over the
burner.

2 pounds beef rib steak
2 shallots
Basic Red Wine marinade
  (page 76)
¾ pound fresh small mushrooms
2 green onions

4 cups dry red wine,
  or as needed
Béarnaise Sauce (page 54)
Curried Yogurt (page 46)
Horseradish with Sour Cream
  (page 59)

1. Cut the beef into thin strips. Peel and chop the shallots. Place the meat and the shallots in a shallow glass dish and pour the marinade over. Refrigerate and marinate the beef for 1 hour. Remove any excess marinade.
2. Wipe the mushrooms with a damp cloth. Remove the stems. Chop the green onions.
3. Heat the wine on the stove or in the fondue pot. Make sure not to fill the pot more than ⅔ full. Stir in the green onions. Keep the wine simmering throughout the meal.
4. Use dipping forks to spear the beef strips and mushroom caps. Cook in the wine for 3 to 4 minutes until cooked through. Serve with the sauces for dipping.

Bacchus Fondues

Named after the Roman god of wine, Bacchus fondues replace oil with alcohol in the fondue pot. In addition to white and red wine, rice wine, sherry, and beer may all be used. Frequently, the alcohol is combined with vegetable or chicken broth. Like cheese fondues, Bacchus fondues work best with a dry wine, but feel free to experiment with your favorite spicy red wine or mulled wine. Steer clear of spirits such as rum, as they can ignite when heated. Serve Bacchus fondues with an assortment of dipping sauces and garnishes.

Beef Carpaccio

8 ounces beef tenderloin, sliced
   paper thin
4 plum tomatoes, fresh or
   canned
2 tablespoons extra-virgin olive
   oil

¼ cup lemon juice
2 tablespoons freshly cracked
   black pepper
Pesto Mayonnaise (page 62)
1 jar capers

Serves 4

To give guests
more dipping
options, serve
with the
dressing in
Vegetables
with Boiled
Salad Dressing
(page 162).

1. Keep the beef chilled until ready to serve. Wash the tomatoes, pat dry, and cut into wedges.
2. Place the beef between pieces of plastic wrap lightly oiled with the olive oil. Pound with a mallet to thin the beef even further. Remove the beef from the wrap and brush with the lemon juice. Sprinkle with the freshly cracked black pepper.
3. Cut the beef into medium-sized pieces that can be comfortably skewered with a dipping fork. Place on a large serving platter. Garnish with the tomato wedges.
4. Place the Pesto Mayonnaise in a cheese or dessert fondue bowl in the middle of the table. Invite guests to skewer the beef slices and dip them into the Pesto Mayonnaise. Serve with the capers.

Heating Oil-Based Fondues

Fondue pot burners aren't designed to generate the high heat needed for cooking in oil. Unless you have an electric fondue set, never try to heat the oil using only the fondue pot's heat source. Instead, add the oil to the fondue pot and heat on the stove. When the oil is hot, transfer the fondue pot to the tabletop burner.

Porcupine Meatballs in Broth

Serves 4

When guests have finished eating the meatballs, ladle out the broth, flavored with the cooked food.

Sweet and Sour Sauce with Tomato Paste (page 70)
8 fresh basil leaves
6 leaves romaine lettuce
1 pound ground beef
½ teaspoon celery salt

3 tablespoons onion, finely chopped
¼ cup cooked rice
2 tablespoons tomato paste
Simple Beef Broth (page 84)
Sour Cream and Mustard Dip (page 65)

1. Warm the Sweet and Sour Sauce over low heat.
2. Chop the fresh basil leaves. Wash and dry the romaine lettuce leaves. With your hands, mix together the ground beef, basil leaves, celery salt, onion, cooked rice, and tomato paste. Shape the ground beef mixture into 18 meatballs the size of golf balls.
3. Heat the broth on the stove or in the fondue pot. Make sure not to fill the pot more than ⅔ full. Keep the broth simmering throughout the meal.
4. Serve the meatballs on the romaine lettuce leaves. Skewer the meatballs so that the skewer comes out the other side of the meatball. Cook the meatball in the hot broth for 5 to 6 minutes until it is cooked through. Serve with the dipping sauces.

Freezing Broth

Here's a handy trick if you frequently use chicken broth in recipes. Pour the cooled broth into ice cube trays, freeze, and then place in individual zipper-lock bags. Each frozen cube holds approximately 1 ounce of broth.

Basic Marinated Chicken Fondue

Mediterranean Chicken
   Marinade (page 74)

1 pound skinless, boneless
   chicken breasts
5 cups oil, or as needed

Serves 4

Aioli (page 48), Speedy Garlic Mayonnaise (page 65), and plain ketchup are all good choices for dips to accompany this simple dish.

1. Let the marinade sit for 1 hour before coating chicken.
2. Wash the chicken breasts and pat dry. Cut into 1-inch cubes. Place in a glass dish. Pour the marinade over the chicken, cover, and refrigerate for 1 hour.
3. Drain the marinade from the chicken and pat dry with paper towels.
4. Add the oil to the fondue pot, making sure it is not more than half full. Heat the pot on a stove element over medium-high heat.
5. When the oil is hot, move the fondue pot to the table and set up the burner. Skewer the chicken cubes so that the skewer goes right through the meat. Cook the chicken cubes in the hot oil for 2 to 3 minutes, until they are browned and cooked through.

Marinated Chicken Wings

2 pounds chicken wings
⅔ cup Mediterranean Chicken
   Marinade (page 74)

4–5 cups oil, or as needed

Serves 4–6

For a complete meal, serve with salad and cooked rice or a vegetable side dish.

1. Rinse the chicken wings and pat dry. Cut through the wings at the joints.
2. Place the wings in a shallow glass dish and brush with the marinade on both sides. Refrigerate the chicken and marinate for 1 hour. Pat dry and remove any excess marinade.
3. Add the oil to the fondue pot, making sure it is not more than half full. Heat the pot on a stove element over medium-high heat.
4. When the oil is hot, move the fondue pot to the table and set up the burner. Use dipping forks or metal skewers to skewer the chicken wings. Cook in the hot oil until the wings are browned and cooked through.

Tandoori-Style Chicken Wings

Serves 4

Both yogurt and sour cream take the edge off a hot tandoori spice mix. If using the lemon, cut into wedges and serve with the dipping sauces. Serve with rice.

2 pounds chicken wings
Instant Tandoori Rub (page 77)
1 cup sour cream
1 cup plain yogurt
2 teaspoons lemon juice
5 cups oil, or as needed
1 lemon, optional

1. Rinse the chicken wings and pat dry. Cut through the wings at the joint. Rub the Tandoori Rub into the chicken.
2. Combine the sour cream with the yogurt. Stir in the lemon juice. Place in individual serving dishes and refrigerate until ready to serve.
3. Add the oil to the fondue pot, making sure it is not more than half full. Heat the pot on a stove element over medium-high heat.
4. When the oil is hot, move the fondue pot to the table and set up the burner. Use dipping forks or metal skewers to skewer the chicken wings. Cook in the hot oil until the wings are browned and cooked through. Drain on paper towels or use a tempura rack if desired. Serve with the yogurt and sour cream mixture for dipping.

Tantalizing Tandoori

Northern India's most famous dish, tandoori chicken takes its name from the oven in which it is traditionally cooked. Made of clay with an opening at the bottom for adding charcoal fuel, tandoor ovens produce intense heat that helps seals in the flavor of grilled lamb and chicken dishes. Tandoors are also used for baking bread. Naan, a type of flatbread, is traditionally made by slapping the bread dough against the oven's clay walls.

Chicken Egg Rolls

4 ounces chicken meat
1 teaspoon Chinese cooking wine
¼ teaspoon sesame oil
2 teaspoons water
1 tablespoon plus 1 teaspoon
   oyster sauce
1 teaspoon soy sauce
½ teaspoon sugar
½ carrot

4 dried Chinese mushrooms
1 tablespoon bamboo shoots,
   shredded
2 tablespoons plus 1 teaspoon
   red bell pepper, finely diced
4 cups oil, or as needed
10 egg roll wrappers
4 tablespoons cornstarch mixed
   with 2 tablespoons water

Yields 10 Egg Rolls

Serve as an appetizer with Basic Marinated Chicken Fondue (page 97), or other oil-based chicken fondues.

1. Chop the chicken meat. Add the Chinese cooking wine and a few drops of sesame oil and marinate the chicken for 30 minutes. Mix together the water, oyster sauce, soy sauce, and sugar. Set aside.

2. Wash or rinse all the vegetables and drain thoroughly. Grate the carrot until you have 2 tablespoons plus 1 teaspoon. Soak the Chinese dried mushrooms in warm water for at least 20 minutes to soften. Squeeze out the excess water, remove the stems, and thinly slice. Mix together the grated carrot, mushrooms, bamboo shoots, and bell pepper.

3. Add 2 tablespoons vegetable oil to a frying pan. When oil is hot, add the chicken. Fry until it changes color, then add the vegetables. Mix in the sauce and bring to a boil. Drizzle with the remaining sesame oil. Cool.

4. To prepare the egg rolls, lay a wrapper in front of you so that it forms a square. Use your fingers to brush all the edges of the wrapper with the cornstarch-and-water mixture. Place a heaping tablespoon of filling in the middle. Fold the top of the wrapper over the filling, fold the bottom half over the top, and seal the edges with more cornstarch and water. Seal the side edges, fold over, and seal again. Continue preparing the remainder of the egg rolls.

5. Add the remainder of the oil to the fondue pot, making sure it is not more than half full. Heat the pot on the stove over medium-high heat. When the oil is hot, move the fondue pot to the table and set up the burner. Deep-fry the egg rolls, two at a time, until they turn golden. Drain.

Serves 4

This adaptation of traditional Asian hot pot is made with garden vegetables and chicken broth.

2 skinless, boneless chicken
   breasts (about 10 ounces
   each)
1 green bell pepper
1 red bell pepper
2 zucchini
2 stalks celery
1 tomato

2 portobello mushrooms
6 cups Homemade Chicken
   Broth (page 81)
2 slices ginger
Sour Cream and Mustard Dip
   (page 65)
½ cup hot chili sauce

1. Rinse the chicken and pat dry. Cut into thin strips.
2. Wash all the vegetables and drain thoroughly. Cut the bell peppers in half, remove the stem and seeds, and cut into bite-sized cubes. Cut the zucchini and the celery into 1-inch pieces. Cut the tomato into 6 to 8 wedges. Thinly slice the portobello mushrooms.
3. Heat the broth on the stove with the ginger slices and bring to a boil. Transfer enough broth to fill the fondue pot about ⅔ full. Set the fondue pot on the burner, with enough heat to keep the broth simmering throughout the meal. (Keep the remaining broth warm on the stove to use as needed.)
4. Use dipping forks to spear the chicken and vegetables and cook in the hot broth. Serve with the mustard dip and the hot chili sauce for dipping.

Or, Transform into a Vegetarian Fondue

To turn Chicken and Vegetables Bathed in Broth into a vegetarian dish, simply replace the chicken with tofu. Prepare the tofu by draining it to remove any excess water; then cut it into bite-sized cubes and cook it in a vegetable broth with the vegetables. Despite its reputation for tasting bland, tofu is nutritious and can be quite flavorful—it acts like a sponge, soaking up the flavor of the food it is cooked with. For best results, use firm or medium-firm tofu, as both will hold their shape in the broth.

Chicken with Curried Rice

3 cups cooked chicken meat
½ pound fresh spinach leaves
2 tablespoons olive oil
¼ onion, peeled and chopped
2 cups long-grain rice
8 cups Homemade Chicken
  Broth (page 81)

¾ teaspoon curry powder
¾ teaspoon ground cumin
⅔ cup raisins
Curried Yogurt (page 46)
1 cup plain yogurt

Serves 4

This tastes
delicious
served with
Spicy Apple
Chutney
(page 52) or
Sweet
Banana
Chutney
(page 47).
Feel free to
substitute
cooked
turkey for
the chicken.

1. Cut the chicken into bite-sized pieces that can be easily speared with a dipping fork. Set aside. Wash the spinach and drain thoroughly.
2. Heat the olive oil in a frying pan over low heat. Add the chopped onion and cook until soft. Add the rice and sauté for 5 minutes until it turns shiny and is heated through.
3. Add 3 cups of broth to the rice. Add the curry powder, ground cumin, and raisins. Bring the rice to a boil, uncovered, on medium heat. Cover, turn down the heat, and boil until cooked through, stirring occasionally. Keep the rice warm over low heat.
4. Bring the remaining 5 cups of broth to a boil on the stove. Add the spinach and simmer briefly. Set the fondue pot on the burner, with enough heat to keep the broth simmering throughout the meal. Cook the chicken and spinach leaves briefly in the broth (use a fondue dipping basket for the spinach leaves if desired). Serve with the Curried Yogurt and plain yogurt for dipping. Eat with the curried rice.

Curry in a Hurry

Invented by the British colonists wanting to reproduce the taste and flavor of genuine Indian curries, commercial curry powder is a mix of dry spices. Ingredients commonly used in curry powder include chilies, cayenne pepper, turmeric (to give the powder a golden color), coriander, and cumin. However, each brand of curry powder will contain a different mixture of spices—try out several until you find one that you like.

Chicken Bourguignonne

Serves 4–6

Serve with salad, crusty bread, and an assortment of pickled onions, olives, and other garnishes for a complete meal.

4 skinless, boneless chicken breasts (about 6 ounces each)
Mediterranean Chicken Marinade (page 74)
8 ounces fresh small mushrooms
2 green bell peppers
2 red bell peppers
6 cups oil, or as needed
Lemon-Soy Dressing (page 68)
Freshly ground black pepper, as needed

1. Rinse the chicken breasts and pat dry. Cut into cubes about 1 inch thick. Place the cubed chicken in a shallow glass dish and brush the marinade over with a pastry brush. Refrigerate and marinate the chicken for 1 hour.
2. Wipe the mushrooms clean with a damp cloth. Dry and cut each mushroom in half.
3. Wash the bell peppers and dry thoroughly. Cut in half, remove the seeds, and cut into cubes between ¾ and 1 inch thick.
4. Add the oil to the fondue pot, making sure it is not more than half full. Heat the pot on a stove element over medium-high heat. When the oil is hot, move the fondue pot to the table, set on the burner, and maintain the heat.
5. Set the chicken and vegetables on serving dishes at the table. Use metal skewers with wooden handles and invite guests to spear 1 pepper, mushrooms, and a chicken cube and cook in the hot oil until the chicken changes color and is cooked through. Drain on paper towels or a tempura rack if desired. Serve with the Lemon-Soy Dressing and freshly ground black pepper for dipping.

Spicy Fried Chicken with Mushrooms

12 skinless, boneless chicken
   thighs
Simple Chicken Rub (page 78)
4 potatoes
2 green bell peppers
2 red bell peppers

¾ pound fresh small mush-
   rooms
7 cups oil, or as needed
Speedy Garlic Mayonnaise
   (page 65)
Lemon-Soy Dressing (page 68)
Horseradish Cream (page 60)

Serves 4–6

Be careful when adding the chicken to the hot oil, as the seasonings may cause splattering. Feel free to reduce the amount of vegetables if serving 4 people.

1. Rinse the chicken thighs, pat dry, and cover with the chicken rub. Cut into cubes.
2. Boil the potatoes for about 15 minutes over medium-low heat, until they can be pierced with a fork but are not too soft. Drain thoroughly, and cut lengthwise into pieces approximately ¾ inch thick.
3. Wash the bell peppers and dry thoroughly. Cut in half, remove the seeds, and cut into strips approximately ¾ inch thick. Wipe the mushrooms with a damp cloth and cut off the stems.
4. Add the oil to the fondue pot, making sure it is not more than half full. Heat the pot on a stove element over medium-high heat. When the oil is hot, move the fondue pot to the table, set on the burner, and maintain the heat.
5. Set the chicken cubes, mushrooms, potatoes, and bell peppers on the table. Use dipping forks or metal skewers with wooden handles to spear 1 or more pieces of food and cook in the hot oil until cooked. Be sure to cook the chicken until it changes color. Drain on paper towels or a tempura rack if desired. Serve with the Speedy Garlic Mayonnaise for the chicken, Lemon-Soy Dressing for the mushrooms, and Horseradish Cream for the potatoes. (Eat the peppers as is or with the dip of your choice.)

Chicken Hot Pot Style

Serves 4

Serve with a number of savoury dips, including Asian sesame seed oil, hot chili sauce, soy sauce, and Basic Chinese Hot Mustard (page 56).

4 skinless, boneless chicken
   breasts
8 ounces cellophane noodles
6 ounces bok choy
2 green onions
3 slices ginger

1 garlic clove
1 8-ounce can bamboo shoots
1 8-ounce can water chestnuts
Basic Mongolian Hot Pot Broth
   (page 84)

1. Cut the chicken into 1-inch cubes. Place on a serving tray on the table, along with dipping sauces. Make sure to give each guest an individual soup bowl when setting the table.
2. Rinse the cellophane noodles and cover with warm water for 15 minutes to soften. Drain thoroughly. If desired, cut the noodles into thirds for easier handling.
3. Wash the bok choy and green onions and drain. Separate the bok choy stalks and leaves. Shred the leaves and cut the stalks into slices about 1 inch thick. Chop the green onions and ginger. Smash and peel the garlic. Rinse the canned bamboo shoots and water chestnuts in warm running water; drain thoroughly.
4. Heat the broth on the stove and bring to a boil. Add the vegetables and bring to a boil again. Transfer enough broth to fill the fondue pot about ⅔ full. Set the fondue pot on the burner, with enough heat to keep the broth simmering throughout the meal. (Keep the remaining broth warm on the stove to use as needed.)
5. Ladle a small portion of the broth with vegetables into the soup bowls. Invite guests to use chopsticks or dipping forks to cook the chicken in the hot pot. Dip the cooked chicken in dipping sauces, or enjoy with the bowls of broth. Use a dipping basket to remove the vegetables.
6. When the meat and vegetables are gone, add the noodles to the broth. Ladle out a bowl for each guest.

Fondue Tandoori Chicken

2 tablespoons ground car-
damom
2 teaspoons ground coriander
1 teaspoon ground cumin
2 teaspoons ground cinnamon
1/4 cup plain yogurt
1/4 cup sour cream

4 skinless, boneless chicken
breasts (about 7 ounces
each)
2 teaspoons lemon juice
5 cups oil, or as needed
2 cups Marvelous Mango
Chutney (page 50)

Serves 4

Leftover
tandoori
chicken
makes a
great filling
for flatbread
wraps. Just
combine the
cooked
chicken and
yogurt/sour
cream mix-
ture with
lettuce and
a few slices
of raw
onion.

1. Blend together the ground cardamom, ground coriander, ground cumin, and ground cinnamon. Combine the yogurt and sour cream. Add 2 teaspoons of the spice mixture to the yogurt and sour cream. Store the remainder of the spice mixture in a sealed container to use another time.
2. Rinse the chicken breasts and pat dry. Use a knife to make cuts in the chicken. Rub 4 teaspoons of the yogurt and sour cream all over the chicken (use more than 4 teaspoons if necessary). Refrigerate and marinate the chicken overnight.
3. Stir the lemon juice into the remainder of the yogurt and sour cream. Cover and refrigerate until needed.
4. Cut the chicken into bite-sized cubes. Add the oil to the fondue pot, making sure it is not more than half full. Heat the pot on a stove element over medium-high heat.
5. When the oil is hot, move the fondue pot to the table and set up the burner. Skewer the chicken cubes so that the skewer goes right through the meat. Cook the chicken cubes in the hot oil for 2 to 3 minutes, until they are browned and cooked through. Serve with the yogurt and sour cream for dipping. Eat with the chutney.

Thai Coconut Chicken Soup

Serves 4

Hot jalapeño pepper gives this soup a sharp bite—feel free to substitute cayenne pepper or a mild chili sauce. This tastes delicious served with rice cooked in coconut milk.

4 skinless, boneless chicken breasts (about 7 ounces each)
¼ cup unsweetened coconut milk
2 teaspoons fish sauce
1 teaspoon lime juice
2 teaspoons brown sugar
2 garlic cloves, peeled
2 teaspoons turmeric
½ small yellow onion

1 jalapeño pepper
1 tomato
10 fresh small mushrooms
2 tablespoons olive oil
2 cups coconut milk
2 cups Homemade Chicken Broth (page 81)
2 slices ginger
1 teaspoon lime juice

1. Rinse the chicken and pat dry. Use a knife to make cuts in the surface. Combine the ¼ cup coconut milk, fish sauce, 1 teaspoon lime juice, brown sugar, whole garlic cloves, and turmeric. Place the chicken in a shallow glass dish and pour the marinade over. Refrigerate and marinate the chicken for at least 2 hours.

2. Preheat the oven to 350°F. Cut the marinated chicken into thin strips. Bake the chicken for 30 minutes or until cooked through.

3. Peel and chop the onion. Cut the chili pepper in half lengthwise and remove the seeds. Cut the tomato into wedges. Wipe the mushrooms clean with a damp cloth and slice.

4. Heat the olive oil in a saucepan over medium-low heat. Add the chopped onion and jalapeño pepper. Simmer on low heat for 5 minutes. Do not let the onion or pepper burn.

5. Add the 2 cups of coconut milk and the broth. Bring to a boil. Add the tomato, ginger, and mushrooms (or reserve the mushrooms to use as dippers, so that they soak up less of the spicy broth). Stir in the lime juice. Bring back to a boil. Transfer the broth to the fondue pot. Set the fondue pot on the burner, with enough heat to keep the broth simmering throughout the meal. (Keep the remaining broth warm on the stove to use as needed.) Dip the chicken into the broth and warm briefly. Ladle out the vegetables in the soup.

Bacchus Chicken Fondue

1½ pounds skinless, boneless
   chicken breasts
¼ yellow onion
12 fresh small mushrooms
1 red bell pepper
1 orange bell pepper
1 garlic clove
2 parsley sprigs
2 green onions

2 tablespoons olive oil
2 cups dry white wine
2 cups chicken broth
Béarnaise Sauce (page 54)
Aioli (page 48)
French Pistou with Cheese
   (page 66)
1 French baguette, sliced

Serves 4

French
pistou
makes an
excellent
side dish for
this version
of a Bacchus
fondue,
made with
white wine
and chicken
broth.

1. Rinse the chicken breasts. Pat dry and cut into thin strips. Chop the yellow onion. Wipe the mushrooms with a damp cloth and remove the stems. Wash the bell peppers, dry, and cut into strips. Peel and crush the garlic clove. Chop the parsley. Cut the green onions into thirds.
2. Heat the olive oil in a medium saucepan. Add the onion and garlic. Sauté until the onion is tender.
3. Add the white wine and chicken broth. Bring to a boil. Add the parsley sprigs and green onion; turn down to a simmer. Transfer the wine mixture to the fondue pot and set on the burner. Keep the wine mixture barely simmering throughout the meal.
4. Skewer the chicken strips and cook in the wine mixture for 3 to 4 minutes, until the chicken is cooked through. Cook the mushrooms and peppers in the wine mixture. Serve with the Béarnaise Sauce and Aioli for dipping. Eat with the French Pistou and the sliced baguette. Add other garnishes, side dishes, and condiments as desired.

Chicken with Coconut Rice

Serves 4

Coconut milk lends a sweet flavor to plain white rice. Serve with Mint and Cilantro Chutney (page 48).

4 skinless, boneless chicken breasts (about 7 ounces each)
3¼ cups coconut milk, divided
2 teaspoons fish sauce
5 teaspoons lime juice, divided
4 teaspoons brown sugar, divided
2 garlic cloves, crushed

2 tablespoons olive oil
½ small onion, peeled and chopped
2 cups long-grain rice
5 cups oil, or as needed
½ cup freshly ground black pepper
Thai Peanut Sauce (page 56)

1. Rinse the chicken and pat dry. Use a knife to make cuts in the surface. Place the chicken in a shallow glass dish. Combine ¼ cup coconut milk, fish sauce, 1 teaspoon lime juice, 2 teaspoons brown sugar, and the crushed garlic. Pour the marinade over the chicken. Refrigerate the chicken and marinate overnight. Remove any excess marinade. Cut the chicken into bite-sized cubes.
2. Heat the olive oil in a frying pan over low heat. Add the chopped onion and cook until soft. Add the rice and sauté for 5 minutes until it turns shiny and is heated through.
3. Combine 3 cups coconut milk with 4 teaspoons lime juice and 2 teaspoons brown sugar. Add to the rice. Bring the rice to a boil, uncovered, on medium heat. Cover, turn down the heat, and boil until cooked through, stirring occasionally. Keep the rice warm over low heat.
4. Add the oil to the fondue pot, making sure it is not more than half full. Heat the pot on a stove element over medium-high heat.
5. When the oil is hot, move the fondue pot to the table and set up the burner. Skewer the chicken cubes so that the skewer goes right through the meat. Cook the chicken cubes in the hot oil for 2 to 3 minutes, until they are browned and cooked through. Serve with the freshly ground black pepper and peanut sauce for dipping. Eat with the coconut rice.

Poached Chicken in Wine with Sweet Herbs

*1½ pounds skinless, boneless
   chicken breasts*
*3 portions Sweet Herb Mix
   (page 47)*
*5 cups dry white wine,
   or as needed*

Béarnaise Sauce (page 54)
*Quick and Easy Blender
   Hollandaise Sauce (page 49)*

Serves 4

It's not essential to strain the wine-and-herb mixture through a sieve before cooking, but be sure to remove the bay leaf.

1. Rinse the chicken breasts. Pat dry and cut into thin strips. Refrigerate until needed.
2. Add the Sweet Herb Mix to the wine and leave for 2 hours.
3. Strain the wine through a sieve to remove the herbs. Heat the wine on the stove in a saucepan or directly in the fondue pot. Transfer to the fondue pot if necessary, making sure not to fill the pot more than ⅔ full. Keep the wine simmering throughout the meal.
4. Use a dipping fork or metal skewer with a wooden handle to thread the chicken strips. Cook in the wine for 3 to 4 minutes, until the chicken is cooked through. Serve with the Béarnaise Sauce and Quick and Easy Blender Hollandaise Sauce for dipping. Add other garnishes, side dishes, and condiments as desired.

Cooking Marinated Meat in Oil

Cooking marinated meat in oil can be a bit tricky. Despite your best intentions, you may find oil splattering. If this happens, try using a fondue dipping basket and cooking the meat in batches. While this method isn't as much fun as using individual dipping forks, it's safer for guests since you control the cooking process.

Chicken and Spinach with Tarragon

Serves 4

For added flavor, let the black peppercorns and other seasonings sit in the wine mixture for up to 2 hours before preparing the fondue.

1½ pounds skinless, boneless chicken breasts
1 tablespoon fresh tarragon, chopped
Quick and Easy Blender Hollandaise Sauce (page 49)
6 tablespoons olive oil, divided
2 shallots, peeled and chopped
2 cups dry white wine

2 cups chicken broth
12 black peppercorns
1 teaspoon ground cloves
1 teaspoon celery salt
2 pounds fresh spinach
2 garlic cloves
1 cup Parmesan cheese, shredded

1. Rinse the chicken breasts. Pat dry and cut into thin strips. Refrigerate until needed. Stir the fresh tarragon into the Quick and Easy Blender Hollandaise Sauce and refrigerate until needed.
2. Heat 2 tablespoons olive oil in a medium saucepan. Add the shallots and sauté until tender. Add the wine and chicken broth to the sautéed shallots. Add the black peppercorns, ground cloves, and celery salt. Bring to a boil. Strain the liquid through a fine-mesh sieve.
3. Wash the spinach leaves, dry thoroughly, and coarsely chop. Peel and crush the garlic. Heat the remaining 4 tablespoons olive oil in a frying pan. Add the crushed garlic and cook for about 1 minute. Add the spinach and sauté briefly, tossing the leaves. Serve the spinach on a plate surrounded by the shredded Parmesan cheese.
4. Reheat the strained wine mixture on the stove either in a saucepan or directly in the fondue pot. Transfer to the fondue pot if necessary, move to the table, and set on the burner. Keep the liquid simmering throughout the meal.
5. Use a dipping fork or metal skewer with a wooden handle to thread the chicken strips. Cook in the wine mixture for 3 to 4 minutes, until the chicken is cooked through. Serve with the Quick and Easy Blender Hollandaise Sauce for dipping. Eat with the spinach and cheese. Add other garnishes, side dishes, and condiments as desired.

Coq au Vin Fondue

1½ pounds skinless, boneless
  chicken breasts
2 carrots
10 fresh small mushrooms
2 shallots
1 garlic clove
2 bay leaves
2 sprigs thyme
2 sprigs parsley

1½ tablespoons olive oil
4 cups Burgundy wine, or as
  needed
Light Horseradish Dressing
  (page 49)
Quick Honey Mustard (page 60)
Sour Cream and Mustard Dip
  (page 65)

Serves 4

The name
"coq au vin"
means
"chicken in
wine,"
which
makes this
popular
French dish
perfect for a
Bacchus
fondue.

1. Rinse the chicken breasts. Pat dry and cut into thin strips. Peel the carrots; blanch briefly in boiling water. Drain thoroughly and thinly slice. Wipe the mushrooms with a damp cloth and slice. Peel and chop the shallots. Peel and slice the garlic clove.

2. Gather together the bay leaves, thyme, and parsley in a piece of cheesecloth about 6 inches by 6 inches. Use a piece of string to tie the cheesecloth and attach a cork to the other end of the string. (This makes it easier to remove the herb bouquet from the fondue.)

3. Heat the olive oil in a medium saucepan. Add the shallots and sauté until tender. Add the garlic. Add the Burgundy to the sautéed shallots. Lower in the spice bag. Bring to a boil. Remove the spice bag and transfer the liquid to the fondue pot. Keep the liquid simmering throughout the meal.

4. Use a dipping fork or metal skewer with a wooden handle to thread the chicken strips. Cook in the wine until the chicken is cooked through. Skewer the mushrooms and carrots and cook as desired. Serve with the sauces for dipping.

CHAPTER 6

Pork and Lamb Fondues

Ham, Cheddar, and Walnut Fondue

Serves 4

For a more romantic atmosphere, transfer the cooked cheese to a chocolate fondue pot and serve over an open flame.

1 pound Cheddar cheese
1½ tablespoons cornstarch
1 garlic clove
2 tablespoons butter or margarine
2 tablespoons onion, chopped
½ cup sour cream

1 teaspoon lemon juice
1 cup ham, chopped
2 tablespoons walnuts, chopped
1 French baguette, cut into cubes

1. Finely dice the Cheddar cheese. Toss with the cornstarch and set aside. Smash the garlic, peel, and cut in half.
2. Rub the garlic around the inside of a medium saucepan. Discard. Melt the butter and add the chopped onion. Cook briefly, and stir in the sour cream.
3. Stir in the lemon juice. Add the cheese, a handful at a time. Stir the cheese continually in a sideways figure eight pattern. Wait until the cheese is completely melted before adding more. Don't allow the fondue mixture to boil.
4. After half the cheese has melted, stir in ½ cup of the cooked ham. When the cheese is completely melted, stir in the remainder of the ham. Add the walnuts.
5. Transfer to a fondue pot and set on the burner. Serve with the baguette cubes for dipping.

Make Your Own Marinade

It's easy to create your own marinade recipe. The one essential ingredient in a marinade is an acid. Acids such as wine, lemon juice, and vinegar act to tenderize the meat. Vegetable oil is frequently added to spread the flavor more quickly, but it isn't essential. The remaining ingredients are up to you! Feel free to experiment by adding your favorite herbs, spices, or even peanut butter.

Deep-Fried Wieners

12 wieners
¼ cup cornstarch

4 cups oil, or as needed
Basic Batter (page 79)

Serves 4–6

Serve with
Sweet and
Sour Sauce
(page 70),
Quick Honey
Mustard (page
60), or
Worcestershire
sauce for
dipping.

1. Dust the wieners lightly with cornstarch. Place a skewer or stick through each wiener and place on a serving tray at the table.
2. Add the oil to the fondue pot, making sure it is not more than half full. Heat the pot on a stove element over medium-high heat. When the oil is hot, move the fondue pot to the table and set up the burner.
3. Invite guests to coat the wieners in the batter and cook in the hot oil until the batter turns golden brown. Drain on paper towels if desired.

Hearty Sausage Fondue

10–12 pork sausages
4 cups oil, or as needed
Horseradish Cream (page 60)

Horseradish with Sour Cream
(page 59)

Serves 6

Cooking
sausages in a
fondue pot is
a great way to
add fun to the
evening
family meal.

1. Thaw the sausages if necessary and pat dry. Cut into 2-inch pieces. Add the oil to the fondue pot, making sure it is not more than half full. Heat the pot on a stove element over medium-high heat. When the oil is hot, move the fondue pot to the table and set up the burner.
2. Use dipping forks to spear the sausages. Cook in the hot oil, turning occasionally, until they are browned and cooked through. Drain on paper towels if desired. Serve with the dipping sauces.

Two Pot Sausage Fondue

Serves 4

This recipe combines a standard cheese fondue with an oil-based fondue. Another option is simply to fry the sausages in a skillet, and then serve with the cheese fondue.

8 Italian sausages
¾ pound Gorgonzola cheese
¾ pound mozzarella cheese
1 garlic clove
1¼ cups milk
2 tablespoons butter

2 tablespoons flour
1 tablespoon cornstarch
2 tablespoons cream
1 teaspoon nutmeg
4 cups oil, or as needed

1. Thaw the sausages if necessary and pat dry. Cut into bite-sized pieces and set aside. Finely dice the Gorgonzola and mozzarella cheeses. Smash the garlic, peel, and cut in half.
2. Warm the milk in a small saucepan. In a separate medium saucepan, rub the garlic around the inside and then discard the garlic. Melt the butter in the saucepan with the garlic and stir in the flour. Add 1 cup of the warmed milk. Cook over low heat for about 10 minutes, whisking to form a creamy sauce.
3. Add the cheese to the milk mixture, a handful at a time. Stir the cheese continually in a sideways figure eight pattern. Wait until the cheese is completely melted before adding more. Don't allow the fondue mixture to boil. Add the remaining ¼ cup of milk as needed.
4. When the cheese is melted, dissolve the cornstarch in the cream and add to the fondue, stirring. Turn up the heat until it is just bubbling and starting to thicken. Stir in the nutmeg. Transfer to a fondue pot and set on the burner.
5. Add the oil to a second fondue pot designed for oil cooking, making sure it is not more than half full. Heat the pot on a stove element over medium-high heat.
6. When the oil is hot, move the fondue pot to the table and set up the burner. Use dipping forks to spear the sausage pieces and dip into the hot oil. Cook until browned. Dip the sausages into the cheese fondue.

Tandoori Pork

1 large yellow onion
½ teaspoon paprika
1 cup milk
½ cup cornstarch
1½ pounds pork tenderloin
⅔ cup Instant Tandoori Rub
   (page 77)

1 zucchini
5 cups oil, or as needed
Tempura Batter (page 78)
2 cups soy sauce
1⅓ cups plain yogurt

Serves 4

As an alternative to plain yogurt, feel free to serve guests the yogurt mixture accompanying the Tandoori-Style Chicken Wings (page 98) for dipping.

1. Peel the onion and cut into rings. Toss with the paprika. Soak in the milk for at least 1 hour, making sure all the onion pieces are covered. Drain the onion pieces and dust with the cornstarch.

2. Rub the pork with the Instant Tandoori Rub and cut into cubes. Cut the zucchini into pieces at least ½ inch thick.

3. Add the oil to the fondue pot, making sure it is not more than half full. Heat the pot on a stove element over medium-high heat. When the oil is hot, move the fondue pot to the table and set up the burner. Keep the heat high.

4. Coat the onion rings with the batter and drop the battered onion rings into the oil. Use a dipping basket if necessary. Cook briefly, turning occasionally, until they turn golden brown. Remove and drain on paper towels.

5. Use dipping forks to spear the seasoned pork and the zucchini and cook in the hot oil. Make sure the pork is cooked through. Provide each guest with a small bowl filled with ½ cup soy sauce, and another bowl filled with ⅓ cup yogurt, for dipping.

Reusing Fondue Oil

Some fondues, like Classic Beef Bourguignonne (page 88), can use large quantities of oil. Fortunately, fondue cooking oil can be reused. Just cool, strain if necessary, and refrigerate. Throw out the oil if it begins to smell, darkens in color, or starts smoking when heated.

Pork "Satay" Fondue

Serves 3–4

For extra flavor, reserve the marinade, boil for 5 minutes, and use as a dipping sauce with the shrimp.

12 large shrimp
2 teaspoons salt
1½ pounds pork tenderloin
2 garlic cloves
1 cup coconut milk
2 tablespoons plus 2 teaspoons lime juice

1 tablespoon plus 1 teaspoon red curry paste
3 teaspoons brown sugar
5 cups oil, or as needed
Thai Peanut Sauce (page 56)

1. Peel and devein the shrimp. Dissolve the salt in a bowl filled with 3 cups of warm water. Soak the hrimp in the water for 5 minutes. Drain. Cut the pork into cubes approximately 1 inch thick.
2. Smash, peel, and mince the garlic cloves. Combine the garlic with the coconut milk and lime juice. Stir in the red curry paste and brown sugar.
3. Lay out the pork in a shallow glass dish. Pour just over half of the coconut-milk marinade over the pork cubes. Refrigerate and marinate the pork for 1 hour. Mix the remaining marinade with the shrimp and marinate for 15 minutes. Remove any excess marinade from the pork and shrimp.
4. Add the oil to the fondue pot, making sure it is not more than half full. Heat the pot on a stove element over medium-high heat. When the oil is hot, move the fondue pot to the table and set up the burner. Keep the heat high.
5. Use dipping forks to spear the pork and shrimp. Cook in the hot oil—the shrimp will cook more quickly than the pork will. Serve with the peanut sauce for dipping.

Satay—More Than Asian Shish Kebab

Contrary to popular belief, satay is not merely the Asian version of shish kebab. Shish kebab strives to be a complete "meal on a stick," loaded with bite-sized cubes of meat and garden vegetables such as bell peppers. By contrast, only meat is found on a wooden satay skewer. But that doesn't mean satay tastes bland—fiery red chilies or tart lime juice can lend flavor to the meat.

Bacon and Water Chestnut Appetizer

24 whole water chestnuts,
  fresh or canned
12 slices bacon

4 cups oil for deep-frying,
  or as needed
1 cup white sugar

Yields 24 appetizers

Cooked bacon tastes delicious topped with white sugar. Ketchup and soy sauce can also be served for dipping.

1. If using fresh water chestnuts, peel, rinse, and drain. If using canned water chestnuts, rinse with warm running water and drain thoroughly.
2. Cut the bacon slices in half. Wrap each piece of bacon around a water chestnut, and use a toothpick to secure. Place the water chestnuts on a serving tray.
3. Add the oil to the fondue pot, making sure it is not more than half full. Heat the pot on a stove element over medium-high heat. When the oil is hot, move the fondue pot to the table and set up the burner.
4. Use dipping forks to spear the water chestnuts and cook briefly in the hot oil. Dip the cooked water chestnuts and bacon in the sugar.

Pork Balls in Coconut and Lime

12 ounces ground pork
¼ cup coconut flakes
6 teaspoons lime juice
2 teaspoons fish sauce

3 pineapple chunks, finely
  minced
2 cups coconut milk
½ cup light cream

Serves 4

These can be a little messy, so be sure to provide plenty of napkins! You can also make the pork balls ahead of time and serve them cold with a dipping sauce.

1. In a medium bowl, combine the ground pork with the coconut flakes, lime juice, fish sauce, and minced pineapple. Mix together thoroughly.
2. Use your hands to form the ground pork mixture into 10–12 balls the size of golf balls.
3. Place the coconut milk in the fondue pot and bring to a boil. Turn down to a simmer and add the cream. Place the fondue pot on the table and set up the burner. Keep the liquid simmering while cooking the pork balls.
4. Use dipping forks to skewer the pork balls. Cook in the fondue until the pork is cooked through (about 5 to 7 minutes).

Sweet and Sour Pork Fondue

Serves 4

For an interesting combination of flavors, serve with Oriental Vegetable Salad with Mediterranean Dressing (page 147) and rice or noodles.

1½ pounds pork tenderloin
Sweet and Sour Marinade
  (page 75)
¼ pound baby carrots
2 red bell peppers
2 green bell peppers
2 cups pineapple chunks,
  canned or fresh

1 cup pineapple juice
½ cup red wine vinegar
6 tablespoons sugar
6 tablespoons tomato paste
5 cups oil, or as needed
¾ cup firmly packed brown
  sugar

1. Cut the pork into bite-sized cubes. Toss with the marinade. Place in a shallow glass dish, refrigerate, and marinate for 1 hour.
2. Blanch the carrots and bell peppers briefly in boiling water. Drain thoroughly. Cut the peppers in half, remove the seeds, and cut into bite-sized cubes. Cut the baby carrots in half. If using canned pineapple chunks, drain and dry thoroughly.
3. Warm the pineapple juice and red wine vinegar in a small saucepan on low heat. Add the sugar, stirring to dissolve. Add the tomato paste and bring to a boil, stirring to make a smooth sauce. Add the baby carrots to the sauce. Keep warm on low heat. (The peppers can be added to the sauce or cooked in the oil.)
4. Add the oil to the fondue pot, making sure it is not more than half full. Heat the pot on a stove element over medium-high heat. When the oil is hot, move the fondue pot to the table and set up the burner. Keep the heat high.
5. Use dipping forks to spear and cook the pork cubes until lightly browned. Spear the pineapple slices and cook until lightly browned. Drain on paper towels if desired. Dip the pork into the sweet and sour sauce and the pineapple chunks into the brown sugar.

Sausages in Broth

9 ounces cooked summer
   sausage
9 ounces cooked knockwurst
9 ounces cooked bratwurst
1 pound asparagus spears
½ small yellow onion

2 tablespoons olive oil
5 cups Vegetable Broth (page
   83), or as needed
Lemony Horseradish (page 57)
Horseradish Cream (page 60)

Serves 4

Fresh
uncooked
sausages can
also be used
in this recipe.
Cook the
sausages in
boiling water
for 5 minutes
before using.

1. Cut the summer sausage in half and cut each half into 3 wedges. Cut the knockwurst and bratwurst into pieces about 2 inches thick. Blanch the asparagus briefly in boiling water, and drain thoroughly. Cut the asparagus into 2-inch pieces. Peel and chop the onion.
2. Heat the olive oil in a medium saucepan on low heat. Add the chopped onion and sauté until the onion is soft and translucent.
3. Add the broth to the cooked onion and bring to a boil. Transfer enough broth to fill the fondue pot about ⅔ full. Set the fondue pot on the burner, with enough heat to keep the broth simmering throughout the meal. (Keep the remaining broth warm on the stove to use as needed.)
4. Use dipping forks to spear the sausages and asparagus and cook in the hot broth. Serve with the horseradish sauces for dipping. Ladle out the cooked onion and serve with the sausages.

Dips and Sauces—the Main Event

Dips, sauces, and other seasonings are indispensable to oil-based fondues such as Mixed Meat Hot Pot (page 168) and Classic Beef Bourguignonne (page 88). When choosing dips, aim for contrast in color, texture, and taste. For example, when serving Chinese hot pot, make sure guests have options besides fiery hot mustard. In general, count on serving at least three dipping sauces with each fondue.

Ham Roll-Ups

Serves 4

For an interesting variety of hors d'oeuvres, serve with Deep-Fried Cheese (page 42) and Fried Three Mushrooms (page 161).

8 ounces cream cheese
1 green onion, diced
1 teaspoon Worcestershire sauce
8 ounces cooked ham, sliced
2 eggs
1 tablespoon milk
$1/4$ teaspoon black pepper
4 cups oil, or as needed
Quick and Easy Batter (page 80)
Quick Honey Mustard (page 60)

1. Combine the cream cheese with diced green onion and Worcestershire sauce. Mix together thoroughly and refrigerate until needed.
2. Cut each slice of ham into strips approximately 1 inch thick. Roll up the slices. If necessary, secure with a toothpick.
3. Beat the eggs with the milk and black pepper. Make sure the egg is beaten thoroughly.
4. Add the oil to the fondue pot, making sure it is not more than half full. Heat the pot on a stove element over medium-high heat. When the oil is hot, move the fondue pot to the table and set up the burner. Keep the heat high.
5. Use dipping forks to spear the rolled-up ham slices, removing the toothpicks if using. Dip into the egg wash, and then coat with the batter. Cook the rolled-up ham in the hot oil until the batter is browned. Serve with the honey mustard and cream cheese mixture for dipping.

Cocktail Wieners

24 cocktail wieners
Sweet and Sour Sauce with
    Tomato Paste (page 70)

4 cups chicken broth
Seafood Cocktail Sauce
    (page 46)

Serves 6

Cocktail
wieners make
a quick
fondue on
nights you
don't feel like
marinating
meat or
slicing
vegetables.

1. Cut each cocktail wiener in half and set aside.
2. Add the orange marmalade to the Sweet and Sour Sauce with Tomato Paste. Keep warm over low heat.
3. Heat the broth on the stove and bring to a boil. Transfer enough broth to fill the fondue pot about ⅔ full. Set the fondue pot on the burner, with enough heat to keep the broth simmering throughout the meal. (Keep the remaining broth warm on the stove to use as needed.)
4. Use dipping forks to spear the cocktail wieners and cook in the hot broth. Serve with the sauces for dipping.

Lamb Kebabs with Sun-Dried Tomatoes

2 cups oil-packed sun-dried
    tomatoes
1¾ pounds lean lamb
¼ cup fresh mint leaves
4 cups olive oil, or as needed

1½ cups Yogurt and Dill
    Dressing (page 63)
Bruschetta with Roma
    Tomatoes (page 246)

Serves 4

Serve with
Yogurt and
Dill Dressing
for dipping
and eat with
the
bruschetta
and the sun-
dried toma-
toes.

1. Drain the tomatoes and chop. Cut the lamb into bite-sized cubes. Place the lamb on a serving platter surrounded by the mint leaves.
2. Add the oil to the fondue pot, making sure it is not more than half full. Heat the pot on a stove element over medium-high heat. When the oil is hot, move the fondue pot to the table and set up the burner. Keep the heat high. Use dipping forks to spear the lamb cubes. Cook in the hot oil until browned.

Indian Curried Lamb

Serves 4

For best results, make the spiced yogurt dip at least 1 day ahead of time, to allow the flavors to blend.

2 tablespoons cardamom seeds
2 teaspoons ground coriander
4 teaspoons ground cumin, divided
2 teaspoons ground cinnamon
1¼ cups plain yogurt, divided
¼ cup sour cream
3 teaspoons curry powder
1 teaspoon freshly cracked black pepper
1 teaspoon turmeric
1½ pounds lean lamb
4 potatoes
1 red bell pepper
1 green bell pepper
1 tomato
1 tablespoon lemon juice
5 cups oil, or as needed

1. Crush the cardamom seeds with a mortar and pestle. Blend together the cardamom, ground coriander, 1 teaspoon ground cumin, and ground cinnamon. Combine ¼ cup of the yogurt with the sour cream. Add 2 teaspoons of the spice mixture to the yogurt and sour cream. Store the remainder of the spice mixture in a sealed container to use another time. Refrigerate the yogurt dressing until needed.

2. Blend together the curry powder, 3 teaspoons ground cumin, black pepper, and turmeric. Rub into the lamb. Cut the lamb into bite-sized cubes. Boil the potatoes on medium-low heat for about 15 minutes, until they can be pierced with a fork but are not too soft.

3. Wash the red and green peppers, remove the seeds, and cut into cubes. Wash and chop the tomato. Stir the lemon juice into the remaining 1 cup of yogurt. Combine the yogurt with the peppers and chopped tomato and refrigerate until ready to serve.

4. Add the oil to the fondue pot, making sure it is not more than half full. Heat the pot on a stove element over medium-high heat. When the oil is hot, move the fondue pot to the table and set up the burner. Keep the heat high.

5. Use dipping forks to spear the lamb cubes. Cook in the hot oil until browned. Serve with the spiced yogurt mixture for dipping. Eat with the boiled potatoes and the pepper, tomato, and yogurt salad.

Fish and Shellfish Fondues

Lemony Ginger Cod

Serves 4

This fish dish goes well with Yogurt and Dill Dressing (page 63), Quick and Easy Tartar Sauce (page 57), and Seafood Cocktail Sauce (page 46).

1½ pounds fresh or frozen cod fillets
¾ cup Lemony Ginger Marinade (page 73)

4 cups oil, or as needed
Parsley for garnish

1. Rinse the cod, pat dry, and cut into cubes at least 1 inch thick. Marinate for 30 minutes in the Lemony Ginger Marinade.
2. Add the oil to the fondue pot, making sure it is not more than half full. Heat the pot on a stove element over medium-high heat. When the oil is hot, move the fondue pot to the table and set up the burner.
3. Spear the fish cubes with a dipping fork and cook in the hot oil until browned. Garnish with parsley. Serve with lemon juice or homemade dipping sauces as desired.

Fish Bathed in Broth

Serves 4–6

For extra flavor, add the shrimp shells while warming the broth. Remove before serving.

20 medium shrimp
2 teaspoons salt
1 pound fish fillets (such as cod, sole, or flounder)

Fish Broth (page 85)
Quick and Easy Tartar Sauce (page 57)

1. Peel and devein the shrimp, leaving the tail on. Fill a bowl with 3 cups of warm water, add the salt, and stir until it dissolves. Add the shrimp and leave in the warm water for 10 minutes. Rinse in cold water, drain, and pat dry with paper towels. Cut the fish fillets into bite-sized pieces.
2. Heat the broth on the stove and bring to a boil. Bring to the table and set up the burner. Be sure to keep the broth at a boil throughout the meal. Use a dipping fork to spear the shrimp and fish. Cook the fish and shrimp in the hot broth. Serve with the tartar sauce for dipping.

Bacon-Wrapped Shrimp

18 large raw tiger shrimp,
   peeled and deveined, tails on
6 slices raw bacon
⅓ cup fresh baby dill

4 cups oil, or as needed
¼ cup lemon juice
¼ cup sugar

Serves 4–6

Holding a fondue party for a crowd? Serve this tasty appetizer with Angels on Horseback (page 130) and Bacon and Water Chestnut Appetizer (page 119).

1. Rinse the shrimp in cold water, drain thoroughly, and pat dry.
2. Remove any excess fat off the bacon and cut each piece into thirds. Take about ¼ teaspoon of the baby dill and place on the shrimp. Wrap a piece of bacon around the shrimp 2 to 3 times. Continue with the remainder of the shrimp. Place on a serving platter on the table.
3. Add the oil to the fondue pot, making sure it is not more than half full. Heat the pot on a stove element over medium-high heat. When the oil is hot, move the fondue pot to the table and set up the burner.
4. Use dipping forks to spear the shrimp. Cook in the hot oil for about 30 seconds. Serve with the remaining dill, lemon juice, and sugar for dipping.

How to Devein Shrimp

The purpose of deveining a shrimp is to remove the gray intestinal tract running down its back. The tract is frequently filled with dirt or sand, which can add an unpleasant gritty taste. To devein, peel the shrimp and cut a slit down the center of its back. Pull out the vein. Use the same procedure to devein prawns.

Mediterranean Salmon with Pesto

Serves 6

Serve with Roasted Red Peppers (page 150) and Italian bread brushed with olive oil for a complete Mediterranean meal.

1½ pounds fresh salmon
    steaks
4 cups olive oil, or as needed
Italian Pesto with Basil and
    Pine Nuts (page 61)

Cilantro and Mint Dressing
    (page 62)
1 jar capers

1. Rinse the salmon, pat dry, and cut into cubes at least 1 inch thick.
2. Add the oil to the fondue pot, making sure it is not more than half full. Heat the pot on a stove element over medium-high heat. When the oil is hot, move the fondue pot to the table and set up the burner.
3. Spear the salmon cubes with a dipping fork and cook briefly until browned all over. Serve with the pesto and dressing for dippers, and the capers as a garnish.

Shrimp with Peppercorn Dip

Serves 4–6

Did you know? Shrimp is the most popular shellfish in the United States.

24 large raw shrimp
2 tablespoons black peppercorns
2 tablespoons white peppercorns

4 cups oil, or as needed
¼ cup freshly squeezed lemon
    juice

1. Peel the shrimp, including the tails, and devein. Rinse the shrimp in cold water, drain thoroughly, and pat dry.
2. Use a pepper grinder to grind the black and white peppercorns. Combine in a small serving bowl. Place the shrimp on a large serving platter.
3. Add the oil to the fondue pot, making sure it is not more than half full. Heat the pot on a stove element over medium-high heat. When the oil is hot, move the fondue pot to the table and set up the burner.

Teriyaki Marinated Salmon

¾ cup Quick and Easy Teriyaki
    Marinade (page 74)
Yogurt and Dill Dressing
    (page 63)
Speedy Garlic Mayonnaise
    (page 65)
1½ pounds fresh salmon
    steaks

1 cup baby carrots
8 ounces sugar snap peas
8 ounces fresh small mush-
    rooms
4 cups oil, or as needed

Serves 4

If substi-
tuting reg-
ular carrots
for baby car-
rots, be sure
to blanch
them before
using in the
fondue.

1. Prepare the marinade, the yogurt dressing, and the mayonnaise at least 1 hour ahead of time. Refrigerate the dressing and mayonnaise until ready to serve.
2. Rinse the salmon, pat dry, and cut into cubes at least 1 inch thick. Marinate the salmon for 1 hour.
3. Wash the vegetables and drain thoroughly. Blanch the peas briefly in boiling water and then plunge into ice water and drain thoroughly. Cut the mushrooms into 2 to 3 slices, but don't slice too thinly.
4. Add the oil to the fondue pot, making sure it is not more than half full. Heat the pot on a stove element over medium-high heat. When the oil is hot, move the fondue pot to the table and set up the burner.
5. Spear the salmon pieces with a dipping fork and cook briefly in the hot oil, turning occasionally, until browned all over (less than 1 minute). Cook the mushrooms and carrots briefly. Dip the carrots and sugar snap peas into the yogurt dressing or the mayonnaise. The teriyaki salmon and mushrooms can be dipped or enjoyed as is.

Angels on Horseback

Serves 6

36 canned Pacific oysters
12 slices raw bacon
6 eggs

1 cup bread crumbs
4½ cups oil, or as needed

For a fancier presentation, use fresh shucked oysters and serve on the half shell. Adjust the amount of bacon and bread crumbs as necessary.

1. Dry the canned oysters thoroughly. Cut any excess fat off the bacon and cut each piece into thirds. Wrap a piece of bacon around each oyster and secure with a toothpick.
2. Place each egg in a small bowl and beat lightly. Place the bacon-wrapped oysters on a serving plate and give each guest a bowl with a beaten egg. Place the bread crumbs in a bowl beside the oysters.
3. Add the oil to the fondue pot, making sure it is not more than half full. Heat the pot on a stove element over medium-high heat. When the oil is hot, move the fondue pot to the table and set up the burner.
4. Use dipping forks to spear the oysters. Invite guests to dip the oyster into the beaten egg and then into the bread-crumb coating. Cook the oysters until the bread crumbs turn a golden brown (about 1 minute).

Storing Bivalves

Both oysters and mussels are live animals and need air to breathe. Storing them in a sealed plastic bag or airtight container will lead to asphyxiation. Instead, cover the oysters and mussels with a damp cloth or paper towels and keep refrigerated. Stored in this manner, they should last for up to 2 days.

Easy Seafood in Broth Dinner

2 cups frozen broccoli and
   cauliflower
20 frozen breaded shrimp

10 frozen fish sticks
4 cups chicken broth

Serves 4–6

1. Thaw the frozen broccoli and cauliflower and pat dry. Place the frozen seafood and vegetables on a large platter.
2. Heat the chicken broth in a fondue pot over a stove element. Bring to a boil, then move the fondue pot to the table and set up the burner. Keep the broth simmering throughout the meal. Use a dipping fork to spear the fish and vegetables and cook in the hot broth.

Serve with
Quick and
Easy Tartar
Sauce (page
57), lemon
juice, and
ketchup
for dipping.

Tempura Shrimp

¾ pound (15–20) large shrimp
¼ cup flour
1 lemon

Tempura Batter (page 78)
4 cups oil, or as needed

Serves 4

1. Peel and devein the shrimp, leaving the tail on. Rinse the shrimp in cold water and pat dry with paper towels.
2. Lightly dust the shrimp with the flour and set on a serving plate. Cut the lemon into wedges. Garnish the shrimp with the lemon wedges. Place the batter in a separate bowl.
3. Add the oil to the fondue pot, making sure it is not more than half full. Heat the pot on a stove element over medium-high heat. When the oil is hot, move the fondue pot to the table and set up the burner. Use dipping forks to spear the shrimp and dip into the batter. Cook in the hot oil until golden brown. Drain on paper towels if desired.

Serve with
freshly
ground black
pepper and
Lemon-Soy
Dressing
(page 68) or
Yogurt and
Dill Dressing
(page 63).

Elegant Butterflied Shrimp in Liqueur

Serves 4–6

If you find the orange liqueur flavor too strong, replace ½ cup of liqueur with ½ cup of orange juice.

4 garlic cloves

1 pound fresh asparagus spears

24 large raw shrimp, peeled and deveined, tails on

2 tablespoons butter

1 cup cream

1 cup orange liqueur (such as Grand Marnier)

½ teaspoon nutmeg

½ cup fresh baby dill

¼ cup cayenne pepper

1. Smash and peel the garlic. Trim the ends off the asparagus, cook in boiling salted water until tender, and drain thoroughly. Cut into 2-inch pieces.
2. Rinse the shrimp in cold water and pat dry with paper towels. To butterfly the shrimp, make an incision lengthwise down the back. Cut down as deeply as possible without cutting right through the shrimp. Halfway down the back, make two parallel cuts on the left and right of the incision. Flatten down the four quarters as much as possible. Place the butterflied shrimp on a large serving platter with the asparagus pieces.
3. In a medium saucepan, melt the butter on low heat. Add the garlic and cook on low heat in the melting butter for 2 to 3 minutes. Add the cream. Carefully add the orange liqueur to the warmed cream. Stir in the nutmeg, baby dill, and the cayenne pepper.
4. Transfer the dish to a fondue pot and set on the burner at the table. Use dipping forks to spear the shrimp and cook in the fondue until they change color. Eat with the asparagus (if desired, the asparagus can be dipped briefly into the fondue).

Fish in White Sauce

2 pounds fresh fish fillets
  (such as sole)
Lemony Ginger Marinade
  (page 73)

1⅓ cups White Sauce for
  Seafood (page 64)
4 cups oil, or as needed

Serves 6–8

Serve with Fried Mushrooms (page 148), Milk Bathed Onion Rings (page 154), or Roasted Red Peppers (page 150) for a complete meal.

1. Pat the fish dry and cut into bite-sized cubes. Place the fish in a shallow glass dish. Pour the marinade over and marinate the fish for 15 minutes. Remove any excess marinade. Prepare the white sauce and keep warm over low heat.
2. Add the oil to the fondue pot, making sure it is not more than half full. Heat the pot on a stove element over medium-high heat. When the oil is hot, move the fondue pot to the table and set up the burner.
3. Use dipping forks to spear the fish cubes and cook very briefly (about 15 seconds) in the hot oil. Dip into the white sauce.

Tempura Oysters

12 fresh oysters
Tempura Batter (page 78)

4 cups oil, or as needed

Serves 3–4

This recipe doesn't really need a dipping sauce. However, if you want to serve one, lemon or lime juice, teriyaki sauce, and soy sauce would all be good choices.

1. Shuck the oysters, rinse in warm water, and drain thoroughly. Prepare the batter.
2. Add the oil to the fondue pot, making sure it is not more than half full. Heat the pot on a stove element over medium-high heat. When the oil is hot, move the fondue pot to the table and set up the burner. Use dipping forks to spear the oysters and dip into the batter. Cook in the hot oil until golden brown. Drain on paper towels if desired.

Chinese-Style Butterfly Shrimp

Serves 4–6

Feel free to use Chinese rice wine or dry sherry in place of the cooking wine if you have it.

1 pound large shrimp
2 teaspoons Chinese cooking wine
½ teaspoon sugar
2 eggs
1 teaspoon five-spice powder

⅔ cup bread crumbs
4 cups oil, or as needed
½ teaspoon freshly ground black pepper
½ teaspoon freshly ground white pepper

1. Peel the shrimp but leave the tail on. Cut a slit along the back, being careful not to cut through. Open the two cut halves to form a butterfly shape. If there is a black sand vein, remove it.
2. Rinse the shrimp in cold water and pat dry. Marinate in the cooking wine and sugar for 15 minutes.
3. Lightly beat the eggs. In a separate bowl, mix the five-spice powder with the bread crumbs.
4. Add the oil to the fondue pot, making sure it is not more than half full. Heat the pot on a stove element over medium-high heat.
5. When the oil is hot, move the fondue pot to the table and set up the burner. Grab the shrimp by the tail and dip into the egg, then coat with the bread crumbs. Spear the shrimp with the dipping fork and cook in the hot oil until golden brown. Drain on paper towels if desired. Dip lightly into the black or white pepper.

Tiger Shrimp

Found in Asia, tiger shrimp take their name from the distinctive black and gray stripes running across their back. Tiger shrimp have a milder flavor than pink or brown shrimp do. For best results, use with highly seasoned dishes such as Chinese-Style Butterfly Shrimp.

Breaded Red Snapper

8 slices fresh bread (to make
  2 cups crumbs)
4 tablespoons fresh baby dill
  leaves, chopped
⅛ teaspoon each salt and
  pepper
1 pound fresh red snapper fillets
¼ cup Quick and Easy Teriyaki
  Marinade (page 74)

2 eggs
½ medium yellow onion
4½ cups oil, or as needed
Seafood Cocktail Sauce
  (page 46)
Quick and Easy Tartar Sauce
  (page 57)

Serves 4

Deep-frying
in bread
crumbs
seals in the
juices of the
red snapper,
and gives it
a crispy
coating.
Enjoy with
or without
the dipping
sauces.

1. Cut the crusts off the bread and process in the food processor. Add the dill leaves and salt and pepper and process again.
2. Pat the red snapper fillets dry and cut into bite-sized cubes. Place the fish in a shallow glass dish. Pour the marinade over and marinate the fish for 15 minutes. Remove any excess marinade.
3. Lightly beat the eggs and place in a small bowl at the table, alongside the bread crumbs. Peel and chop the onion.
4. Add the oil to the fondue pot, making sure it is not more than half full. Heat the pot on a stove element over medium-high heat. When the oil is hot, move the fondue pot to the table and set up the burner.
5. Place the chopped onion in a dipping basket in the oil. Fry briefly and then remove. Use dipping forks to spear the fish cubes. Dip into the egg wash and coat with the bread crumbs. Fry in the hot oil until the bread crumbs turn golden brown (about 30 seconds). Dip into the cocktail or tartar sauce. Eat with the fried onion.

Nutritious Fish Facts

Nothing beats fish for providing an excellent source of protein and vitamins. Light-fleshed fish, such as sole and cod, is both high in protein and low in fat. Dark-fleshed fish such as swordfish is an excellent source of fatty acids such as omega-3. Besides promoting brain function, fatty acids are believed to reduce the risk of heart attack.

Le Grand Aioli

Serves 4–6

This French dish featuring Aioli garlic sauce is traditionally served on special occasions such as a family picnic or New Year's Eve.

1 pound salted cod
4 medium beets
4 red-skinned potatoes
1 cup baby carrots

1 pound green beans
1 pound mussels
8 hard-boiled eggs
Aioli (page 48)

1. The day before serving the meal, place the salted cod in cold water. Soak for 24 hours, changing the water several times.
2. One hour before the meal is to be served, preheat the oven to 350°F. Wrap the beets in foil and bake for 1 hour, or until the beets are tender.
3. Blanch the remaining vegetables in boiling salted water. Begin with the potatoes. When they are nearly tender, add the carrots and green beans. Peel and julienne the carrots. Cut the potatoes into bite-sized chunks.
4. Poach the cod in boiling water for 15 minutes. Drain thoroughly and break into pieces. Rinse the mussels under cold water, scrubbing the shells with a stiff brush. Poach in boiling water for 4 to 5 minutes. Drain thoroughly. Peel the hard-boiled eggs and cut into halves.
5. To serve, place the Aioli in a cheese fondue serving dish. Arrange the vegetables on a serving platter. Place the hard-boiled eggs on top. Serve the cod and mussels on another platter. Use dipping forks to spear the vegetables and seafood and dip into the aioli.

Aioli Origins

Aioli is believed to have originated in the French region of Provence, where a lack of grazing land for cows meant that residents had to find an alternative to butter. The word aioli is a combination of the French words for garlic and oil. Like mayonnaise, aioli is made by whisking oil with egg yolks until the mixture emulsifies. Aromatic garlic adds a distinctive taste.

Poached Mussels and Prawns in Wine

12 mussels
2 teaspoons salt
12 prawns, peeled and
   deveined
2 garlic cloves
1/4 yellow onion
2 tablespoons olive oil
1 cup dry white wine
1 cup clam juice

1/4 cup cream
1/4 teaspoon pepper
2 tablespoons fresh parsley,
   chopped
Quick and Easy Blender
   Hollandaise Sauce (page 49)
Seafood Cocktail Sauce
   (page 46)

Serves 4

You could also cook the mussels at the table with the shrimp—keep the wine mixture boiling, and not just simmering, while the mussels cook, and double the amount of broth.

1. Under cold running water, scrub the mussels with a stiff brush to remove any dirt. Soak the mussels in cold water for 5 minutes. Rinse and repeat. Steam the mussels in boiling water for 5 minutes until they open. Rinse and remove from the shells. Throw out any mussels that don't open. Dissolve the salt in 3 cups of warm water. Rinse the prawns in the warm water for 5 minutes and pat dry.
2. Smash the garlic cloves, peel, and chop. Peel and chop the onion. Heat the olive oil on low heat in a fondue pot or a medium saucepan. Add the onion and cook briefly. Add the chopped garlic cloves and cook on low heat until the onion is soft.
3. Turn up the heat to medium-low and add the wine. Warm briefly and add the clam juice. Add the cream. Stir in the pepper and chopped parsley.
4. Transfer the broth to the fondue pot if necessary; set the fondue pot on the table and set up the burner. Place the mussels and prawns on a serving platter. Use dipping forks to spear the seafood and cook in the hot broth. Serve with the sauces for dipping.

Five Flavor Fish Stew

¾ *pound large shrimp*
1 *pound light fish fillets*
   (such as cod)
4 *large white potatoes*
¾ *pound asparagus spears*
2 *celery stalks*
1 *garlic clove*

1 *shallot*
2 *tablespoons olive oil*
1 *cup white wine*
4 *cups Fish Broth (page 85)*
Speedy Garlic Mayonnaise
   (page 65)
½ *cup five-spice powder*

1. Peel and devein the shrimp, leaving the tails on. Rinse the shrimp in cold water, drain, and pat dry. Rinse the fish, pat dry, and cut into bite-sized pieces.
2. Cook the potatoes in boiling water until they can be pierced easily with a fork but are not overly tender. Cool and cut into chunks. Blanch the asparagus spears briefly in boiling water. Drain thoroughly. Cut the spears into 1-inch pieces. Cut the celery stalks diagonally into 1-inch slices. Smash, peel, and chop the garlic clove. Chop the shallot.
3. Heat the olive oil on low heat in a fondue pot or a medium saucepan. Add the shallot and cook briefly on low heat. Add the garlic clove. Turn up the heat to medium-low and add the wine and the broth. Bring to a boil. Transfer the broth to the fondue pot if necessary; set the fondue pot on the table and set up the burner. Set the temperature high enough to keep the broth simmering throughout the meal.
4. Place the shrimp, fish, potatoes, celery, and asparagus on serving platters. Use dipping forks to spear the seafood and asparagus and dip into the hot broth. (The potatoes and celery can be dipped into the broth or eaten as is.) Serve with the mayonnaise and five-spice powder for dipping.

Five-Spice Powder

Intriguing five-spice powder encompasses all five flavors: sweet, sour, bitter, salty, and pungent. The secret ingredients are fennel, cloves, cinnamon, star anise, and Szechwan peppercorns.

Deep-Fried Mussels

1 pound mussels (about 16)
$\frac{1}{3}$ cup flour
Tempura Batter (page 78)
4 cups oil, or as needed

Seafood Cocktail Sauce
 (page 46)
Lemon-Soy Dressing (page 68)

Frying bat-
tered mus-
sels provides
a cheaper
alternative to
oysters when
you want to
add a bit of
protein to a
tempura veg-
etable dish.

1. Under cold running water, scrub the mussels with a stiff brush to remove any dirt. Soak the mussels in cold water for 5 minutes. Rinse and repeat. Steam the mussels in boiling water for 5 minutes until they open. Rinse and remove from the shells. Throw out any mussels that don't open.
2. Dry the mussels thoroughly. Lightly dust with flour and set on a serving platter. Prepare the batter.
3. Add the oil to the fondue pot, making sure it is not more than half full. Heat the pot on a stove element over medium-high heat. When the oil is hot, move the fondue pot to the table and set up the burner. Keep the oil hot throughout the meal.
4. Spear the mussels with a skewer or dipping fork and coat with the batter. Cook in the hot oil until the batter turns golden brown. Serve with the sauces for dipping.

Safe Cooking with Mussels

Live animals such as mussels and oysters can pick up bacteria. For safety's sake, use fresh mussels within 2 days. Be sure to check mussels for freshness: tap shells that are slightly opened, and throw the mussels out if the shells don't close. Boil or steam mussels for about 5 minutes, and throw out any shells that don't open.

Cod in Herbed Batter

Serves 4–6

This recipe is also good with haddock, flounder, and other firm, white-fleshed fish.

2 pounds frozen cod fillets
2 zucchini
2 tomatoes
1 fresh lemon
1 16-ounce can artichokes
2 eggs
1 teaspoon salt
1 teaspoon pepper

5 cups oil, or as needed
Herbed Seafood Batter
   (page 80)
Seafood Cocktail Sauce
   (page 46)
Quick and Easy Tartar Sauce
   (page 57)
Lemon-Soy Dressing (page 68)

1. Thaw the cod fillets, dry, and cut into bite-sized pieces. Wash the zucchini, peel, and slice diagonally. Wash the tomatoes. Cut the tomatoes and lemon into wedges. Drain the artichokes and dry.
2. Lightly beat the eggs. Stir in the salt and pepper.
3. Add the oil to the fondue pot, making sure it is not more than half full. Heat the pot on a stove element over medium-high heat. When the oil is hot, move the fondue pot to the table and set up the burner. Keep the oil hot throughout the meal.
4. Use a wooden skewer or dipping fork to spear the fish pieces. Dip into the beaten egg and coat with the batter. Cook in the hot oil until the batter turns golden brown. Spear the artichokes and cook briefly. Serve with the lemon wedges and the sauces for dipping. Eat with the tomatoes and zucchini.

Oil Temperatures

The oil temperature for cooking fondue should be between 350°F and 375°F. The easiest way to measure the temperature is to use a deep-fry thermometer with a clamp. Simply clamp the thermometer to the side of the fondue pot. Besides knowing when the oil is hot enough to use, the thermometer will tell you if the temperature drops too low once the fondue pot is on the table.

Fish and Chips

4 large potatoes
1½ pounds frozen fish sticks
4½ cups oil, or as needed

Seafood Cocktail Sauce
    (page 46)
Quick and Easy Tartar Sauce
    (page 57)

Serves 6

Don't have
time to pre-
pare a dip-
ping sauce?
Serve this
recipe with
all the stan-
dard fish-
and-chip
condiments,
including
ketchup,
lemon juice,
and salt.

1. Boil the potatoes for about 15 minutes on medium-low heat, until they
   can be pierced with a fork but are not too soft. Drain thoroughly, and
   cut lengthwise into pieces approximately ¾ inch thick. Place the potatoes and fish sticks on a serving platter.
2. Add the oil to the fondue pot, making sure it is not more than half full.
   Heat the pot on a stove element over medium-high heat. When the oil
   is hot, move the fondue pot to the table and set up the burner.
3. On a skewer, place 2 fish sticks and 2 potato slices, alternating. Lay
   the skewer crosswise in the hot oil so that both the fish sticks and
   the potatoes cook evenly. If desired, drain on paper towels after
   cooking. Serve with the sauces for dipping.

What Is Flash Freezing?

*Flash freezing is a process whereby fishermen can freeze fish within hours of
catching them at sea. Taking mere seconds, flash freezing freezes the water
inside the tissues of the fish, preserving its flavor. While fresh fish is normally
superior to frozen, flash-frozen fish will have a better flavor than fresh fish that
is several days old by the time it reaches the market.*

Butterfly Prawns Dipped in Lemon Pepper

Serves 4–6

Lemon pepper combines tart lemon with black pepper, garlic, and other seasonings. Use to enhance the taste of seafood in cooking.

2 garlic cloves
2 lemons
24 large prawns, raw or
    cooked

4 cups oil, or as needed
3 tablespoons lemon pepper

1. Smash and peel the garlic cloves. Cut the lemons into wedges.
2. Peel the prawns but leave the tail on. Cut a slit along the back, being careful not to cut through. Open the two cut halves to form a butterfly shape. If there is a black sand vein, remove it. Rinse the prawns in cold water and pat dry.
3. Add the oil to the fondue pot, making sure it is not more than half full. Heat the pot on a stove element over medium-high heat. When the oil is hot, add the garlic cloves. Brown and then remove them from the pot. Move the fondue pot to the table and set up the burner.
4. Place the butterflied prawns on a serving plate, with the lemon wedges as a garnish. Use dipping forks to spear the prawns and cook in the hot oil until golden brown. Drain on paper towels if desired. Dip into the lemon pepper.

Bread Cubes in Oil Fondues

Bread does double duty in an oil fondue. First, adding a bread cube to the heating oil will tell you when it's ready to use. Hot oil will sizzle all around the cube. At the table, adding a bread cube to the fondue pot helps prevent oil splatters: The bread absorbs moisture coming from excess marinade or meat or vegetables that are not thoroughly dry.

Teriyaki Fish Fry

1 pound fresh red snapper
  fillets
¾ pound fresh flounder fillets
2 portions Quick and Easy
  Teriyaki Marinade (page 74)
6 potatoes
2 green bell peppers
1 red onion

2 shallots
3 tablespoons olive oil
2 fresh lemons
4½ cups oil, or as needed
Seafood Cocktail Sauce
  (page 46)
Homemade Tartar Sauce
  (page 55)

Serves 4

Teriyaki
marinade
doubles as a
dipping
sauce in
this recipe.
Quick and
Easy Tartar
Sauce (page
57) can be
used in
place of the
homemade
version.

1. Pat the fish fillets dry and cut into pieces roughly 2 inches long
   and 1 inch wide. Place the fish in shallow glass dishes, keeping the
   snapper and flounder separate. Set 1 portion of the Quick and Easy
   Teriyaki Marinade aside to serve as a dipping sauce. Pour just over
   half of the remaining portion of the marinade over the red snapper,
   and the rest over the flounder. Marinate the fish for 15 minutes.
   Remove any excess marinade.
2. Boil the potatoes on medium-low heat for about 15 minutes, until they
   can be pierced with a fork but are not too soft. Drain thoroughly.
   Wash the green peppers, drain thoroughly, and cut into bite-sized
   cubes. Peel and chop the onion and shallots.
3. Heat the olive oil in a frying pan. Sauté the onion and shallots until
   soft. Keep warm. Cut the lemons into wedges.
4. Add the oil to the fondue pot, making sure it is not more than half
   full. Heat the pot on a stove element over medium-high heat. When
   the oil is hot, move the fondue pot to the table and set up the
   burner. Keep the oil hot throughout the meal.
5. Spear the fish on wooden skewers, with the ends sticking through.
   Cook the fish and the green bell peppers briefly in the hot oil. Serve
   with the lemon wedges and the sauces and teriyaki marinade for dipping. Eat with the potatoes and sautéed onion and shallots.

CHAPTER 8
Vegetable Fondues and Side Dishes

Cheesy Tomato Fondue

Serves 6

Feel free to substitute fresh or dried basil and tarragon leaves for the thyme and oregano.

½ pound Swiss Emmenthal cheese
½ pound Gruyère cheese
4 medium tomatoes
½ teaspoon thyme
¼ teaspoon oregano
Salt and pepper to taste

1 garlic clove, smashed, peeled, and cut in half
1 cup dry white wine
2 teaspoons lemon juice
1½ tablespoons cornstarch
2 tablespoons water
Bruschetta Fondue Cubes with Vegetables (page 247)

1. Preheat the oven to 350°F. Finely dice the cheese. Wash the tomatoes, dry, and cut off the stems. Peel and cut each tomato into 8 equal slices.
2. Mix the tomato slices with the thyme, oregano, and salt and pepper. Lay the slices flat on a baking tray and bake for approximately 25 minutes, making sure that the bottoms of the tomatoes don't burn.
3. While the tomatoes are baking, prepare the cheese fondue. Rub the garlic around the inside of a medium saucepan. Discard. Add the wine to the pan and cook on low heat. Don't allow the wine to boil.
4. When the wine is warm, stir in the lemon juice. Add the cheese, a handful at a time. Stir the cheese continually in a sideways figure eight pattern. Wait until the cheese is completely melted before adding more. Don't allow the fondue mixture to boil.
5. When the cheese is melted, dissolve the cornstarch in the water and add to the cheese. Turn up the heat until it is just bubbling and starting to thicken. Transfer to a fondue pot and set on the burner. Serve with the baked tomato slices and bruschetta cubes for dipping.

Marinated Tomatoes

4 tomatoes
2 green onions
¼ cup olive oil
2 tablespoons lemon juice
2 tablespoons balsamic vinegar

2 tablespoons water
1 teaspoon sugar
2 teaspoons cracked coriander
1 tablespoon cranberry juice,
  optional

Serves 6–8

Serve as a side dish with Chèvre Fondue (page 31), Brie and Pesto (page 44), or Bagna Cauda (page 165).

1. Peel the tomatoes and cut into thin slices. Thinly slice the green onions.
2. Whisk together the olive oil, lemon juice, balsamic vinegar, water, sugar, coriander, and cranberry juice. Place in a jar and shake well to blend the ingredients. If not using the marinade immediately, seal the jar and refrigerate until ready to use.
3. Pour the marinade over the tomatoes and green onions.

Oriental Vegetable Salad with Mediterranean Dressing

1 8-ounce can bamboo shoots
1 red pepper
1 garlic clove
2 tablespoons olive oil
1 tablespoon balsamic vinegar

½ teaspoon sugar
Fresh ground black pepper
  to taste
Parsley sprigs

Serves 4

Balsamic vinegar's tart flavor nicely complements Oriental vegetables. Feel free to substitute baby corn for the bamboo shoots.

1. Rinse the bamboo shoots in warm running water and drain thoroughly. Remove the stem and seeds from the red pepper and cut into thin strips. Smash, peel, and mince the garlic. Place the vegetables in a bowl.
2. Combine the olive oil, balsamic vinegar, sugar, and black pepper. Toss with the vegetables. Garnish with the parsley.

Batter-Fried Broccoli

¾ *pound broccoli*
¼ *cup flour*

4 cups oil for deep-frying
Tempura Batter (page 78)

(page 78)

Serves 4

For added flavor, encourage guests to season the broccoli with salt and pepper before eating.

1. Steam the broccoli and drain thoroughly. Chop into pieces so that approximately 1 inch of the stalk is connected to the floweret. This will make it easier to keep the broccoli from sliding off the dipping fork into the hot oil. Lightly dust the broccoli with the flour.
2. Add the oil to the fondue pot, making sure it is not more than half full. Heat the pot over medium-high heat. When the oil is hot, move the fondue pot to the table, set up the burner, and maintain the heat.
3. To cook, place a broccoli piece on a dipping fork and coat with batter. Feel free to use your fingers to lightly cover the broccoli with the batter. Dip into the hot oil and cook briefly until the coating turns golden brown. Drain on paper towels or a tempura rack.

Fried Mushrooms

30 mushrooms
4½ cups oil, or as needed

Serves 6

Juicy when heated, cooked mushrooms don't require any extra seasoning. Serve with Tempura Oysters (page 133) or a beef fondue cooked in oil.

1. Wipe the mushrooms clean with a damp cloth. Dry and cut into slices approximately ½ inch thick.
2. Add the oil to the fondue pot, making sure it is not more than half full. Heat the pot on a stove element over medium-high heat.
3. When the oil is hot, move the fondue pot to the table, set on the burner, and maintain the heat. Use a dipping fork to cook the mushroom slices briefly in the hot oil until golden. Drain on paper towels or a tempura rack.

Autumn Harvest Vegetables

6 ounces broccoli

4 potatoes

12 fresh large mushrooms

¼ cup cornstarch

4½ cups oil, or as needed

Basic Batter (page 79)

Fresh ground black pepper and
  white pepper

Serves 6

Cooking the
vegetables
first gives
them a nice
crisp texture
when deep-
fried. Serve
with Fried
Potato Skins
(page 153)
for a com-
plete meal.

1. Steam the broccoli, and drain thoroughly. Boil the potatoes on medium-low heat for about 15 minutes, until they can be pierced with a fork but are not too soft. Wipe the mushrooms with a damp cloth.
2. Cut the steamed broccoli into pieces so that approximately 1 inch of the stem is attached to the floweret. Cut the potato lengthwise into slices approximately ¾ inch thick. Cut the mushrooms into slices approximately ½ inch thick. Dust the prepared vegetables lightly with the cornstarch.
3. Add the oil to the fondue pot, making sure it is not more than half full. Heat the pot on a stove element over medium-high heat.
4. When the oil is hot, move the fondue pot to the table, set up the burner, and maintain the heat. Using a dipping fork, dip the vegetables into the batter and cook briefly in the hot oil until they turn golden brown. Remove from the dipping fork and drain on paper towels or a tempura rack. Dip into the black and white pepper.

Don't Forget the Dieters!

When serving a selection of meat and vegetable tempura dishes, try serving extra vegetables that aren't coated in cornstarch. This gives guests the option of cutting down on calories by deep-frying some of the vegetables without batter or simply enjoying them raw. Another idea is to include an assortment of low-calorie dips, such as yogurt, lemon juice, or soy sauce.

Roasted Red Peppers

Serves 6

For added flavor, toss with extra olive oil and balsamic vinegar prior to serving.

3 red bell peppers
2 yellow bell peppers
1 orange bell pepper

1 teaspoon balsamic vinegar
1 teaspoon olive oil

1. Place the peppers side down (not standing up) on a broiling pan. Brush the top side of the peppers with the balsamic vinegar. Turn over and brush the other side with the olive oil. Broil the peppers for about 20 minutes, turning frequently, until the skins are blackened and charred.
2. Place the peppers in a sealed plastic bag. Leave the peppers in the bag for at least 10 minutes. Remove from the bag and peel off the skins. Remove the stems and the seeds. To serve, cut into cubes or lengthwise into strips.

Roasted Pepper Dip

Yields ⅔ cup

Feel free to experiment by adding herbs such as fresh basil or oregano, but take care not to overpower the smoky flavor of the red peppers.

1 garlic clove
3 tablespoons onion, chopped
2 tablespoons olive oil
2 red bell peppers

½ teaspoon sugar
½ teaspoon lemon juice
¼ teaspoon ground cumin, or to taste

1. Smash, peel, and chop the garlic clove. Cook the garlic and onion in the olive oil.
2. Roast the red peppers (see Roasted Red Peppers), remove the peel and seeds, and cut into cubes. Process with the garlic and onion in the blender. Add the sugar, lemon juice, and ground cumin. Process again briefly, keeping the texture a bit chunky, like a salsa.

Asian Vegetables with Vinaigrette Dressing

1 8-ounce can baby corn
1 red bell pepper
½ cup mung bean sprouts
1 tablespoon olive oil
2 tablespoons soy sauce

1 teaspoon sugar
1 teaspoon rice vinegar
¼ teaspoon ginger juice,
  or to taste

Serves 4

Ginger juice is easy to make—just grate a few slices of ginger and squeeze out the juice with your fingers.

1. Rinse the baby corn in warm running water. Wash the red pepper and mung bean sprouts. Drain all the vegetables well. Remove the stem and seeds from the red pepper and cut into cubes. Place in a large bowl.
2. Combine the olive oil, soy sauce, sugar, rice vinegar, and ginger juice. Toss the vegetables with the dressing. Let the salad sit for about 30 minutes before serving.

Sweet Peppers and Herbs

1 potato, boiled
1 tablespoon balsamic vinegar
1 teaspoon olive oil
3 tablespoons onion, chopped
1 garlic clove, minced
1 tablespoon fresh cilantro,
  chopped

1 tablespoon fresh parsley,
  chopped
2 mint leaves, chopped
2 large red bell peppers,
  roasted

Serves 4

This zesty side dish makes a nice accompaniment to less-highly seasoned meat and seafood fondues. Serve with Fish Bathed in Broth (page 126).

1. Cut the potato into thin strips. Mix together the balsamic vinegar, olive oil, chopped onion, minced garlic, cilantro, parsley, and mint leaves. Add to the potato strips, tossing.
2. Peel the roasted peppers, cut off the stems, and remove the seeds. Cut the peppers into thin strips. Combine with the other ingredients. Cover and refrigerate until ready to serve.

Fried Mashed Potatoes

Yields 16–18 potato balls

This recipe turns left-over mashed potatoes into a fun fondue dish! Serve with sour cream for dipping.

4 medium potatoes
3 tablespoons butter or margarine
½ cup plus 3 tablespoons milk, divided
¼ teaspoon paprika

¼ teaspoon salt
½ cup flour
⅛ teaspoon garlic powder
Pepper to taste
5 cups oil, or as needed

1. Wash and peel the potatoes. Cook in boiling salted water until they are tender and pierce easily with a fork.
2. Place the potatoes in a bowl and add the butter or margarine, 3 table-spoons milk, paprika, and a pinch of salt. Use a potato masher or fork to mash the potatoes until they are fluffy. Roll into balls. Place on a tray lined with wax paper and freeze overnight.
3. To prepare the batter, mix together the flour, garlic powder, pepper, and remaining salt. Stir in 1 tablespoon vegetable oil. Slowly add ½ cup milk, stirring constantly, until it forms a runny batter.
4. Add the oil to the fondue pot, making sure it is not more than half full. Heat the pot on a stove element over medium-high heat. When the oil is hot, move the fondue pot to the table and set up the burner. Keep the heat high.
5. Roll the mashed potato balls in the batter and drop into the hot oil. Cook for about 4 minutes, turning occasionally, until they turn a deep golden brown and are cooked through. Remove with a slotted spoon and drain on paper towels.

Fried Potato Sticks

4 large potatoes
5 cups oil, or as needed

Freshly ground black pepper
and white pepper

Serves 4–6

This simple dish makes a filling snack or side dish. For a hearty breakfast, serve with Welsh Rarebit (page 178).

1. Boil the potatoes for about 15 minutes on medium-low heat, until they can be pierced with a fork but are not too soft. Drain thoroughly, and cut lengthwise into pieces approximately ¾ inch thick.
2. Add the oil to the fondue pot, making sure it is not more than half full. Heat the pot on a stove element over medium-high heat. When the oil is hot, move the fondue pot to the table and set up the burner. Keep the heat high.
3. Using a dipping fork, dip the potato slices briefly into the oil. Drain on paper towels or a tempura rack. Season with black or white pepper as desired before eating.

Fried Potato Skins

4 baking potatoes
¼ teaspoon ground white pepper

¼ teaspoon paprika
4½ cups oil, or as needed

Serves 4

Serve as is, with standard potato toppings such as sour cream and chives, or with Speedy Garlic Mayonnaise (page 65) for dipping.

1. Bake the potatoes at 425°F until they are tender and pierce easily with a fork. Cool. Cut the potatoes in half. Cut each half lengthwise into 3 to 4 sections. Scoop out most of the pulp, so that only ⅛ to ¼ inch remains. Discard the pulp or use in another recipe. Sprinkle half the potato skins with the ground white pepper, and the remaining half with the paprika. Add more seasoning if desired.
2. Add the oil to the fondue pot, making sure it is not more than half full. Heat the pot on a stove element over medium-high heat. When the oil is hot, move the fondue pot to the table and set up the burner. Keep the heat high.
3. Using a dipping fork, briefly dip the potato slices into the oil until browned.

Milk Bathed Onion Rings

Serves 4–6

If you have one, a dipping basket is perfect for cooking the onion rings. Serve with Speedy Garlic Mayonnaise (page 65) and ketchup for dipping.

1 large yellow onion
½ teaspoon paprika
1 cup milk

½ cup cornstarch
Tempura Batter (page 78)
4½ cups oil, or as needed

1. Peel the onion and cut into rings. Toss with the paprika. Soak in the milk for at least 1 hour, making sure all the onion pieces are covered.
2. Drain the onion pieces and dust with the cornstarch. Coat with the batter.
3. Add the oil to the fondue pot, making sure it is not more than half full. Heat the pot on a stove element over medium-high heat. When the oil is hot, move the fondue pot to the table and set up the burner. Keep the heat high.
4. Drop the battered onion rings into the oil. Cook briefly, turning occasionally, until they turn golden brown. Remove and drain on paper towels.

Pepper Medley

Serves 6

Even thick green peppers become tender when gently simmered in broth.

2 red bell peppers
2 green bell peppers
2 orange bell peppers

4 cups Vegetable Broth
(page 83)
½ cup soy sauce

1. Wash the peppers and drain thoroughly. Remove the seeds and stems, and cut into bite-sized cubes.
2. Heat the broth in the fondue pot over a stove element. Bring to the table and set up the burner. Add the peppers and simmer until tender. Remove the peppers with a slotted spoon. If desired, ladle the broth into individual serving bowls. Serve with the soy sauce for dipping.

Garden Vegetables with White Sauce

2 tablespoons olive oil
¼ onion, peeled and chopped
2 cups long-grain rice
5 cups Homemade Chicken
  Broth (page 81), divided

1 cup snow peas
1 cup baby carrots
2 green peppers
White Sauce for Vegetables
  (page 64)

Serves 4–6

To turn into a complete meal, add 1 pound of cleaned and deveined shrimp and increase the amount of broth in the fondue pot to 4 cups.

1. Heat the olive oil in a frying pan on low heat. Add the chopped onion and cook until soft. Add the rice and sauté for 5 minutes until it turns shiny and is heated through.
2. Add 3 cups of the broth. To cook the rice, bring to a boil, uncovered. Cover, turn down the heat, and cook until cooked through.
3. Wash the snow peas, carrots, and green peppers; drain thoroughly. Cut the peppers in half, remove the seeds and stems, and cut into bite-sized cubes.
4. Heat the remaining 2 cups of broth in a fondue pot over a stove element. Bring to the table and set up the burner. Add the vegetables to the broth, using a dipping basket if you have one. Simmer the vegetables until tender. If not using a dipping basket, remove with a slotted spoon.
5. Serve the vegetables with the warmed sauce for dipping. Eat with the rice. At the end of the meal, serve the cooked broth if desired.

Storing Homemade Broth

If you're planning to use it over the next day or two, leftover broth can be stored in a sealed container in the refrigerator. For longer periods, it needs to be frozen. Cool the broth and place in a plastic freezer container or zipper-locked bag, making sure neither is more than ¾ full. Place the bag or container in the freezer. When ready to use, simply allow the broth to return to room temperature.

French Green Beans
with Fondue Béchamel Sauce

Serves 6

Serve with baked chicken thighs coated with Simple Chicken Rub (page 78) for a complete meal.

Fondue Béchamel Sauce
  (page 67)
3 cups canned French-style
  green beans

2 cups Homemade Chicken
  Broth (page 81)

1. Warm the sauce on low heat, without allowing to come to a boil.
2. Drain the green beans. Bring the broth to a boil. Add the green beans and gently simmer for about 10 minutes.
3. Pour the fondue sauce over the beans and serve.

Cream of Celery Soup

Serves 4

For extra flavor, garnish with parsley sprigs and 2 tablespoons of Parmesan cheese.

1 stalk celery
1 green onion
1 tablespoon butter or margarine
1/4 cup yellow onion, chopped

2 10-ounce cans cream of
  celery soup
10 ounces chicken broth
10 ounces water
Salt and pepper to taste

1. Wash the celery. Cut the celery and green onion into 1-inch slices on the diagonal.
2. On a stove element, melt the butter in the fondue pot, add the chopped onion, and cook until tender. Mix in the cream of celery soup, chicken broth, and water and heat through. Season with the salt and pepper.
3. Bring the fondue pot to the table and set on the stand. Add the celery and green onion to the soup and simmer briefly until tender. Allow everyone to serve themselves or ladle the soup into individual serving bowls.

Tomato Soup Fondue

12 ounces beef broth
8 ounces water
2 10-ounce cans tomato soup
8 ounces Cheddar cheese,
  shredded

¼ teaspoon celery salt
Salt and pepper to taste
Toasted Pita Chips (page 244)

Serves 4

Don't have pita chips on hand? This also tastes delicious served with warm crusty bread.

1. Bring the beef broth and water to a boil in the fondue pot on the stove. Stir in the tomato soup and heat through. Keeping the heat on medium-low, gradually stir in the shredded Cheddar cheese, a handful at a time. Stir in the celery salt and salt and pepper.
2. Bring the fondue pot to the table and set up the burner. Allow everyone to serve themselves or ladle the soup into individual serving bowls. Dip the pita chips into the soup.

Fried Asparagus and Zucchini

2 zucchini
1 pound asparagus spears
4 cups oil, or as needed

Speedy Garlic Mayonnaise
  (page 65)
½ cup soy sauce

Serves 4

Find that deep-frying softens the pulpy center of the zucchini too much for your taste? Simply remove that section before cooking.

1. Wash the zucchini and dry thoroughly. Cut on the diagonal into pieces at least ½ inch thick. Blanch the asparagus briefly in boiling water. Drain thoroughly, and cut into 2-inch pieces.
2. Add the oil to the fondue pot, making sure it is not more than half full. Heat the pot on a stove element over medium-high heat. When the oil is hot, move the fondue pot to the table and set up the burner.
3. Spear the vegetables with a dipping fork and cook briefly in the hot oil. Serve with Garlic Mayonnaise and soy sauce for dipping.

Vegetable Spring Rolls

Yields 6

To make this a vegetarian dish, use vegetarian "oyster" sauce that is flavored with mushrooms.

1 cup fresh mung bean sprouts
½ carrot
4 dried Chinese mushrooms
1 tablespoon bamboo shoots, shredded
2 tablespoons plus 1 teaspoon red pepper, finely diced
1 tablespoon plus 1 teaspoon oyster sauce
2 teaspoons water
½ teaspoon sugar
1 teaspoon soy sauce
5 cups oil, or as needed
8–10 spring roll wrappers
4 tablespoons cornstarch mixed with 2 tablespoons water

1. Wash or rinse all the vegetables and drain thoroughly, particularly the mung bean sprouts. Grate the carrot until you have 2 tablespoons plus 1 teaspoon. Soak the dried Chinese mushrooms in warm water for at least 20 minutes to soften. Squeeze out the excess water, remove the stems, and thinly slice. Mix together the mung bean sprouts, grated carrot, mushrooms, bamboo shoots, and diced red pepper.
2. Mix together the oyster sauce, water, sugar, and soy sauce. Set aside.
3. Heat 1½ tablespoons vegetable oil in a frying pan. When oil is hot, add the vegetables. Mix in the sauce and bring to a boil.
4. To prepare the spring rolls, lay a wrapper in front of you so that it forms 2 triangles. Use your fingers to brush the edges of the wrapper with the cornstarch-and-water mixture. Place a full tablespoon of filling in the middle. Roll up the wrapper, tucking in the edges, and seal with more cornstarch and water. Prepare the remaining spring rolls in the same way.
5. Add the remaining oil as needed to the fondue pot, making sure it is not more than half full. Heat the pot on a stove element over medium-high heat. When the oil is hot, move the fondue pot to the table and set up the burner. Deep-fry the spring rolls, two at a time, until they turn golden (3 to 4 minutes). Drain on paper towels.

Tempura Vegetables

6 ounces lotus root
1 pound daikon radish
1 green pepper
1 Western eggplant (about 10 ounces)
⅓ cup flour

Tempura Batter (page 78)
4½ cups oil, or as needed
Yogurt and Dill Dressing (page 63)
½ cup soy sauce, optional

Serves 6

Soft eggplant, crunchy daikon radish, and crisp lotus root give this dish an interesting variety of textures.

1. Wash all the vegetables. Cut the ends off the lotus root. Scrape the skin off the lotus root and daikon radish with a potato peeler, and cut into slices about ½ inch thick. Cut the green pepper in half, remove the stem and seeds, and cut into 1-inch cubes. Peel the eggplant and cut into sticks about ½ inch thick and 3 inches long.
2. Dust all the vegetables lightly with the flour before setting on the table for dipping. (Some flour will probably be left over.) Prepare the batter.
3. Add the oil to the fondue pot, making sure it is not more than half full. Heat the pot on a stove element over medium-high heat. When the oil is hot, move the fondue pot to the table and set up the burner.
4. Invite guests to spear the vegetables with a dipping fork and coat with the batter. Cook the vegetables in the hot oil until golden brown. Try to vary which vegetables are cooked to allow for different cooking times—the eggplant will take up to 4 minutes, while the peppers will cook quite quickly. Serve with the Yogurt and Dill Dressing and soy sauce for dipping.

Daikon Radish

It's hard to believe that the large, white radish featured in numerous Asian dishes tastes nearly identical to the small, round, red radishes found in Western supermarkets. Also called icicle radish because of its white color and shape, a mature daikon radish can grow up to 20 inches long. Daikon makes a frequent appearance in Japanese cuisine. Grated radish is a popular garnish, while sliced daikon is often used in sunomono, a Japanese cucumber salad.

Parsnip Soup

Serves 4

Fruit dippers aren't only for dessert fondues. Sweet pears and savory vegetables make an interesting combination in this dish.

4 pears
4 parsnips
½ yellow onion
1 garlic clove
4 cups Vegetable Broth (page 83)

¾ teaspoon curry powder
¼ teaspoon salt
Pepper to taste
2 tablespoons parsley, chopped

1. Wash the pears, remove the stems, and cut into bite-sized pieces. Wash and peel the parsnips. Cut diagonally into ½-inch pieces. Peel and chop the onion. Smash, peel, and chop the garlic clove.
2. Heat the broth in the fondue pot over a stove element. Add the parsnips, onion, garlic, curry powder, salt, and pepper to the broth. Simmer for at least 15 minutes, or until parsnips are tender. Stir in the parsley.
3. Transfer the fondue pot to the table and set up the burner. Use dipping forks to spear the pears and dip into the soup.

Vegetable Medley

Serves 4

This makes a nice change from the usual cheese fondue.

½ pound broccoli
½ pound cauliflower
2 carrots
½ green pepper
½ red pepper

Vegetable Broth (page 83)
Lemon-Soy Dressing (page 68)
Sour Cream and Mustard Dip
  (page 65)

1. Blanch the broccoli and cauliflower briefly in boiling water and drain thoroughly. Remove the stems and cut the flowerets into bite-sized pieces.
2. Peel and dice the carrots. Blanch briefly in boiling water and drain.
3. Cut the green and red peppers into bite-sized pieces.
4. Heat the broth in the fondue pot over a stove element. Bring to a boil and then transfer the fondue pot to the table and set up the burner. Use dipping forks to spear the vegetables and cook in the hot broth. Serve with the dressing and the dip.

Fried Three Mushrooms

20 *fresh small mushrooms*
6 *portobello mushrooms*
4 *oyster mushrooms*
4½ *cups oil, or as needed*

Horseradish with Sour Cream
(page 59)
½ *cup balsamic vinegar*

Serves 4

This makes a flavorful side dish for beef fondues such as Classic Beef Bourguigno nne (page 88).

1. Wipe the mushrooms with a damp cloth. If desired, remove the feathery "gills" from underneath the cap of the portobello and oyster mushrooms.
2. Remove the stems from all the mushrooms. Slice the small mushrooms. Cut the portobello and the oyster mushrooms into bite-sized squares or rectangles (this will give them a better surface area for cooking in hot oil).
3. Add the oil to the fondue pot, making sure it is not more than half full. Heat the pot on a stove element over medium-high heat. When the oil is hot, move the fondue pot to the table and set up the burner.
4. Spear the mushrooms with a dipping fork. Cook for approximately 20 seconds in the hot oil until the mushrooms are lightly browned but not burned. (If not cooked long enough, they can taste oily.) Drain on paper towels. Serve with the Horseradish with Sour Cream and balsamic vinegar for dipping.

Marvelous Mushrooms

Large and with feathery brown "gills" underneath the cap, portobello mushrooms are known for their strong earthy flavor. While all mushrooms exude liquid when heated, portobello mushrooms exude more than most, making them very flavorful when cooked. Gray with white gills, oyster mushrooms have a more subtle flavor. Both can easily hold their own against a strong dip like Horseradish with Sour Cream.

Vegetables with Boiled Salad Dressing

4 carrots
4 celery stalks
2 tomatoes
1 head romaine lettuce
8 tablespoons butter
½ cup white vinegar

4 eggs
½ cup sugar
½ teaspoon cayenne pepper
2 tablespoons Dijon mustard
½ cup light cream or
    half-and-half

Serves 6

This easy recipe trans- forms salad dressing into a fondue. Feel free to sub- stitute other seasonal vegetables to use in the salad.

1. Wash all the vegetables and drain thoroughly. Peel the carrots and cut lengthwise into thin slices about 2 inches long. Cut the celery the same way. Cut the tomatoes into wedges. Separate the romaine lettuce leaves. Arrange the carrots, celery, and tomato wedges on the lettuce and place on a large serving platter.
2. To prepare the boiled dressing, melt the butter in a small saucepan. Place the vinegar in the top half of a double boiler or in a metal bowl over water that is just barely simmering.
3. Slowly add the eggs and melted butter to the warmed vinegar. Whisk constantly until the mixture thickens (this can take several minutes). Once the mixture has thickened, whisk in the sugar, cayenne pepper, and Dijon mustard. Remove from the heat and whisk in the cream.
4. Pour the boiled dressing into a cheese fondue dish. Serve hot or cold. Use dipping forks to spear the salad vegetables and dip into the dressing.

Dijon Mustard

Created in the eighteenth century by Jean Naigeon, Dijon mustard is named after the region in France where it was created. The distinctive flavor of Dijon mustard comes from combining spicy brown mustard seeds with the juice from unripened grapes. Prior to that time, vinegar was used. Today, Dijon-style mus- tard is manufactured throughout the world.

CHAPTER 9
Ethnic Fondues

Mexican Fondue with Guacamole Dip

Serves 4–6

Jalapeño peppers give this dish bite without the over-powering heat associated with stronger peppers.

¾ *pound Cheddar cheese*
¾ *pound Monterey Jack cheese*
3 *fresh green jalapeño peppers*
1 *garlic clove*
1½ *cups beer*

3 *teaspoons lemon juice*
1 *tablespoon cornstarch*
3 *tablespoons cognac*
1 *bag tortilla chips*
Guacamole (page 58)

1. Shred the Cheddar and Monterey Jack cheeses. Wash the peppers, cut lengthwise, remove the seeds, and chop.
2. Smash the garlic, peel, and cut in half. Rub the inside of a medium saucepan with the garlic. Add the beer and warm on medium-low heat, being careful not to bring to a boil. When the beer has warmed, stir in the lemon juice.
3. Add the cheese, a handful at a time. Stir the cheese continually in a sideways figure eight pattern. Don't allow the fondue mixture to boil.
4. When the cheese is nearly melted, turn up the heat until it is just bubbling. Dissolve the cornstarch in 2 tablespoons of cognac and add to the fondue, stirring quickly to thicken. Add the remaining table-spoon of cognac. Transfer to a fondue pot and set on the burner. Serve with the tortilla chips for dipping and accompany with the Guacamole dip.

Fondue Beer

It may be tempting, but don't add your favorite strong beer to the fondue mix. Stronger beers can overpower the cheese flavor. Use a weaker beer or a light beer.

Bagna Cauda—Italian Fondue

1 small head broccoli
1 small head cauliflower
2 cardoon stalks (or 2 celery
   stalks)
1 fennel bulb
2 red peppers
1 zucchini

4 ounces anchovies
4 garlic cloves
4 tablespoons butter
½ cup olive oil
4 tablespoons cream
1 loaf Italian bread, sliced

Serves 4

Feel free to hold the bread underneath the dipped vegetables to catch any excess sauce. Then, enjoy the sauce-laden bread!

1. Wash the vegetables. Blanch the broccoli, cauliflower, and cardoon stalks briefly in boiling water and drain thoroughly. Cut all the vegetables and fennel bulb into bite-sized pieces.
2. Drain and separate the anchovies. Smash, peel, and mince the garlic.
3. Melt the butter and keep warm on low heat.
4. Heat the olive oil in a frying pan over low heat. Add the garlic. Cook on low heat for a few minutes, and then add the anchovies. Continue to cook on low heat, gently mashing the anchovies and mixing together with the garlic. Add the melted butter. Stir in the cream.
5. Transfer the Bagna Cauda to a fondue pot and set on the burner. Serve with the vegetables—or with your own favorite combination of mixed vegetables—for dipping. Eat with the sliced bread.

Bagna Cauda

The name of the dish says it all: "Bagna cauda" comes from the Italian words bagno caldo, meaning "warm bath." Garlic and butter combine with golden olive oil to make a flavorful warm sauce, while anchovies take the place of salt as a seasoning. Originating in the mountain regions of southern Italy, bagna cauda makes a frequent appearance at buffet dinners on Christmas Eve. Traditionally, one of the vegetables served with bagna cauda is cardoon, a white-stalked vegetable with sharp edges that resembles celery. Cardoons can be hard to find, and celery may be used as a substitute.

Fondue Chinoise

Serves 6

For a complete meal, serve with side dishes such as Asian Vegetables with Vinaigrette Dressing (page 151).

2 pounds filet of beef
Chinese Beef Broth (page 83)
Horseradish Cream (page 60)

Basic Chinese Hot Mustard
    (page 56), prepared just
    before serving
Marvelous Mango Chutney
    (page 50)

1. Cut the beef into very thin slices, approximately 2 inches long.
2. Heat the broth on the stove and bring to a boil. Transfer enough broth to fill the fondue pot about ⅔ full. Set the fondue pot on the burner, with enough heat to keep the broth simmering throughout the meal. (Keep the remaining broth warm on the stove to use as needed.)
3. Invite guests to spear the sliced beef with a dipping fork and cook briefly in the broth until cooked according to individual taste. Serve with the Horseradish Cream and mustard for dipping. Eat with the chutney.

Marinated Fondue Chinoise

Serves 4–6

Sesame oil's nutty flavor makes it a popular addition to Asian marinades. For an added touch, serve with sesame seeds as a garnish.

2 pounds beef flank steak
1 green onion
¼ cup soy sauce
3 tablespoons dry sherry
2 tablespoons sesame oil

Chinese Beef Broth (page 83)
Hot Pot Dip for Beef (page 68)
Golden Hot Mustard (page 63)

1. Cut the beef into very thin slices. Cut the green onion into thirds. Place the beef in a shallow glass dish and marinate the beef in the soy sauce, sherry, sesame oil, and green onion in the refrigerator for 1 hour.
2. Heat the broth on the stove and bring to a boil. Transfer enough broth to fill the fondue pot about ⅔ full. Set the fondue pot on the burner, with enough heat to keep the broth simmering throughout the meal. (Keep the remaining broth warm on the stove to use as needed.)
3. Spear the sliced beef with a dipping fork and cook briefly in the broth to individual taste. Serve with the dipping sauces.

Classic Mongolian Hot Pot

3 pounds lean lamb
6 Chinese dried mushrooms
8 ounces cellophane noodles
1 head Napa cabbage
1 bunch fresh spinach (approx-
    imately ½ pound)
Basic Mongolian Hot Pot Broth
    (page 84)

Extra Hot Pot Dipping Sauce
    (page 67)
Nut-Free Hot Pot Dipping Sauce
    (page 69)
6 eggs

Serves 6

Serve with an assort-ment of dips, including Golden Hot Mustard (page 63), soy sauce, salt, pepper, and freshly ground white pepper.

1. Cut the lamb into paper-thin slices, about 2½ inches long.
2. Soak the dried mushrooms in warm water for 20 minutes. Squeeze out the excess water and cut into thin slices. Soak the cellophane noodles in warm water to soften. Drain and cut into thirds for easier use.
3. Wash the cabbage, drain, and remove the stem. Cut each leaf in half lengthwise, and then slice thinly. Wash the spinach and drain.
4. Heat the broth on the stove and bring to a boil. Add the dried mush-rooms. Transfer enough broth to fill the fondue pot about ⅔ full. Set the fondue pot on the burner, with enough heat to keep the broth sim-mering throughout the meal. (Keep the remaining broth warm on the stove to use as needed.)
5. Invite guests to spear the sliced lamb with a dipping fork and cook briefly in the broth until cooked according to individual taste. Serve with the dipping sauces. When the lamb is gone, cook the noodles, cabbage, and spinach in the hot broth. When all the food is gone, poach the eggs in the broth.

Don't Skimp on the Seasonings!

In addition to specially prepared dips like Extra Hot Pot Dipping Sauce, feel free to serve one-pot dishes with an assortment of spicy seasonings. Hot chili paste, sesame seed paste, and even fermented bean curd give guests a variety of fiery options.

Mixed Meat Hot Pot

Serves 4–6

Adding an egg to the hot pot broth allows guests to finish the meal with a nourishing bowl of egg drop soup.

2 teaspoons salt
1 pound fresh large shrimp, peeled and deveined
1 pound fresh red snapper fillets
2 skinless, boneless chicken breasts (about 8 ounces each)
1 pound bok choy
2 green onions
1 bunch cilantro
Basic Mongolian Hot Pot Broth (page 84)
3 slices ginger
Extra Hot Pot Dipping Sauce (page 67)
Sesame Dipping Paste (page 69)
1 egg

1. Dissolve the salt in 3 cups of warm water. Soak the shrimp in the water for 5 minutes. Drain and pat dry. Cut the red snapper and chicken breasts into thin strips.
2. Wash the vegetables and drain. Separate the bok choy stalks and leaves. Shred the leaves and cut the stalks into slices about 1 inch thick. Chop the green onions. Chop the cilantro and use to garnish the shrimp.
3. Heat the broth on the stove and bring to a boil. Add the bok choy, green onions, and ginger. Bring to a boil again. Transfer enough broth to fill the fondue pot about ⅔ full. Set the fondue pot on the burner, with enough heat to keep the broth simmering throughout the meal. (Keep the remaining broth warm on the stove to use as needed.)
4. Ladle a small portion of the broth with vegetables into the soup bowls. Invite guests to use chopsticks or dipping forks to cook the chicken and seafood in the hot pot. Dip the cooked food in dipping sauces, or enjoy with the bowls of broth.
5. When the food is gone, swirl an egg into the broth to make egg drop soup. Serve each guest a bowl of the soup.

Provolone "Fonduta"

1 pound provolone cheese
1¼ cups milk
4 egg yolks
¼ cup half-and-half or light cream

2 tablespoons butter
½ teaspoon nutmeg
¼ teaspoon cinnamon
Salt and pepper to taste

1. Finely dice the provolone cheese. Place the cheese and the milk in a saucepan and leave for 1 hour.
2. Heat the milk and cheese on low heat, without bringing to a boil, until the cheese turns creamy. Whisk in the egg yolks, half-and-half, and butter. Keep whisking until the mixture thickens, but not to the point where the egg starts scrambling. Stir in the nutmeg, cinnamon, and salt and pepper.
3. Transfer to a fondue pot and set on the burner. Serve with toasted Italian bread for dipping.

Serves 4–6

If desired, have guests ladle the fonduta from the fondue pot into individual serving bowls.

Greek Fondue

¾ cup milk
¾ pound ricotta cheese
½ pound feta cheese
¾ tablespoon cornstarch
1 garlic clove, peeled
2 teaspoons lemon juice

¼ teaspoon dried oregano
¼ teaspoon dried basil
Toasted Pita Chips (page 244)
Bruschetta with Roma
    Tomatoes (page 246)

Serves 4–6

Serve with an assortment of olives, pickles, and vegetables marinated with Greek salad dressing.

Mix ¼ cup of the milk with the ricotta cheese and set aside. Crumble the feta cheese and toss with the cornstarch. Cut the garlic in half. Rub the garlic around the inside of a medium saucepan. Discard. Add the remaining ½ cup of milk and warm on medium-low heat. Stir in the lemon juice. Add the ricotta cheese mixture and the feta cheese, stirring continuously. Don't let the cheese boil. When the cheese is fully melted, turn up the heat until it is just bubbling and starting to thicken. Stir in the oregano and basil. Serve with the pita chips and bruschetta for dipping.

Japanese Sukiyaki

Serves 4

Food is dipped in a sweet-and-spicy sauce instead of broth in this popular Japanese one-pot meal.

16 ounces beef sirloin steak
1 pound firm or medium-firm
  tofu
6 ounces cellophane noodles
1 small Napa cabbage

10 oyster mushrooms
4 eggs
2 tablespoons cooking oil,
  or as needed
Sukiyaki Sauce (page 66)

1. Cut the beef into paper-thin slices, no more than 3 inches long. Drain the tofu and cut into cubes. Soak the noodles in warm water for 15 minutes to soften, and drain thoroughly. If desired, cut the noodles in half to make them more manageable. Wash the cabbage, drain, and shred the leaves. Wipe the mushrooms with a damp cloth, and cut into bite-sized pieces.

2. Set a sukiyaki pan or large electric frying pan in the middle of the table. When setting the table, make sure each guest has a small bowl containing a beaten egg.

3. Heat 2 tablespoons of oil in the pan. Brown the meat in the oil. Add the tofu, vegetables, mushrooms, and noodles. Pour the Sukiyaki Sauce over. Invite guests to use chopsticks to retrieve the cooked food and dip into the beaten egg.

Serving Sukiyaki

Known as the friendship dish, sukiyaki is Japan's most famous one-pot food. The word sukiyaki combines suki, meaning "plow," and yaki, meaning "to broil." According to legend, the dish was invented by farm laborers who would use a spade or plow to grill their food over an open fire after a hard day's work in the fields.

Sukiyaki with Rice

1 small Napa cabbage
1 cup fresh mung bean
   sprouts
10 fresh small mushrooms
1 pound flank steak
1 block firm tofu

4 cups cooked rice
2 tablespoons vegetable oil,
   or as needed
¾ cup soy sauce
¼ cup sake
4 tablespoons sugar

Serves 4

For a more authentic touch, replace the cooking oil with 2 pieces of beef suet or lard and rub over the bottom of the sukiyaki pot or frying pan.

1. Wash the cabbage and mung bean sprouts and drain thoroughly. Wipe the mushrooms with a damp cloth. Slice the mushrooms and shred the cabbage leaves. Cut the steak into paper-thin slices, no more than 3 inches long. Drain the tofu and cut into cubes.
2. Give each guest a small bowl with 1 cup of the cooked rice to eat with the food. Set a sukiyaki pan or large electric frying pan in the middle of the table.
3. Heat the cooking oil in the pan. Add ½ of the beef and lightly braise it. Add ½ of the mushrooms, cabbage, and tofu, putting each in their own section. Add as much of the soy sauce, sake, and sugar as desired. When the food is almost cooked, add ½ of the bean sprouts. Either serve the cooked food to the guests or invite them to serve themselves. Repeat with the remaining half of the food. Eat with the cooked rice.

Sukiyaki Styles

The Japanese have developed two main styles of preparing sukiyaki sauce. Mixing the sauce ingredients together before adding them to the pot is typical of the way sukiyaki is prepared in eastern Japan's Kanto region. In the Kansai region of central Japan, the sauce ingredients are normally added separately.

Spicy Hot Pot for a Crowd

Serves 8

To cut down on spiciness, serve ¼ cup of Worcestershire sauce and ¼ cup of hot chili sauce as dipping sauces on the side instead of adding them to the broth.

2 teaspoons salt
1 pound prawns or large
   shrimp, cleaned and deveined
3 large skinless, boneless
   chicken breasts (about
   10 ounces each)
2 pounds fish fillets
10 fresh oysters
8 Chinese dried mushrooms
4 stalks celery
2 bunches spinach

Extra Hot Pot Dipping Sauce
   (page 67)
Nut-Free Hot Pot Dipping Sauce
   (page 69)
12 cups Basic Mongolian Hot
   Pot Broth (page 84)
4 garlic cloves, peeled
4 tablespoons Worcestershire
   sauce
1 teaspoon hot chili sauce
10 eggs

1. Dissolve the salt in 3 cups of warm water. Rinse the prawns in the water for 5 minutes, and pat dry. Cut in half lengthwise. Cut the chicken and fish fillets into very thin slices. Shuck the oysters, rinse in warm water, and dry thoroughly.

2. Soak the dried mushrooms in warm water for 20 minutes to soften. Cut into thin slices. Wash the spinach and celery and drain thoroughly. Cut the celery into bite-sized pieces on the diagonal.

3. Place the chicken, seafood, celery, and spinach, on the table, along with dipping sauces. Give each guest an individual soup bowl.

4. Heat the broth on the stove with the mushrooms and garlic cloves and bring to a boil. Stir in the Worcestershire sauce and hot chili sauce. Transfer enough broth to fill the fondue pot about ⅔ full. Set the fondue pot on the burner, with enough heat to keep the broth simmering throughout the meal. (Keep the remaining broth warm on the stove to use as needed.)

5. Use chopsticks or dipping forks to cook the chicken, seafood, and celery in the hot pot. Dip the cooked food in dipping sauces, or enjoy with the bowls of broth. When the food is gone, add the spinach to the broth. Ladle out a small bowl for each guest. Poach the eggs in the remaining broth.

Shabu-Shabu

1 8-ounce can bamboo shoots
1 small Napa Cabbage
4 leeks
2 large carrots
1 block medium-firm tofu
1½ pounds sirloin beef

Lemon-Soy Dressing (page 68)
Instant Dashi (page 85) or
    Vegetable Broth (page 83),
    as needed
4 cups cooked rice

Serves 4–6

The Japanese version of Mongolian hot pot, shabu-shabu is also cooked in a mild-flavored broth.

1. Rinse the bamboo shoots in warm running water. Wash the cabbage, leeks, and carrots. Drain all the vegetables thoroughly. Chop the leeks and shred the cabbage. Peel and dice the carrots.
2. Drain the tofu and cut into bite-sized cubes. Cut the beef into paper-thin slices. Arrange the meat, tofu, and vegetables separately on a large platter. Serve the Lemon-Soy Dressing in individual serving bowls.
3. Heat the dashi or broth on the stove and bring to a boil. Transfer enough broth to fill the fondue pot about ⅔ full. Set the fondue pot on the burner, with enough heat to keep the broth simmering throughout the meal. (Keep the remaining broth warm on the stove to use as needed.)
4. Invite guests to cook the meat, tofu, and all the vegetables except for the bamboo shoots in the broth, and then dip into the dressing. Replenish the broth as needed. Serve the rice with the food. When the food has been eaten, add the bamboo shoots to the broth, cook briefly, and then ladle out the soup.

Shabu-Shabu—The Perfect Party Dish

Although sukiyaki is more popular, shabu-shabu is a better choice when you're cooking for a crowd. Instead of merely watching, guests have fun cooking the food themselves. Furthermore, if you're using more than one sukiyaki pan or frying pan, it may be difficult to coordinate cooking times so that everyone eats together.

Shabu-Shabu with Noodles

Serves 4

The sweet, mellow flavor of warmed sake makes it an ideal accompaniment for shabu-shabu and other Japanese one-pot dishes.

2 ounces cellophane noodles
2 leeks
2 carrots
1 small Napa Cabbage
10 shiitake mushrooms
1½ pounds sirloin beef

Sesame Dipping Paste (page 69), prepared in advance to allow flavors to blend
Instant Dashi (page 85) or Vegetable Broth (page 83), as needed
½ cup grated daikon radish

1. Soak the cellophane noodles in warm water to soften. Drain thoroughly and chop into quarters. Wash the vegetables and drain thoroughly. Chop the leeks and peel and dice the carrots. Shred the cabbage. Wipe the mushrooms with a damp cloth and slice thinly.
2. Cut the beef into paper-thin slices. Arrange the meat, vegetables, and noodles separately on a large platter. If desired, set out the sesame dip in individual serving bowls.
3. Heat the dashi or broth on the stove and bring to a boil. Transfer enough broth to fill the fondue pot about ⅔ full. Set the fondue pot on the burner, with enough heat to keep the broth simmering throughout the meal. (Keep the remaining broth warm on the stove to use as needed.)
4. Invite guests to cook all the meat and vegetables and then dip into the dipping sauce. Serve with the grated daikon radish. Replenish the broth as needed. When the food has been eaten, add the noodles to the broth, cook briefly, and then ladle out the soup.

Cellophane Noodles

Made from mung bean starch, cellophane noodles are famous for puffing up when deep-fried. When added to soup or broth, they soak up the flavor of the foods they are cooked with.

Classic Fonduta

1 truffle
1¼ pounds Fontina cheese
1¾ cups milk
4 egg yolks
⅓ cup light cream

2½ tablespoons butter
Salt and freshly ground white
    pepper to taste
1 loaf Italian bread, sliced and
    toasted

Serves 4–6

Cheese soft-
ened in milk
forms a rich,
creamy sauce
when heated.
Warm toasted
bread makes
an excellent
accompani-
ment.

1. Cut the truffle into thin shavings and set aside. Finely dice the Fontina cheese. Place the cheese and the milk in the saucepan. Let the cheese soak for at least 4 hours.
2. Drain the milk from the cheese, reserving 1¼ cups. Heat the reserved milk on low heat, without bringing to a boil. Place the warmed milk and the soaked cheese in a metal bowl on top of a saucepan half-filled with boiling water (or in the top half of a double boiler). Heat over low heat, stirring, until the cheese turns creamy. Whisk in the egg yolks, cream, and butter. Keep whisking until the cheese forms strings. Let it sit for a minute until it just begins to thicken, but not to the point where the egg starts scrambling. Stir in the salt and white pepper.
3. Transfer to a fondue pot and set on the burner. Just before serving, sprinkle the shaved truffle slices over the fondue. Serve with the toasted bread for dipping.

Greek Fondue with Alcohol

¾ pound Emmenthal cheese
½ pound feta cheese
1 garlic clove
1¼ cups plus 2 tablespoons
   dry white wine

1 tablespoon lemon juice
1½ tablespoons cornstarch
Marinated Tomatoes (page 147)
Toasted Flatbread (page 245)

Serves 4–6

Mild Emmenthal balances the strong flavor of feta cheese in this recipe. Add more spice by sprinkling fresh herbs such as dill or thyme over the fondue just before serving.

1. Finely dice the cheeses. Smash the garlic clove, peel, and cut in half.
2. Rub the garlic around the inside of a medium saucepan. Discard. Add 1¼ cups wine to the pan and cook on medium-low heat. Don't allow the wine to boil.
3. When the wine is warm, stir in the lemon juice. Add the cheese, a handful at a time. Stir the cheese continually in a sideways figure eight pattern. Wait until the cheese is completely melted before adding more. Don't allow the fondue mixture to boil.
4. Dissolve the cornstarch in the remaining 2 tablespoons of wine. When the cheese is melted, stir in the cornstarch-and-wine mixture. Turn up the heat until the cheese is just bubbling and starting to thicken. Transfer to a fondue pot and set on the burner. Serve with the Marinated Tomatoes as a side dish and the flatbread for dipping.

Slicing Meat for Hot Pot

Cutting meat into the thin slices needed for hot pot cooking can be difficult. One option is to have the meat sliced at the butcher shop. Another is to freeze the meat for approximately 1 hour before using. Frozen meat is much easier to cut.

Vietnamese Beef Hot Pot

16 ounces tenderloin beef or
   any tender cut
1 teaspoon freshly ground
   black pepper
2 teaspoons sugar
1 cucumber
3 green onions
1 head lettuce
1 bunch fresh coriander
24 rice paper wrappers

8 ounces rice vermicelli noodles
1 cup mung bean sprouts
1 jar pickled onions
1 bunch fresh mint leaves
⅓ cup nuoc mam fish sauce
½ cup Asian hoisin sauce
Lemon-Soy Dressing (page 68)
¼ cup crushed peanuts
Vietnamese Beef Broth (page
   82), as needed

Serves 4

Like Beef
Carpaccio
(page 95),
paper-thin
beef is sea-
soned with
spices and
chilled in
this recipe.

1. Cut the beef into paper-thin slices, or have it cut at the butcher shop.
   Sprinkle lightly with the black pepper and sugar. Refrigerate until needed.
2. Wash or rinse all the vegetables and drain thoroughly. Peel the
   cucumber and cut lengthwise into thin slices no more than 2 inches
   long. Cut the green onions into 2-inch slices. Break the lettuce into
   individual leaves. Chop the coriander leaves.
3. Dip the rice paper wrappers briefly in warm water to dampen. Rinse
   the rice vermicelli and cover with warm water for 15 minutes to
   soften. Drain thoroughly. Place the lettuce, cucumber, mung bean
   sprouts, pickled onions, coriander, and mint leaves on a large serving
   platter, with the rice paper wrappers in the middle. Set out the nuoc
   mam fish sauce, hoisin sauce, Lemon-Soy Dressing, and crushed
   peanuts for dipping.
4. Heat the broth on the stove and bring to a boil. Add the green
   onions and softened noodles. Transfer enough broth to fill the fondue
   pot about ⅔ full. Set the fondue pot on the burner, with enough heat
   to keep the broth simmering throughout the meal.
5. Encourage guests to take a rice paper wrapper and add a selection of
   vegetables. Use dipping forks to spear the beef. Cook the beef in the
   hot broth and place on top of the vegetables lying on the wrapper.
   Roll up the wrapper and dip into the dipping sauces. At the end of
   the meal, ladle out the broth with the noodles.

Welsh Rarebit

Serves 3–4

For an added touch, pour a small amount of beer around the edges of the toast before dipping into the cheese.

1 loaf bread
1 pound aged Cheddar cheese
2 tablespoons butter or margarine

1½ cups beer or ale
½ teaspoon cayenne pepper
1 teaspoon dry mustard
Salt and pepper to taste

1. Toast the bread and cut into cubes. Finely dice the Cheddar cheese.
2. Melt the butter in a saucepan on medium-low heat. Add the beer and warm, making sure it doesn't boil. When the beer is warm, add the cheese, a handful at a time. Stir the cheese continually in a sideways figure eight pattern. Wait until the cheese is completely melted before adding more. Don't allow the fondue mixture to come to a boil.
3. When the cheese is melted, turn up the heat until it is just bubbling and starting to thicken. Stir in the cayenne, dry mustard, and salt and pepper. Transfer to a fondue pot and set on the burner. Serve with the toasted bread cubes for dipping.

Welsh Rarebit—The First Fondue?

Classic fondue may be a Swiss invention, but a Welsh dish combining melted cheese and liquor can be traced back several centuries. A popular tavern dish, Welsh rarebit consists of Cheddar cheese, ale, and seasonings baked and poured over toast. In Britain's Yorkshire County, you can get a heartier version of Welsh rarebit (also called Welsh rabbit) made with poached eggs. It's easy to adapt Welsh rarebit for fondue purposes by using the toast as a dipper. For a nonalcoholic version, substitute 1 cup of milk for the ale and replace the cayenne and dry mustard with nutmeg.

Saucy French Fondue

¾ pound Emmenthal cheese
¼ pound Gruyère cheese
1½ tablespoons flour
1½ cups dry white wine

2 teaspoons lemon juice
French Pistou with Cheese
  (page 66)
1 baguette, cut into cubes

Serves 6

French pistou is really Italian pesto without the pine nuts. Try using it wherever you would use a pesto sauce.

1. Finely dice the cheeses and toss with the flour.
2. Warm the wine in a saucepan on medium-low heat. Don't allow the wine to boil. Remove ¼ cup of the wine and keep warm on low heat in a separate saucepan.
3. When the wine is warm, stir in the lemon juice. Add the cheese, a handful at a time. Stir the cheese continually in a sideways figure eight pattern. Wait until the cheese is completely melted before adding more. Don't allow the fondue mixture to boil.
4. When the cheese is melted, turn up the heat until it is just bubbling and starting to thicken. Stir in the pistou. Add the remaining ¼ cup of wine if necessary. Transfer to a fondue pot and set on the burner. Use dipping forks to dip the bread cubes into the cheese.

What Is Crème Fraîche?

Valued for its sharp flavor and velvety texture, crème fraîche is made by adding bacteria to pasteurized cream, in a process similar to making yogurt. A French invention, crème fraîche can be hard to find in North America. However, a homemade version can be made by combining heavy cream with buttermilk (see French Crème Fraîche Fondue, page 216).

Italian Pesto Fondue with Ham

Serves 6

To add extra flavor to this recipe, replace the bell peppers with Roasted Red Peppers (page 150).

8 ounces cooked ham
8 ounces prosciutto
8 ounces fresh small mushrooms
2 red bell peppers
4–6 cups olive oil, or as needed

Italian Pesto with Basil and Pine Nuts (page 61)
1 loaf Italian bread, cubed, or Bruschetta Fondue Cubes with Vegetables (page 247)

1. Roll up the ham and prosciutto and cut into bite-sized pieces. Wipe the mushrooms with a damp cloth. Cut the mushrooms in half. Remove the seeds and stems from the red peppers, and cut the peppers into cubes.
2. Add the oil to the fondue pot, making sure it is not more than half full. Heat the pot on a stove element over medium-high heat. When the oil is hot, move the fondue pot to the table and set up the burner.
3. Use dipping forks to spear the rolled-up slices of ham and prosciutto and the vegetables. Cook in the hot oil. Serve with the pesto and the Italian bread or bruschetta cubes.

Storing Pesto

If you enjoy pesto's strong flavor, you may want to prepare a large quantity ahead of time for future use. To make, follow the basic pesto recipe, leaving out the cheese and garlic. Place in a jar, cover with a thin film of olive oil, seal, and store in the refrigerator. Pesto stored in this manner will last for weeks. When ready to use, add the cheese and garlic and process the pesto until creamy, adding more olive oil if necessary.

Italian Pesto Fondue with Cheese

¼ *pound Fontina cheese*
½ *pound Gruyère cheese*
1 *tablespoon cornstarch*
½ *teaspoon dried oregano*
1 *garlic clove, peeled and*
  halved

1 *cup dry white wine*
2 *teaspoons lemon juice*
½ *cup Italian Pesto with Basil*
  and Pine Nuts (page 61)
1 *package soft breadsticks*

Serves 4–6

Versatile pesto complements many different types of cheese, including Italian Fontina.

1. Finely dice the Fontina and Gruyère. Mix the cornstarch with the oregano. Toss the cheese with the cornstarch mixture.
2. Rub the garlic around the inside of a medium saucepan. Discard. Add the wine to the saucepan and warm on medium-low heat. Don't allow the wine to boil. Remove ¼ cup of the wine and keep warm on low heat in a separate saucepan.
3. When the wine is warm, stir in the lemon juice. Add the cheese, a handful at a time. Stir the cheese continually in a sideways figure eight pattern. Wait until the cheese is completely melted before adding more. Don't allow the fondue mixture to boil.
4. When the cheese is melted, turn up the heat until it is just bubbling and starting to thicken. Stir in the pesto. Add the remaining ¼ cup of wine if necessary. Transfer to a fondue pot and set on the burner. Serve with the soft breadsticks for dipping.

Mild Bagna Cauda

Serves 4

In this regional variation, the anchovies are rinsed, reducing the salty taste. For a lighter version, leave out the cream.

½ cup mushroom caps
1 small head broccoli
1 small head cauliflower
2 red peppers
1 zucchini
2 stalks celery
4 ounces anchovies
4 garlic cloves
1 white truffle
½ cup olive oil
4 tablespoons butter
4 tablespoons light or heavy cream
Basic Bruschetta (page 246)

1. Wipe the mushrooms clean with a damp cloth and wash the other vegetables. Blanch the broccoli and cauliflower briefly in boiling water and drain thoroughly. Cut the vegetables into bite-sized pieces.
2. Rinse the anchovies, drain, and separate. Smash and peel the garlic cloves, leaving the cloves whole. Thinly slice the truffle.
3. Heat the olive oil and butter in a frying pan over low heat. Add the garlic cloves. Cook over very low heat for 10 minutes, and then add the anchovies. Continue to cook on low heat, gently mashing the anchovies and mixing together with the garlic. Add the cream.
4. Transfer the Bagna Cauda to a fondue pot and set on the burner. Serve with the vegetables for dipping, or with your own favorite combination of mixed vegetables. Eat with the bruschetta.

Cooking Vegetables in Broth

The main thing to watch when cooking vegetables in a broth fondue is the cooking time. Thicker, denser vegetables such as broccoli and carrots take 4 to 5 minutes to become tender, while leaf vegetables such as lettuce and bok choy take mere seconds. One option with soft vegetables is to add them all at once and then ladle them into individual soup bowls with the broth, leaving guests to dip the other vegetables.

Korean Bulgogi Hot Pot

1½ pounds beef flank steak
2 tablespoons soy sauce
1½ teaspoons sugar
1½ tablespoons rice vinegar
1½ teaspoons sesame oil
½ large daikon radish
4 large carrots

1 cucumber
2 green onions
1 8-ounce can baby corn
1 bunch cilantro sprigs
4 cups cooked rice
6 cups Simple Beef Broth
   (page 84)

Serves 4

Distilled white vinegar can be substituted for the rice vinegar in this recipe. Serve with soy sauce and Korean kimchi for dipping.

1. Cut the beef into paper-thin slices. Combine the soy sauce, sugar, rice vinegar, and sesame oil in a small bowl. Add the beef and marinate for at least 30 minutes.
2. Wash all the vegetables and drain. Peel the daikon radish. Cut in half and then into slices about 2½ inches long. Do the same with the carrots. Peel and slice the cucumber on the diagonal into slices about 1 inch thick. Chop the green onions. Rinse the baby corn in warm water and drain.
3. Place the marinated beef and vegetables on separate serving platters. Garnish the vegetables with the cilantro. Serve each guest an individual bowl half-filled with cooked rice.
4. Heat the broth on the stove, and bring to a boil. Add the meat and vegetables and bring to a boil again. Transfer enough broth to fill the fondue pot about ⅔ full. Set the fondue pot on the burner, with enough heat to keep the broth simmering throughout the meal. (Keep the remaining broth warm on the stove to use as needed.)
5. At the table, allow the hot pot to cook for another 5 minutes. Ladle a small portion of the broth with meat and vegetables into the soup bowls over rice. Invite guests to use chopsticks to eat the food.

Classic Tiramisu

4 egg yolks
4 tablespoons sugar
4 ounces semisweet chocolate
1 pound mascarpone cheese
8 tablespoons Marsala wine

2 tablespoons espresso or strong hot coffee
2 teaspoons powdered hot chocolate
1 tablespoon cornstarch
24 ladyfingers

1. Whisk the egg yolks with the sugar and set aside. Grate the chocolate and set aside.
2. Whisk the mascarpone with 6 tablespoons Marsala wine. Combine with 1 tablespoon of the espresso in a metal bowl and place on top of a saucepan half-filled with simmering water. Melt the mixture on low to medium-low heat, stirring frequently and making sure that it doesn't boil.
3. When the mascarpone has melted and has a texture close to pudding, stir in the hot chocolate. Dissolve the cornstarch in 2 tablespoons Marsala wine and stir into the fondue. Whisk in the egg yolks to thicken.
4. Transfer the fondue mixture to the fondue pot and set on the burner. Keep warm on low heat. Just before serving, sprinkle with the grated chocolate. Brush the ladyfingers with the remainder of the coffee and serve with the fondue for dipping.

Marvelous Mascarpone

Famous for its rich, buttery flavor, mascarpone has a texture similar to pudding's when cooked. It is the main ingredient in Classic Tiramisu, Italy's famous dessert made with chocolate and espresso. Unripened and with a fat content of over 75 percent, mascarpone tastes like a richer version of ricotta cheese. Experiment by adding a few tablespoons to your favorite chocolate fondue recipe.

Toblerone Fondue with Orange Liqueur

Serves 4–6

Chocolate
and orange
make an
unbeatable
combina-
tion. For a
kid's ver-
sion, simply
leave out
the liqueur.

1 pound fresh strawberries
2 tablespoons freshly squeezed
orange juice
4 3.5-ounce (100-gram)
Toblerone milk chocolate bars

⅔ cup half-and-half or light
cream
4 teaspoons Grand Marnier
liqueur

1. Wash and drain the strawberries on paper towels. Remove the hulls.
   Lightly sprinkle the orange juice over the drained strawberries.
2. Break the Toblerone bars into pieces. Combine the cream and
   Toblerone pieces in a metal bowl and place on top of a saucepan
   half-filled with simmering water. Melt the mixture on low to medium-
   low heat, stirring frequently. Make sure that it doesn't boil.
3. Carefully add the Grand Marnier to the heated chocolate, 1 teaspoon
   at a time. Transfer the chocolate mixture into the fondue pot and set
   on the burner.
4. Keep warm on low heat. Use dipping forks to dip the strawberries into
   the chocolate fondue.

Dipping Tips

*When using dipping forks, unless the recipe instructions state differently, draw
the dipped fruit right through the chocolate. In addition to making sure the fruit
is entirely covered, this helps prevent the chocolate near the bottom of the
fondue pot from burning. When dipping forks aren't used (for example, when
cake or cookies are the dippers), stir the fondue frequently.*

Basic Chocolate Fondue

8 ounces semisweet chocolate
1 cup whipping cream
1 tablespoon liqueur, optional

2 pounds fresh fruit (or 1
pound each fresh fruit and
cake)

Serves 4

Looking for a
creative way
to serve fresh
fruit or left-
over cake?
Both family
and guests
will love this
basic recipe.

1. Break the chocolate into pieces. Combine the whipping cream and chocolate in a metal bowl and place on top of a saucepan half-filled with simmering water. Melt the mixture on low to medium-low heat, stirring frequently. Make sure that it doesn't boil.
2. When the chocolate is melted, stir in the liqueur. Transfer the chocolate mixture into the fondue pot and set on the burner. Keep warm on low heat. Use dipping forks to dip the fruit and/or cake into the fondue.

Basic Chocolate Chip Fondue for Four

1¾ cups chocolate chips
⅓ cup plus 2 tablespoons light
cream

1 tablespoon liqueur, optional
4 cups fresh fruit for dipping

Serves 4

Serve this
easy-to-make
dish with or
without the
liqueur. Feel
free to experi-
ment with dif-
ferent flavors
of baking
chips.

1. Combine the chocolate chips and cream in a metal bowl and place on top of a saucepan half-filled with simmering water. Melt the chocolate on low to medium-low heat, stirring frequently and making sure that it doesn't boil. Stir in the liqueur.
2. Transfer the fondue mixture to the fondue pot and set on the burner. Keep the fondue warm on low heat. Serve with fresh fruit for dipping.

Instant Mocha

Serves 4

Can't find coffee cream? Use regular cream and add one tablespoon of instant coffee to the chocolate mixture during cooking.

8 ounces semisweet chocolate
¾ cup coffee cream
¼ teaspoon nutmeg
1 can pineapple chunks, drained

2 medium oranges, peeled and sliced
Biscuits or biscotti

1. Break the semisweet chocolate into pieces. Combine the coffee cream and chocolate in a metal bowl and place over a saucepan half-filled with simmering water. Melt the chocolate on low to medium-low heat, stirring constantly and not allowing the mixture to boil.
2. When the chocolate is melted, transfer the fondue mixture to the fondue pot and set on the burner. Keep the fondue warm on low heat. Stir in the nutmeg.
3. Serve the fondue with pineapple chunks, sliced oranges, and biscuits or fruit-flavored biscotti for dipping.

Quick and Easy Butterscotch Fondue

Serves 6–8

This dessert tastes delicious served with vanilla ice cream. Biscotti, ladyfingers, or biscuits can also be used for dipping.

4 bananas
3 cups canned pear slices
½ cup light cream
1¾ cups butterscotch chips

3 tablespoons powdered hot chocolate
½ teaspoon vanilla extract
1 tablespoon Kahlua

1. Peel the bananas and slice diagonally. Drain the pear slices and dry on paper towels.
2. Combine the cream and butterscotch chips in a metal bowl and place on top of a saucepan half-filled with simmering water. Melt on low to medium-low heat, stirring constantly. Do not allow the mixture to boil. When the butterscotch chips are completely melted, stir in the hot chocolate, vanilla extract, and the Kahlua.
3. Transfer the fondue mixture to the fondue pot and set on the burner. Keep the fondue warm on low heat. Serve with the fruit for dipping.

Elegant Chocolate Fondue

1 cup light cream
4 heaping tablespoons fresh
   mint leaves, chopped
12 ounces semisweet chocolate

2 tablespoons cognac
Cake, biscuits, or fruit for
   dipping

Serves 4

Mint has a clean, refreshing flavor that combines well with chocolate. If fresh mint leaves are not available, replace the cognac with a peppermint liqueur.

1. In a small saucepan, heat the cream with the mint leaves over low heat for 15–20 minutes, until the mint leaves are tender and the cream almost has a faint greenish color. Strain the cream to remove the mint leaves. Break the chocolate into pieces.
2. Combine the cream and the chocolate in a metal bowl and place over a saucepan half-filled with simmering water. Melt the chocolate on low to medium-low heat, stirring constantly. Do not allow the mixture to boil. Add more cream if necessary.
3. When the chocolate has melted, transfer the fondue mixture to the fondue pot and set on the burner. Keep the fondue warm on low heat. Stir in the cognac. Serve with sponge cake, biscuits, or fresh fruit for dipping. It goes very well with fresh fruit such as apples, pineapples, and bananas, and fruit-flavored biscotti.

Cooking with Chocolate

Cooking with chocolate can be tricky, as it burns quite easily. For best results, never cook chocolate directly over a heating element. Instead, use the top section of a double boiler or place the chocolate in a metal bowl on top of a saucepan partially filled with water that has just begun to simmer. Make sure the simmering water doesn't reach the bottom of the bowl containing the chocolate.

Cinnamon Fondue

Serves 4–6

Adding the cinnamon after the fondue has been removed from the heating agent will help keep the chocolate from seizing up.

1 pound fresh strawberries
8 ounces semisweet chocolate
4 ounces unsweetened chocolate

1 cup heavy cream
1 teaspoon cinnamon

1. Wash and drain the strawberries on paper towels. Remove the hulls. Break the semisweet and unsweetened chocolate into pieces.
2. Combine the cream and chocolate in a metal bowl and place over a saucepan half-filled with barely simmering water. Melt the chocolate on low to medium-low heat, stirring constantly. Do not let the mixture overheat. Add more cream if necessary.
3. When the chocolate has melted, transfer the fondue mixture to the fondue pot and set on the burner. Keep the fondue warm on low heat. Stir in the cinnamon. Serve with the strawberries for dipping.

Cool Yogurt Fondue

Serves 6

This smooth and creamy fondue makes a perfect dessert on warm summer evenings. Feel free to experiment with other types of fresh fruit for dipping.

6 tablespoons unsweetened
* coconut flakes*
3 teaspoons lime juice
3½ tablespoons liquid honey
2 cups plain yogurt

2 peaches
2 apples
3 tablespoons lemon juice
2 bananas

1. Stir the coconut flakes, lime juice, and honey into the yogurt. Chill until ready to serve.
2. Wash the peaches and apples and drain thoroughly. Cut into wedges and lightly cover with the lemon juice. Peel the bananas and cut into 1-inch slices.
3. Use a dipping fork to dip the fruit pieces into the chilled yogurt.

Peanut Butter Fondue

4 large bananas
4 ounces milk chocolate
1 cup chunky peanut butter

1 cup milk
Peanut butter cookies, optional

1. Peel and slice the bananas. Break the chocolate into pieces.
2. Combine the peanut butter, milk, and milk chocolate in a metal bowl and place on top of a saucepan half-filled with simmering water. Melt the chocolate on low to medium-low heat, stirring constantly. Make sure that it doesn't boil.
3. Transfer the fondue mixture to the fondue pot and set on the burner. Keep the fondue warm on low heat. Serve with the bananas and cookies for dipping.

Chunky peanut butter adds texture and flavor to this easy-to-make fondue.

Chocolate Banana Fondue

½ cup half-and-half or light cream
1½ cups semisweet chocolate chips

⅓ cup Sweet Banana Chutney (page 47)
¼ cup crushed peanuts

1. Combine the cream and semisweet chocolate in a metal bowl and place over a saucepan half-filled with simmering water. Melt the chocolate on low to medium-low heat, stirring continuously and making sure it doesn't boil. When the chocolate is melted, stir in the chutney.
2. Garnish the fondue with the crushed peanuts. Keep the fondue warm on low heat while serving. Serve with sliced apples, sliced bananas, and plain biscuits for dipping.

Milk chocolate or Toblerone can be substituted for the semisweet chocolate chips. Use 4 100-gram milk chocolate Toblerone bars and adjust the cream as necessary.

Three Fruit Medley

Serves 6

In this recipe, a traditional chocolate fondue is transformed into a decadent sauce. Feel free to experiment with different fruit combinations.

1 cup fresh strawberries
1 banana
1 cup pineapple chunks
2 tablespoons pineapple juice
  or water

1½ tablespoons brown sugar
1 tablespoon sugar
½ cup light cream
8 ounces semisweet chocolate
  chips

1. Wash the strawberries, cut off the stems, and slice. Peel the banana, cut in half lengthwise, and slice. Lay the sliced strawberries and the pineapple chunks flat in a glass serving dish, with the sliced banana in the middle. If using canned pineapple chunks, reserve 2 tablespoons of the juice. Sprinkle the brown sugar over the pineapple chunks and bananas, and the white sugar over the strawberries. Set aside.

2. Combine the cream and chocolate chips in a metal bowl and place over a saucepan half-filled with simmering water. Melt the chocolate chips on low to medium-low heat, stirring constantly and not allowing the mixture to boil. When the chocolate has melted, stir in the reserved pineapple juice or water. Pour over the pineapple chunks, banana slices, and strawberries. Serve warm.

Preparing Strawberries for a Chocolate Fondue

Make sure you wash the strawberries before removing the stems. Removing the stems first causes the strawberries to fill with water, which can react with the chocolate during dipping.

Harvest Apple Fondue

3–4 large red apples
1½ cups peanuts
½ cup whipping cream
¾ cup semisweet chocolate
   chips

½ cup cinnamon baking chips
2 teaspoons sugar

Serves 6

Sweet Spartan apples work very well in this recipe. Be sure to have extra crushed peanuts on hand.

1. Core the apples and cut into wedges. Refrigerate until ready to use. Crush the peanuts in a blender or food processor.
2. Combine the cream and chips in a metal bowl and place over a saucepan half-filled with simmering water. Melt the chips on low to medium-low heat, stirring continuously and making sure the mixture doesn't boil. Stir in the sugar.
3. Transfer the chocolate mixture to a fondue pot over low heat. Remove the apple slices from the refrigerator and set on the table. Set out individual bowls of crushed peanuts for each person. Dip the apple slices in the fondue and then roll in the crushed peanuts.

Using Fruit in Chocolate Fondue

It tastes great, but fruit dipped in warm chocolate can be a little messy to eat. To keep the chocolate from dripping off, refrigerate the sliced fruit until the fondue is ready to serve. The chocolate cools down when it meets the chilled fruit, making it harden slightly. Another trick is to roll the fruit in crushed peanuts, coconut, or another topping after dipping.

Mexican Chocolate Fondue
with Kahlua and Strawberries

Serves 4–6

For a different flavor, try substituting half the semisweet chocolate with unsweetened chocolate and adding honey to taste.

1 pound fresh strawberries
12 ounces semisweet chocolate
½ cup half-and-half
¾ cup evaporated milk
1 teaspoon ground cinnamon

½ teaspoon nutmeg
¼ teaspoon ground cloves, optional
1 tablespoon Kahlua, or to taste

1. Wash and drain the strawberries on paper towels. Remove the hulls. Break the chocolate into pieces.
2. Combine the chocolate, half-and-half, and evaporated milk in a metal bowl and place on top of a saucepan half-filled with simmering water. Melt the mixture on low to medium-low heat, making sure that it doesn't boil.
3. When the chocolate is melted, stir in the cinnamon, nutmeg, and ground cloves. Stir in the Kahlua.
4. Transfer the fondue mixture to the fondue pot and set on the burner. Keep the fondue warm on low heat. Serve with the strawberries for dipping.

Burned Chocolate Cure

Burning chocolate causes the skin to "seize" and tighten until the texture resembles pudding. To reliquefy burned chocolate, stir 1 or 2 tablespoons of butter into the chocolate mixture.

Spiced Apple Fondue

3 medium Spartan apples
¼ cup half-and-half or light
   cream

1¾ cups semisweet chocolate chips
½ teaspoon cinnamon
2 tablespoons apple schnapps

Serves 6

To prevent
discoloration
and add extra
flavor, lightly
coat the apple
wedges in
pineapple or
lemon juice
and refrig-
erate until
ready to use.

1. Core the apples and cut into wedges. Combine the cream and chocolate chips in a metal bowl and place over a saucepan half-filled with simmering water. Melt the chips on low to medium-low heat, stirring continuously and making sure the mixture doesn't boil.
2. When the chocolate is melted, transfer the fondue mixture to the fondue pot and set on the burner. Stir in the cinnamon and the apple schnapps. Keep the fondue warm on low heat. Serve with the apple wedges for dipping.

Sweet and Sour Tropical Fondue

4 bananas
2 cups tropical dried fruit mix
   (or another dried fruit mix)
¾ cup sour cream

2 tablespoons butter or
   margarine
2 cups chocolate macaroons
2 tablespoons Kahlua

Serves 6–8

For an added
touch, roll the
dipped
banana slices
in grated
coconut
before eating.

1. Slice the bananas and set aside with the dried fruit mix.
2. Combine the sour cream, butter, and chocolate macaroons in a metal bowl and place over a saucepan half-filled with simmering water. Heat the mixture on medium-low heat, stirring constantly. Do not let the mixture boil.
3. When the chocolate is melted, stir in the Kahlua. Transfer the mixture to the fondue pot and set on the burner. Keep the fondue warm on low heat. Serve with the bananas and dried fruit for dipping.

Yin Yang Fondue

Serves 6–8

Did you know? White chocolate's subtle flavor comes from the addition of vanilla extract and other ingredients into the cocoa butter.

8 ounces white chocolate
8 ounces semisweet chocolate
½ cup evaporated milk
½ teaspoon cinnamon

¼ cup kirsch
6 cups mixed apple and cantaloupe slices

1. Break the chocolate into pieces. Combine the white chocolate, semisweet chocolate, and evaporated milk in a metal bowl and place on top of a saucepan half-filled with simmering water. Melt the mixture on low to medium-low heat, making sure that it doesn't boil.
2. When the chocolate has melted, stir in the cinnamon and the kirsch. Transfer the fondue mixture to the fondue pot and set on the burner. Keep the fondue warm on low heat. Serve with the apple and cantaloupe slices for dipping.

Decadent Chocolate Berry Sauce

Serves 6

This decadent dessert goes particularly well with chocolate or a fruit-flavored biscuit, such as raspberry biscotti slices.

2 cups mixed frozen strawberries and blueberries
¼ cup sugar
16 ounces milk chocolate

⅔ cup whipping cream
2 teaspoons lemon juice
Chocolate macaroons and biscuits for dipping, as desired

1. Break up any large frozen strawberries. Simmer the berries in a pot with the sugar for about 10 minutes, until the berries are soft and mushy. Cool and process in a blender or food processor.
2. Break the chocolate into pieces. Combine the milk chocolate and whipping cream in a metal bowl and place on top of a saucepan half-filled with simmering water. Melt the mixture on low to medium-low heat, making sure that it doesn't boil. Stir in the lemon juice and the processed berries.
3. Transfer the fondue mixture to the fondue pot and set on the burner. Keep the fondue warm on low heat. Serve with the chocolate macaroons or biscuits for dipping.

Hot Yogurt Fondue

2 cups plain yogurt
2/3 cup liquid honey
1 teaspoon cinnamon
1 teaspoon lime juice
1 teaspoon lemon juice

1 teaspoon hot chili sauce
2 tablespoons rum
6 cups mixed cantaloupe and
  kiwifruit or other tropical
  fruit slices

Serves 6–8

Don't have time to cook? This fondue can also be served cold. For extra flavor, use banana-flavored yogurt.

1. Combine the yogurt, honey, cinnamon, lime juice, lemon juice, and hot chili sauce in a saucepan and cook over medium-low heat until the yogurt has melted. Stir in the rum.
2. Transfer the fondue mixture to the fondue pot and set on the burner. Keep the fondue warm on low heat. Serve with the tropical fruit for dipping.

Two for One Fondue

1/2 Creamy Caramel Fondue for
  Adults (page 233)
Brandied Peppermint Fondue
  (page 210)

4 tablespoons coconut milk
1 tablespoon kirsch
Pineapple slices and cake
  pieces for dipping

Serves 4

Feel free to warm the coconut milk and kirsch ahead of time but keep the heat low. Like cheese, coconut milk has a tendency to curdle at high temperatures.

1. Combine both fondues and place in a bowl over a saucepan filled with barely simmering water. Add the coconut milk and the kirsch.
2. Transfer the fondue mixture to the fondue pot and set on the burner. Keep the fondue warm on low heat. Serve with the pineapple slices and cake for dipping.

Sweet, Sour, and Spicy Apple

Serves 4–6

In this dish the dippers are cooked in the fondue. This fondue can be enjoyed alone, with ice cream, or with cheese and bread.

2 Spartan apples
¼ teaspoon cinnamon
4 tablespoons honey
2 tablespoons balsamic vinegar
3 tablespoons butter or margarine, divided

1 tablespoon brown sugar
½ cup apple juice
2 teaspoons apple schnapps, optional

1. Wash, core, and cut the apples into thin slices. Toss the sliced apples with the cinnamon. Warm the honey and balsamic vinegar in a medium saucepan.
2. While the honey and vinegar are warming, heat 2 tablespoons of the butter or margarine in a pan. Sauté the apple slices until they are tender. Add the remaining tablespoon of butter and the brown sugar. Cook until the brown sugar has caramelized.
3. Add the apple juice to the honey-and-vinegar mixture. When it has warmed, add the apple slices and heat the mixture. If using the liqueur, stir it in and allow to cook for another few minutes. Transfer to a fondue pot and set up the burner. Use a dipping fork to pick up the apple slices.

Choosing Dipping Fruit

For chocolate fondue, stick with fruit that will hold its shape and texture when pierced with a dipping fork and bathed in warm chocolate. Firm fresh fruits such as bananas, strawberries, and apples are excellent choices. Although kiwifruit and pineapple are less firm, their tart flavor contrasts nicely with the sweet chocolate.

Red, White, and Blue Fondue

4 cups mixed frozen raspberries and blueberries
6 tablespoons sugar
1 tablespoon lemon juice
1 cup plain yogurt

4 teaspoons cornstarch
4 teaspoons water
2 tablespoons kirsch
20–24 ladyfingers

Serves 4

This tasty dessert makes a light but refreshing treat. Dieters need not fear hidden calories in the alcohol—1 tablespoon of kirsch has less than 50 calories.

1. Heat the berries on medium-low heat with the sugar, stirring, until they are mushy. Stir in the lemon juice. Process in a blender or food processor.
2. Return the berries to the saucepan on medium-low heat and add the yogurt. Dissolve the cornstarch in the water and add to the yogurt mixture, stirring to thicken. Stir in the kirsch.
3. Transfer the fondue mixture to the fondue pot and set on the burner. Keep the fondue warm on low heat. Serve with the ladyfingers for dipping.

Kirsch Brandy

The original versions of Swiss fondue wouldn't have been complete without Gruyère cheese, Neuchâtel wine, and kirsch liqueur. A brandy made from distilled cherries, kirsch has a high alcohol content and packs a potent punch in both cheese and chocolate fondues. Still, it is not essential. Feel free to experiment with other types of fruit brandies and liqueurs, or forego spirits entirely.

Doughnut Fondue

Serves 6

Not a fan of doughnuts? This fondue also tastes delicious served with fresh cantaloupe slices for dipping.

8 ounces semisweet chocolate
1 cup cinnamon baking chips
6 tablespoons sour cream
6 tablespoons evaporated milk

¼ cup half-and-half
2 tablespoons butter or margarine
¼ teaspoon ground allspice
Plain doughnuts for dipping

1. Break the chocolate into pieces. Combine the chocolate, baking chips, sour cream, evaporated milk, and half-and-half in a metal bowl and place on top of a saucepan half-filled with simmering water. Melt the mixture on low to medium-low heat, making sure that it doesn't boil. Add the butter or margarine and melt. Stir in the ground allspice.
2. Transfer the fondue mixture to the fondue pot and set on the burner. Keep the fondue warm on low heat. Serve with the doughnuts for dipping. The doughnuts can be eaten whole or cut into pieces and speared with a dipping fork.

Fondue with Tangerines

Serves 6

Feel free to substitute pineapple slices for the tangerines. If using canned pineapple, make sure to dry off the slices to remove excess juice.

6 tangerines
2 cups semisweet chocolate chips

½ cup half-and-half or light cream
1½ tablespoons kirsch

1. Peel the tangerines and dry on paper towels. Combine the chocolate chips and cream in a metal bowl and place on top of a saucepan half-filled with simmering water. Melt the mixture on low to medium-low heat, making sure that it doesn't boil. Stir in the kirsch.
2. Transfer the fondue mixture to the fondue pot and set on the burner. Keep the fondue warm on low heat. Serve with the tangerine slices for dipping.

Sweet Pudding

6 bananas
1½ cups cocoa
6 tablespoons corn syrup
½ cup milk

4 tablespoons sugar
4 tablespoons butter or
    margarine

Serves 6

If the pudding
is too thin,
chill briefly in
the refriger-
ator until it
just begins to
set.

1. Peel the bananas and cut into 1-inch pieces. Combine the cocoa, corn syrup, milk, and sugar.
2. Melt the butter in a medium saucepan. Add the cocoa-and-milk mixture. Bring to a boil and simmer for 10 minutes. Remove and cool. The pudding will thicken as it cools. Serve with the bananas for dipping.

Homemade Butterscotch Fondue

2 cups sugar
½ cup water
4 tablespoons butter
½ cup whipping cream

2 tablespoons corn syrup
½ cup unsalted peanuts, chopped
Marshmallows, fruit, or cake
    for dipping

Serves 6

Stirring the
mixture con-
tinuously
once the
butter and
whipping
cream are
added keeps it
from hard-
ening into
butterscotch
candy.

1. Combine the sugar and water in a medium saucepan and cook on medium heat, stirring to dissolve the sugar. When the sugar is dissolved, turn up the heat and boil the mixture for at least 5 minutes, until the sugar turns a golden color.
2. If the sugar has formed clumps, leave on medium heat and stir to melt the clumps. Once the butterscotch is evenly mixed, remove from the heat and immediately stir in the butter and the whipping cream. Stir vigorously to keep the mixture from hardening. Stir in the corn syrup and the chopped peanuts. Serve unheated in a bowl with the marshmallows, fruit, or cake for dipping.

Serves 4

Ladyfingers become the dippers in the fondue version of this classic Italian dessert. Feel free to substitute a good Marsala wine for the rum.

1 pound mascarpone
¼ cup light cream
¼ cup powdered (confectioners' or icing) sugar
¼ cup strong, fresh brewed espresso coffee

1 tablespoon plus 1 teaspoon powdered hot chocolate
2 teaspoons cornstarch
2 tablespoons rum
4 egg yolks
2 teaspoons cinnamon
24 ladyfingers

1. Combine the mascarpone, light cream, powdered sugar, and 4 teaspoons of the espresso in a metal bowl and place on top of a saucepan half-filled with simmering water. Melt the mixture on low to medium-low heat, stirring frequently and making sure that it doesn't boil.
2. When the mascarpone has melted and has a texture close to pudding, stir in the hot chocolate. Dissolve the cornstarch in the rum and stir into the fondue. Whisk in the egg yolks to thicken.
3. Transfer the fondue mixture to the fondue pot and set on the burner. Keep warm on low heat. Just before serving, sprinkle with the cinnamon. Brush the ladyfingers with the remainder of the espresso and serve with the fondue for dipping.

Terrific Tiramisu

According to legend, tiramisu was created in honor of a visit by an Italian count to the village of Siena in northern Italy. Nicknamed "the Duke's Soup" and "Tuscan Trifle," classic tiramisu consists of alternating layers of espresso-dipped ladyfingers and a mascarpone-based custard. But it also tastes delicious as a fondue!

Fruit Fiesta

1 pound plums
1 medium mango
1 cup water
½ cup sugar

1 teaspoon lemon juice
½ teaspoon ground ginger
½ teaspoon cinnamon

Serves 4–6

Serve with
1 pound of
cubed Swiss
cheese for the
adults, and
sponge cake
or pound cake
for the kids.

1. Wash and drain the fruit. Cut the plums in half, remove the stem and pit, and cut in half again. Cut off the stem of the mango and peel. Cut in half, remove the pit, and cut the flesh into bite-sized chunks.
2. In a medium saucepan, warm the water on medium-low heat. (*Note:* If using canned mangoes or plums, feel free to replace a few table-spoons of the water with the canned fruit juice.) Turn up the heat until nearly boiling and add the sugar, stirring to dissolve. Add the mango and simmer for a few minutes.
3. Add the plums and simmer for 20 minutes more. Stir in the lemon juice, ginger, and cinnamon. Simmer for a few more minutes, then process in a blender or food processor. Transfer the fruit mixture to a fondue pot and set on the burner over medium heat to keep the fruit warm.

A Touch of Lemon

To prevent cut fruit such as apples and pears from discoloring, brush lightly with lemon juice before placing in the refrigerator. If you find the taste of lemon too strong, use a mixture of half lemon juice and half water instead.

Deep-Fried Ice Cream

Serves 6

Coat thoroughly with both the crumb mixture and the batter, and make sure the ice cream is frozen hard before frying.

½ cup graham cracker crumbs
½ teaspoon nutmeg
4 tablespoons plus 2 teaspoons sugar
1 pint vanilla ice cream

Quick and Easy Batter (page 80)
1 teaspoon cinnamon
4 cups oil, or as needed

1. Line a tray with aluminum foil. Place in the freezer while preparing the crumb coating. Combine the graham cracker crumbs, nutmeg, and 1 tablespoon plus 2 teaspoons of the sugar and set aside.
2. Scoop out 6 golf-ball-sized scoops of ice cream. Roll thoroughly in the crumb mixture. Stick a chopstick through the middle of each ball, and place on the frozen tray. Freeze overnight.
3. The next day, prepare the batter. Refrigerate and chill for 30 minutes. Combine the cinnamon with 3 tablespoons of the sugar and set aside. Heat the oil in the fondue pot on the stove, and set on the burner.
4. Take one ice cream ball out of the freezer. If necessary, use a knife to gently dislodge the bottom of the ball from the foil. Use your fingers to completely coat the ball with the batter.
5. If possible, lay the chopstick across the fondue pot, so that half the ice cream is in the hot oil. (This works best with an electric fondue pot.) Otherwise, use a dipping basket to gently lower the ice cream ball until it is submerged halfway in the oil. Cook very briefly, for about 5 seconds, then turn over and cook the other side. Remove and roll in the cinnamon mixture. Continue with the rest of the ice cream balls.

Decadent Mascarpone Fondue

1 pound mascarpone
¼ cup light cream
¼ cup powdered (confectioners' or icing) sugar

4 teaspoons powdered hot chocolate
2 teaspoons cornstarch
2 tablespoons brandy

Serves 4

Rich mascarpone is the Italian alternative to chocolate in dessert fondues. Serve with ladyfingers or biscotti.

1. Combine the mascarpone, cream, and powdered sugar in a metal bowl and place on top of a saucepan half-filled with simmering water. Melt the mixture on low to medium-low heat, stirring frequently and making sure that it doesn't boil.
2. When the cheese has melted and has a texture close to pudding, stir in the hot chocolate. Dissolve the cornstarch in the brandy and stir into the fondue.
3. Transfer the fondue mixture to the fondue pot and set on the burner. Keep warm on low heat.

Sour Cream Fondue

2 cups canned pineapple chunks
1½ cups sour cream

3 tablespoons liquid honey
3 tablespoons pineapple juice (reserved from the can)

Serves 2–4

For added flavor, sprinkle 3 tablespoons of coconut flakes over the fondue before placing in the refrigerator.

Dry the pineapple chunks. Combine the sour cream, honey, and pineapple juice. Chill briefly until the fondue just starts to set. Use dipping forks to dip the pineapple chunks into the sour cream.

Chocolate Zucchini Fondue

Serves 4

Zucchini's firm texture and delicate flavor makes it an excellent dipper in this twist on chocolate cake with zucchini.

4 zucchini
1¾ cups chocolate chips
⅓ cup plus 2 tablespoons evaporated milk
2 teaspoons vanilla extract

1 teaspoon almond extract
1 tablespoon plus 1 teaspoon instant hot chocolate
½ teaspoon cinnamon
1 tablespoon kirsch

1. Wash the zucchini, peel, and cut diagonally into slices approximately ¼–½ inch thick. Cut in half again.
2. Combine the chocolate chips, evaporated milk, vanilla extract, and almond extract in a metal bowl and place on top of a saucepan half-filled with simmering water. Melt the chocolate on low heat, stirring frequently and making sure that it doesn't boil. Stir in the cocoa, cinnamon, and kirsch.
3. Transfer the fondue mixture to the fondue pot and set on the burner. Keep the fondue warm on low heat.

Sweet Orange Liqueur Fondue

Serves 4

Have some leftover fondue? This recipe makes an excellent cake glaze. Just reheat the chocolate mixture over warm water and ice the cake.

1 pound nectarines
1 pound fresh peaches
8 ounces semisweet chocolate
1 cup whipping cream

½ teaspoon almond extract
1 teaspoon vanilla extract
20 mini marshmallows
1 tablespoon Grand Marnier

1. Wash the nectarines and peaches and dry thoroughly. Remove the pits and cut each piece of fruit into 6 to 8 equal wedges.
2. Break the chocolate into pieces. Combine the chocolate, whipping cream, almond extract, vanilla extract, and marshmallows in a metal bowl and place on top of a saucepan half-filled with simmering water. Melt the chocolate on low heat. Stir in the Grand Marnier.
3. Transfer the fondue mixture to the fondue pot and set on the burner. Keep the fondue warm on low heat. Use dipping forks to spear the fruit wedges and draw through the chocolate. Serve with cookies.

Basic Chocolate Chip Fondue for Two

This recipe
yields
1 cup of
chocolate
fondue, which
makes a nice,
light romantic
dessert for
two people.

1¼ cups chocolate chips
⅓ cup light cream

2 teaspoons liqueur
3 cups fresh fruit for dipping

1. Combine the chocolate chips and cream in a metal bowl and place on top of a saucepan half-filled with simmering water. Melt the chocolate on low to medium-low heat, stirring frequently and making sure that it doesn't boil. Stir in the liqueur.
2. Transfer the fondue mixture to the fondue pot and set on the burner. Keep the fondue warm on low heat. Serve with fresh fruit slices for dipping. Use dipping forks to spear the pieces of fruit and draw them through the warm chocolate.

Summer Squash Fondue

Serves 2–4

If you have
extra zucchini
left over,
enjoy the
slices raw. If
you are run-
ning out, just
cut the
remaining
slices in half
one more
time.

2 zucchini
1¼ cups chocolate chips
⅓ cup evaporated milk
1 teaspoon vanilla extract

1 tablespoon instant hot
chocolate
2 teaspoons kirsch, or to taste

1. Wash and peel the zucchini. Cut diagonally into slices approximately ¼–½ inch thick.
2. Combine the chocolate chips, evaporated milk, and vanilla extract in a metal bowl and place on top of a saucepan half-filled with simmering water. Melt the chocolate on low to medium-low heat, stirring frequently and making sure that it doesn't boil. Stir in the cocoa and kirsch.
3. Transfer the fondue mixture to the fondue pot and set on the burner. Keep the fondue warm on low heat. Serve with the sliced zucchini for dipping.

Macaroons Dipped in White Chocolate

30–40 coconut macaroons
2 cups frozen red and blue
   berries
3 tablespoons sugar
1 teaspoon lemon juice
4 ounces white chocolate

2 tablespoons whipping cream
4 teaspoons cornstarch
4½ teaspoons water
2 teaspoons coconut flakes
2 tablespoons cognac

Serves 2

Chilling the macaroons ahead of time makes it easier to place them on the dipping fork prongs and prevents melting when they meet the warm chocolate.

1. One hour before preparing the fondue, place the macaroons in the refrigerator.
2. Break up any large frozen berries, such as strawberries, into pieces. Heat the berries on medium-low heat with the sugar, stirring, until they are mushy. Stir in the lemon juice. Process in a blender or food processor.
3. Break the white chocolate into pieces. Combine the whipping cream and 2 ounces of chocolate in a metal bowl and place on top of a saucepan half-filled with simmering water. Melt the chocolate on low to medium-low heat, stirring frequently and making sure that it doesn't boil.
4. Add the strained berries and add the remaining 2 ounces of white chocolate. Dissolve the cornstarch in the water. When all the chocolate has melted, add the cornstarch-and-water mixture, stirring to thicken. Stir in the coconut and the cognac.
5. Transfer the fondue mixture to the fondue pot and set on the burner. Keep the fondue warm on low heat. Serve with the macaroons for dipping.

Chocolate Macaroons

Reputedly invented by Italian monks in the eighth century, the word "macaroon" is an adaptation of the Venetian word macarpone, meaning "paste." Traditionally, macaroons are made with almond paste. Coconut macaroons substitute shredded coconut for almond paste, and add cocoa or grated chocolate and condensed milk. This gives them a decadent "melt-in-your-mouth" quality.

Almond Orange Fondue

Serves 2

This makes 1 cup of chocolate fondue, perfect for a romantic dessert after a main meal.

3 tangerines
6 ounces semisweet chocolate
¾ cup whipping cream
¼ teaspoon almond extract

¼ teaspoon grated orange peel
2 teaspoons orange liqueur
4 almond cookies

1. Peel the tangerines, separate into segments, and pat dry on paper towels. Break the chocolate into pieces.
2. Combine the whipping cream, chocolate, almond extract, and grated orange peel in a metal bowl and place on top of a saucepan half-filled with simmering water. Melt the chocolate on low to medium-low heat, stirring frequently and making sure that it doesn't boil. Stir in the orange liqueur.
3. Transfer the fondue mixture to the fondue pot and set on the burner. Keep the fondue warm on low heat. Serve with the tangerines and almond cookies for dipping.

Brandied Peppermint Fondue

Serves 2

This recipe makes a fairly thick fondue. To thin, increase the half-and-half up to ½ cup.

8 caramel candies
⅓ cup half-and-half
1 cup semisweet chocolate chips

¾ cup peppermint chips
1½ tablespoons kirsch
15–20 cookies

1. Unwrap the caramel candies. Combine the half-and-half and caramels in a metal bowl and place on top of a saucepan half-filled with simmering water. When the caramels are half-melted, add the chocolate and peppermint chips.
2. Melt the mixture on low heat, stirring continuously, and making sure that it doesn't boil. When the chocolate is melted, stir in the kirsch.
3. Transfer the fondue mixture to the fondue pot and set on the burner. Keep the fondue warm on low heat. Serve with the cookies for dipping.

Honey Almond Flambé

4 3.5-ounce Toblerone Honey and Almond milk chocolate bars

½ cup half-and-half or light cream

2 tablespoons cognac

Banana and pear slices for dipping, as needed

Using cognac lighted on a spoon to ignite the remaining cognac prevents you from having to lean over to light the fondue, which could be dangerous.

1. Break the chocolate into pieces. Combine the chocolate and cream in a metal bowl placed over a saucepan half-filled with boiling water. When the chocolate is melted, transfer the fondue mixture to the fondue pot and set on the burner.
2. Add the cognac on top of the fondue, reserving 1 teaspoon. Fill a dessert spoon with the 1 teaspoon of cognac. Light the cognac on the spoon. Use the lighted cognac to light the brandy on the chocolate. Once the cognac has burned out, the fondue is ready to eat.
3. Keep the fondue warm on low heat. Serve with the fresh fruit slices for dipping.

Toblerone—The Original Chocolate Fondue

Switzerland is famous as the birthplace of cheese fondue, but fewer people realize that a famous Swiss chocolate bar inspired the creation of chocolate-based dessert fondues. The original chocolate dessert fondue was made with Swiss Toblerone, an oversized chocolate bar loaded with honey and almonds. Today, many people still feel Toblerone is the best choice for a chocolate fondue.

Instant Fondue

Serves 2–4

For a more romantic atmosphere, transfer the cooked cheese to a chocolate fondue pot and serve over an open flame.

¼ cup walnuts, finely chopped
2 tablespoons apple schnapps
½ pound Cheddar cheese
Crackers for dipping

1. Preheat the oven to 350°F. Soak the walnuts in the liqueur for at least 15 minutes.
2. Slice the Cheddar and break into chunks. Lay out flat in a shallow greased baking dish. Sprinkle the liquor-soaked walnuts on top.
3. Bake for 3 to 5 minutes, until the cheese melts. (This will happen quite quickly.) Remove and serve in a ceramic fondue pot, with the crackers for dipping.

Deep-Fried Chocolate

Serves 2

The secret to this recipe lies in how the batter is applied—it needs to be thick enough to cover the chocolate, but thin enough to cook quickly.

1 3.5-ounce Toblerone bar
1 egg, lightly beaten
⅓ cup graham cracker crumbs
4½ cups oil, or as needed
¼ cup Tempura Batter (page 78), prepared without the black pepper

1. Break the Toblerone bar into 12 individual pieces. Dip each piece in the beaten egg and then roll in the graham cracker crumbs until coated. Place the chocolate on a tray lined with aluminum foil and freeze for 2 hours.
2. Add the oil to the fondue pot, making sure it is not more than half full. Heat the pot on a stove element over medium-high heat.
3. When the oil is hot, move the fondue pot to the table and set up the burner. Coat the chocolate with the batter, using your fingers. Using a dipping basket or spatula, gently lower the chocolate into the hot oil. Cook very briefly until the batter lightly browns (about 30 seconds). Eat immediately.

Blushing Fondue

½ pound Swiss Emmenthal
  cheese
½ pound Gruyère cheese
1 garlic clove
1 cup dry rosé

2 teaspoons lemon juice
1½ tablespoons cornstarch
2 tablespoons kirsch
½ teaspoon nutmeg
½ loaf French bread, cubed

Serves 2–4

Rosé wine adds a romantic reddish tinge and fruity flavor to a traditional Swiss cheese fondue.

1. Finely dice the Emmenthal and Gruyère cheeses and set aside. Smash the garlic, peel, and cut in half.
2. Rub the garlic around the inside of a medium saucepan. Discard. Add the rosé to the pan and cook on low heat. Don't allow the wine to boil.
3. When the rosé is warm, stir in the lemon juice. Add the cheese, a handful at a time. Stir the cheese continually in a sideways figure eight pattern. Wait until the cheese is completely melted before adding more. Don't allow the fondue mixture to boil.
4. When the cheese is melted, turn up the heat until it is just bubbling and starting to thicken. Dissolve the cornstarch in the kirsch and add to the cheese. Stir in the nutmeg. Transfer to a fondue pot and set on the burner. Serve with the French bread cubes for dipping.

Fast Fondue

Don't want to spend the evening melting cheese or chocolate? Make a fondue broth ahead of time and refrigerate. To prepare, simply return the broth to room temperature and heat in the fondue pot. Provide an assortment of your favorite cold meats and vegetables for dipping. Serve with cheese on the side and finish the meal with wine or beer.

Champagne Fondue

Serves 2–4

This is a perfect recipe for celebrating special occasions such as New Year's Eve. Serve any leftover Brie on crackers with the remainder of the champagne.

1 pound Brie cheese
1 garlic clove
1 cup plus 2 tablespoons dry
   champagne
2 teaspoons lemon juice

2 teaspoons cornstarch
1/8 teaspoon nutmeg, or to taste
1 French bread baguette, cut
   into cubes

1. Cut the Brie into cubes. Smash the garlic, peel, and cut in half. Rub the garlic around the inside of a medium saucepan. Discard. Add 1 cup champagne to the saucepan and warm on medium-low heat. Don't allow it to boil.
2. When the champagne is warm, stir in the lemon juice. Add the cheese, a few cubes at a time. Stir the cheese continually in a sideways figure eight pattern. Wait until the cheese is completely melted before adding more. Don't allow the fondue mixture to boil.
3. Dissolve the cornstarch in the remaining 2 tablespoons of champagne. When the cheese is melted, add the dissolved cornstarch. Turn up the heat until it is just bubbling and starting to thicken. Stir in the nutmeg.
4. Transfer to a fondue pot and set on the burner. Serve with the sliced French baguette cubes for dipping.

Champagne and Chocolate

As romantic as it sounds, a bottle of fine champagne isn't the best way to finish off a romantic dessert fondue served over an open flame. Unfortunately, the acidity level in champagne clashes with sweet chocolate. If you do choose to pair champagne with chocolate, stick to the sweeter varieties such as demi-sec.

Tiramisu for Two

½ pound mascarpone
2 tablespoons light cream
2 tablespoons powdered (confectioners' or icing) sugar
2 tablespoons strong hot
   coffee, divided

2 teaspoons powdered hot
   chocolate
1 teaspoon cornstarch
1 tablespoon rum
2 egg yolks
1 teaspoon cinnamon
12 ladyfingers

Serves 2

This tastes delicious chilled overnight. For an extra treat, sprinkle with grated semisweet chocolate before serving.

1. Combine the mascarpone, cream, powdered sugar, and 2 teaspoons of the coffee in a metal bowl and place on top of a saucepan half-filled with simmering water. Melt the mixture on low to medium-low heat, stirring frequently and making sure that it doesn't boil.
2. When the mascarpone has melted and has a texture close to pudding, stir in the hot chocolate. Dissolve the cornstarch in the rum and stir into the fondue. Whisk in the egg yolks to thicken.
3. Transfer the fondue mixture to the fondue pot and set on the burner. Keep warm on low heat. Just before serving, sprinkle with the cinnamon. Brush the ladyfingers with the remainder of the coffee and serve with the fondue for dipping.

Tiramisu—The Perfect Romantic Pick-Me-Up

According to legend, Venetian courtesans used to build up their strength for the next amorous encounter by enjoying a dish of chilled tiramisu dessert.

French Crème Fraîche Fondue

Serves 2

Plan ahead to make this dessert. The crème fraîche needs to be prepared the day before.

½ cup heavy cream
1 tablespoon buttermilk
2 apples
2 teaspoons lemon juice

8 ounces semisweet chocolate
2 tablespoons coffee liqueur
Biscotti

1. The day before you plan to serve the fondue, make the crème fraîche. Combine the heavy cream and buttermilk in a bowl, cover, and let sit for 24 hours.
2. Wash the apples and dry thoroughly. Cut the apples in half, remove the stems and seeds, and cut each apple into 6 to 8 equal wedges. Lightly brush the wedges with lemon juice and refrigerate.
3. Combine the semisweet chocolate and the crème fraîche in a metal bowl placed on top of a saucepan half-filled with simmering water. Melt the chocolate on low heat, stirring frequently and making sure that it doesn't boil. Stir in the coffee liqueur.
4. Transfer the fondue mixture to the fondue pot and set on the burner. Keep warm on low heat. Serve with the biscotti and apple wedges for dipping.

Chocolate Chip Origins

Massachusetts innkeeper Ruth Wakefield is credited with inventing chocolate chips. In the 1930s, she began serving guests at her Tollhouse Inn cookies made with broken pieces of semisweet chocolate instead of baker's chocolate. The cookies became quite popular, and Nestlé eventually purchased the recipe. In honor of Ruth Wakefield, they named the chocolate chips Toll House Real Chocolate Morsels.

Chocolate-Honey Fondue

4 bananas

4 ounces unsweetened chocolate

⅔ cup sweetened condensed
   milk

2 teaspoons liquid honey

1 tablespoon honey liqueur

1. Peel the bananas and slice. Refrigerate until it is time to use the bananas in the fondue.
2. Combine the unsweetened chocolate, condensed milk, and honey in a metal bowl placed on top of a saucepan half-filled with simmering water. Melt the chocolate on low heat, stirring frequently and making sure that it doesn't boil. Remove from the heat and stir in the honey liqueur.
3. Transfer the fondue mixture to the fondue pot and set on the burner. Keep warm on low heat. Serve with the banana slices for dipping.

Which Fondue Pot to Use?

When it comes to creating a romantic atmosphere to enjoy chocolate fondue by, nothing beats dessert fondue pots. Made of ceramic and with a single candle for the heat source, most will conveniently hold up to 2 cups of chocolate fondue.

Mascarpone with Baked Pears

Serves 2

The firm texture of baked pears makes an interesting contrast to the creamy mascarpone. Serve with hot spiced rum for a romantic dessert for two.

4–6 firm ripe pears
¾ cup apple juice
8 ounces mascarpone
¼ cup corn syrup

⅛ teaspoon nutmeg
¼ teaspoon cinnamon,
  or to taste
3 teaspoons rum

1. Preheat oven to 350°F. Cut the pears in half, remove the stems and seeds, and cut into bite-sized chunks. Place in a 9" × 9" shallow glass dish and pour the apple juice over. Bake for 30 minutes.
2. Combine the mascarpone and corn syrup in a metal bowl and place on top of a saucepan half-filled with simmering water. Melt the mixture on low to medium-low heat, stirring frequently and making sure that it doesn't boil. When the mascarpone has melted and the fondue has the texture of custard, stir in the nutmeg, cinnamon, and rum.
3. Transfer the fondue mixture to a dessert fondue pot and keep warm on low heat over a candle. Use dipping forks to spear the baked pear chunks and dip into the fondue.

Olive Oil Types

Sometimes called "liquid gold," olive oil is valued for both its delicate flavor and its nutritional properties. There are three main types of olive oil. Both virgin and extra-virgin olive oil are made by a process known as cold-pressing, which reduces the acidity. The acidity level of virgin olive oil cannot exceed 3 percent, while extra-virgin olive oil has an acidity level of less than 1 percent. The intense flavor of virgin and extra-virgin olive oils makes them an excellent choice for salad dressings and drizzling on bread. However, regular olive oil should be used in cooking, as it has a higher smoking point.

Peppermint Fondue

4 ounces semisweet chocolate
½ cup peppermint-flavored
   baking chips
3 tablespoons sour cream
6 teaspoons evaporated milk

1 tablespoon butter or
   margarine
1 tablespoon peppermint
   liqueur, or to taste

Serves 2

This fondue tastes excellent with fresh strawberries and sliced kiwifruit for dippers.

1. Combine the semisweet chocolate, peppermint baking chips, sour cream, and evaporated milk in a metal bowl and place on top of a saucepan half-filled with simmering water. Melt the chocolate on low to medium-low heat, stirring frequently and making sure that it doesn't boil. Add the butter or margarine and melt. Stir in the peppermint liqueur.
2. Transfer the fondue mixture to the fondue pot and set on the burner. Keep warm on low heat. Serve with fresh fruit slices for dipping.

Dim Sum for Two

4 frozen gyoza pork potstickers
4 frozen prawn potstickers
2 frozen spring rolls

4½ cups oil, or as needed
Golden Hot Mustard (page 63)
¼ cup soy sauce

Serves 2

Gyoza are the Japanese version of Chinese potstickers. Other choices for dipping sauces include sesame oil, Worcestershire sauce, and peanut sauce.

1. Thaw the potstickers and spring rolls. Pat dry with paper towels to remove any excess moisture.
2. Add the oil to the fondue pot, making sure it is not more than half full. Heat the pot on a stove element over medium-high heat. When the oil is hot, move the fondue pot to the table and set up the burner.
3. Use dipping forks to spear the potstickers and spring rolls. Cook in the hot oil until they turn golden brown. Serve with the mustard and soy sauce for dipping.

Fried Ice Cream
with Decadent Chocolate Sauce

Serves 2

Serve with
biscotti or
cookies to
use as dip-
pers for any
leftover
chocolate
sauce.

Vanilla ice cream
⅓ cup graham cracker crumbs
¾ cup Quick and Easy Batter
   (page 80)
4½ cups oil, or as needed

½ cup semisweet chocolate
   chips
¼ cup evaporated milk
1 tablespoon liquid honey
½ teaspoon vanilla extract

1. Cover a tray with aluminum foil, and place in the freezer. Form 4
   large scoops of ice cream the size of tennis balls. Roll each ball in
   the graham cracker crumbs, making sure it is thoroughly covered. (You
   may have graham cracker crumbs left over.) Stick a chopstick through
   the middle of each ball. Place on the tray and freeze overnight.

2. Chill the batter in the refrigerator for 30 minutes. Heat the oil in the
   fondue pot on the stove, and set on the burner.

3. While the oil is heating, prepare the sauce. Combine the chocolate
   chips, evaporated milk, honey, and vanilla extract in a metal bowl
   placed over a saucepan half-filled with boiling water. Melt the chocolate and allow to cool.

4. Take 1 ice cream ball out of the freezer. If necessary, use a knife to
   gently dislodge the bottom of the ball from the foil. Use your fingers to
   completely coat the ball with the batter. Maneuver the chopstick so that
   only the bottom half of the ice cream is in the hot oil. (Use a spatula
   or dipping basket if necessary.) Cook very briefly, for about 5 seconds,
   then turn over and cook the other side. Remove and dip into the
   chocolate sauce. Continue with the rest of the ice cream balls.

Fried Cheese Cubes

¾ pound Fontina cheese
1 cup bran flakes
2 eggs
1 tablespoon milk

¼ teaspoon paprika
½ teaspoon sugar
4½ cups oil, or as needed
½ cup flour

1. Remove the rind from the cheese and cut into cubes about ¾ inch thick.
2. Crush the bran flakes with a mortar and pestle. Beat the eggs with the milk, paprika, and sugar. Make sure the eggs are thoroughly beaten. Use your hands to mix the crushed bran flakes with the beaten eggs.
3. Add the oil to the fondue pot, making sure it is not more than half full. Heat the pot on a stove element over medium-high heat.
4. When the oil is hot, move the fondue pot to the table and set up the burner. Coat the cheese cubes with the flour. Dip the cheese into the egg mixture, making sure it is thoroughly coated. Spear the cheese with a dipping fork and cook very briefly in the hot oil. Drain on paper towels if desired. Cool and eat.

Choosing Fondue Oil

To help prevent oil splatters, choose oils that can take the high temperatures needed for cooking. Peanut oil and vegetable oils such as canola are good choices. Avoid using olive oil unless specifically called for in the recipe—its distinctive flavor can overpower the food being cooked.

Spring Rolls for Two

Yields 4–6

Serve this light appetizer with a bottle of dry white wine such as a German Riesling.

½ cup baby shrimp
1 tablespoon plus 2 teaspoons oyster sauce
½ tablespoon water
1 tablespoon soy sauce
½ teaspoon sugar
½ cup mung bean sprouts
½ carrot
1 tablespoon canned bamboo shoots

1 large Chinese dried mushroom, sliced, optional
1 green onion
5 cups oil, or as needed
¼ teaspoon sesame oil
4–6 spring roll wrappers
2 tablespoons cornstarch mixed with 1 tablespoon water

1. Rinse the shrimp and pat dry. Cut into tiny pieces. Toss with 2 teaspoons of the oyster sauce and let marinate for 15 minutes. Mix together the water, 1 tablespoon oyster sauce, soy sauce, and sugar. Set aside.
2. Rinse the mung bean sprouts and drain thoroughly. Wash and grate the carrot until you have 2 full tablespoons. Cut the bamboo shoots in half and then cut into very thin slices. Dice the green onion.
3. Add 1½ tablespoons vegetable oil to a frying pan. When oil is hot, add the dried mushroom slices. Fry for about 1 minute, then add the bamboo shoots, bean sprouts, grated carrot, and the green onion. Mix in the soy sauce mixture and bring to a boil. Add the shrimp. Drizzle with the sesame oil. Cool.
4. To prepare the spring rolls, lay a wrapper in front of you so that it forms 2 triangles. Use your fingers to brush the edges of the wrapper with the cornstarch-and-water mixture. Place a full tablespoon of filling in the middle. Roll up the wrapper, tucking in the edges, and seal with more cornstarch and water. Prepare the remaining spring rolls in the same way.
5. Add the oil to the fondue pot, making sure it is not more than half full. Heat the pot on a stove element over medium-high heat. When the oil is hot, move the fondue pot to the table and set up the burner. Deep-fry the spring rolls, two at a time, until they turn golden. Drain on paper towels.

Carpaccio-Style Beef with Pesto Mayonnaise

4 ounces beef tenderloin, sliced paper thin

2 ounces Parmigiano-Reggiano cheese

1 tablespoon olive or vegetable oil

2 tablespoons lemon juice

2 tablespoons extra-virgin olive oil

2 tablespoons freshly cracked black pepper

¼ cup fresh basil leaves, chopped

Pesto Mayonnaise (page 62)

½ Italian or French baguette, sliced

Serves 2–4

Marinating the beef in lemon juice darkens the color, making it appear to be slightly cooked.

1. Keep the beef chilled until ready to use. Shred the Parmigiano-Reggiano cheese.
2. Place the beef between pieces of lightly oiled plastic wrap. Pound with a mallet to thin the beef even further. Remove the beef from the wrap and brush on both sides with the lemon juice. Refrigerate for 1 hour.
3. Cut the beef into thin strips. Lightly brush with the extra-virgin olive oil and sprinkle the cracked black pepper over. Place on a serving dish and garnish with the fresh basil leaves and shredded cheese.
4. Place the mayonnaise in a cheese or dessert fondue bowl in the middle of the table. Skewer the beef slices and dip into the mayonnaise. Eat with the baguette slices.

Beef Carpaccio—Italian Steak Tartare

Beef carpaccio was created in a Venice bar, reportedly to help a patron whose doctor had ordered her to swear off meat. The dish is named after a famous fifteenth-century Venetian painter. While beef carpaccio is similar to steak tartare, it has a more subtle flavor. Most steak tartare recipes call for the meat to be seasoned with Tabasco sauce and Worcestershire sauce.

Caribbean Butterflied Shrimp

Serves 2

Feel free to
use mild or
strong curry
powder,
depending
on your
preference.

12 large raw shrimp, peeled
  and deveined, tails on
2 garlic cloves
1 firm banana
1 tablespoon butter or margarine

½ cup light cream
4 teaspoons lime juice
½ cup rum
¼ teaspoon curry powder
1 cup sweetened coconut
  flakes

1. Rinse the shrimp in cold water and pat dry with paper towels. To butterfly the shrimp, make an incision lengthwise down the back. Cut
   down as deeply as possible without cutting right through the shrimp.
   Halfway down the back, make two parallel cuts on the left and right
   of the incision. Flatten down the 4 quarters as much as possible.
   Place the butterflied shrimp on a large serving platter.
2. Smash and peel the garlic. Peel the banana and cut into slices at least
   ½ inch thick.
3. In a medium saucepan, melt the butter on low heat. Add the garlic
   and cook on low heat in the melting butter for 2 to 3 minutes. Add
   the cream and the lime juice. Carefully add the rum. Stir in the curry
   powder.
4. Transfer the dish to a fondue pot and set on the burner at the table.
   Use dipping forks to spear the shrimp and cook in the fondue until
   they change color. Dip into the coconut flakes. When the shrimp are
   gone, add the banana to the fondue and dip into the coconut flakes.

Half-and-Half Warning

*Made by combining cream with milk, half-and-half can curdle at higher tem-
peratures. While it's safe to use in chocolate dessert fondues, which never reach
the boiling point, use real cream for other recipes.*

Shabu-Shabu for Two

½ pound sirloin beef
½ cup canned bamboo shoots
1 small carrot
½ head Napa cabbage
2 eggs

2 cups cooked rice
Instant Dashi (page 85)
½ cup Lemon-Soy Dressing
  (page 68)

Serves 2

Instead of dashi soup, 3 cups of chicken broth combined with 3 cups of water can be used. Serve with Spring Rolls for Two (page 222) for a complete meal.

1. Cut the meat into paper-thin slices. Rinse the bamboo shoots in warm running water and drain thoroughly. Wash the carrot, peel, and dice. Wash the cabbage leaves and rip into chunks.
2. Place the beef and vegetables on a platter in separate sections. Place each egg in a small bowl and beat. Place the rice in a separate serving bowl.
3. Heat the dashi broth on the stove and bring to a boil. Transfer to the fondue pot. Set the fondue pot on the burner, with enough heat to keep the broth simmering throughout the meal.
4. Cook the meat and carrot in the broth. Dip the cooked food into the dipping sauce and/or the beaten egg. Serve the rice with the food. When the beef and carrot are gone, add the bamboo shoots and cabbage to the broth, cook briefly, and then eat the soup.

Hands-On Dining with Shabu-Shabu

Shabu-shabu is Japanese for "swish swish." Diners use chopsticks to swish the thinly sliced meat around in the hot broth. While the meat cooks in seconds, the vegetables take longer and can be left for a few minutes in the broth. Traditionally, shabu-shabu is made with Kobe beef that comes from cattle fed on a beer-based diet. World-famous for its marbled texture and tender flavor, Kobe beef is also extremely expensive. A good cut of beef sirloin is an acceptable substitute.

Three Aphrodisiac Soup

Serves 2

Did you know? Garlic, oysters, and tomatoes are all considered to be aphrodisiacs in different cultures.

2 Italian sausages
6 canned Pacific oysters
2 garlic cloves
½ cup plus 1 tablespoon white wine
2 tablespoons liquid from the canned oysters

1 teaspoon lemon juice
¾ cup mozzarella cheese, shredded
2 teaspoons cornstarch
¼ teaspoon nutmeg
Bruschetta with Roma Tomatoes (page 246)

1. Fry the sausages, cut into bite-sized pieces, and set aside. Drain the oysters, reserving the liquid, and chop into thin pieces.
2. Smash and peel the garlic cloves. Use half of one to rub the inside of a medium saucepan. Leave the garlic cloves in the saucepan, and add ½ cup of the wine and the oyster liquid. Warm on low heat.
3. When the wine mixture is warmed, stir in the lemon juice. Add the cheese, a handful at a time. Stir the cheese continually in a sideways figure eight pattern. Wait until the cheese is completely melted before adding more. Don't allow the fondue mixture to boil. When the cheese is nearly melted, add the oysters and cook for a few more minutes.
4. Dissolve the cornstarch in the remaining tablespoon of white wine and add to the fondue. Turn up the heat until it is just bubbling and starting to thicken. Stir in the nutmeg. Transfer to a fondue pot and set on the burner. Serve with the bruschetta and the sausages for dipping.

CHAPTER 12
Family Favorites

S'Mores!

Serves 2–4

The addition of evaporated milk turns a campfire favorite into a tasty fondue. This recipe yields just over 1 cup but can easily be doubled.

½ cup evaporated milk
30 mini marshmallows
¾ cup semisweet chocolate chips

⅔ cup graham cracker crumbs
25 regular-sized marshmallows, or as needed for dipping

1. Combine the evaporated milk and mini marshmallows in a metal bowl and place on top of a saucepan half-filled with simmering water. Stir frequently on low heat, making sure the mixture doesn't come to a boil.
2. When the marshmallows are melted, add the chocolate chips. Melt the chocolate on low to medium-low heat, stirring frequently and continuing to make sure the mixture doesn't boil.
3. When the chocolate is melted, stir in the graham cracker crumbs. Transfer the fondue mixture to the fondue pot and set on the burner. Keep the fondue warm on low heat. Serve with the marshmallows for dipping.

S'more, Please!

A favorite snack of the Girl Scouts since the 1920s, s'mores are made by combining chocolate with graham crackers and marshmallows. The name s'mores is reputed to be a shortening of the phrase "give me some more." Traditionally, s'mores are enjoyed around the campfire by placing toasted marshmallows and chocolate on graham crackers. The heat from the marshmallows melts the chocolate.

Chocolate Bar Fondue

6 apples
4 regular-sized Mars bars

½ cup whipping cream

Serves 4

1. Wash the apples, pat dry, and cut into 6 slices each. Refrigerate until ready to use in the fondue.
2. Unwrap the chocolate bars and cut into several pieces. Combine a few pieces of the chocolate with the whipping cream in a metal bowl and place on top of a saucepan half-filled with simmering water. Stir frequently on low heat, making sure the mixture doesn't come to a boil. Continue adding more chocolate, a few pieces at a time, until all the chocolate is melted.
3. Transfer the mixture to the fondue pot and set on the burner. Keep the fondue warm on low heat. Serve with the apple slices for dipping. (This recipe produces 1 cup of chocolate fondue.)

Turn Your Favorite Chocolate Bar into a Fondue

It's easy! Just break the chocolate bar into several pieces, combine with cream, and melt in a metal bowl placed over a saucepan half-filled with barely simmering water. Start with a small amount of cream and add more if needed. (It takes about 2 tablespoons to melt each chocolate bar, depending on the exact size of the bar and the specific ingredients.) Be sure not to let the chocolate boil. For best results, stick with one or possibly two chocolate bar brands.

The caramel flavor in Mars bars combines nicely with tart apple. For a more adult version, add 1 tablespoon of Kahlua or kirsch to the melted chocolate before serving.

Popcorn Fondue

Serves 6–8

For best results, prepare the popcorn twists on the same day you are making the fondue. You could also use it with pieces of rice cakes.

6 cups popcorn twists
6 tablespoons corn syrup
4 tablespoons butter or margarine
8 teaspoons brown sugar

½ teaspoon ground cinnamon
½ teaspoon nutmeg, optional
Creamy Caramel Fondue for Adults (page 233)

1. Preheat the oven to 250°F. Grease a baking tray. Lay the popcorn twists out flat on the tray.
2. Melt the corn syrup, butter, and brown sugar over medium-low heat. Stir in the cinnamon and nutmeg. Pour over the popcorn. Bake for 30 minutes. Cool.
3. Use the popcorn twists as dippers with the caramel fondue.

Gooey Peanut Butter Fondue

Serves 4

Evaporated milk can be used in place of the half-and-half in this recipe.

4 bananas
½ cup plus 2 tablespoons half-and-half
½ cup peanut butter

2 tablespoons semisweet chocolate chips
¼ cup mini marshmallows
Peanut butter cookies, optional

1. Peel the bananas and cut into slices approximately ¾ inch thick.
2. Combine the half-and-half, peanut butter, chocolate chips, and mini marshmallows in a metal bowl and place on top of a saucepan half-filled with simmering water. Melt the chocolate on low to medium-low heat, making sure that it doesn't boil.
3. Transfer the fondue mixture to the fondue pot and set on the burner. Keep the fondue warm on low heat. Serve with the bananas and cookies for dipping.

Minty Chocolate Fondue

½ cup whipping cream
8 ounces chocolate peppermint
  chips

¼ teaspoon vanilla extract
Cake or fruit for dipping

Serves 4

This kid's version of Elegant Chocolate Fondue (page 189) is thick and gooey. Feel free to substitute peanut butter baking chips or semisweet chocolate chips.

1. Warm the whipping cream in a saucepan on low heat. When the cream is warm, add the peppermint chips and melt, stirring continuously. When the chocolate has melted, stir in the vanilla extract.
2. Transfer the fondue mixture to the fondue pot and set on the burner. Keep the fondue warm on low heat. Serve with cake or fruit for dipping.

Berries with White Chocolate

2 cups frozen berries
3 tablespoons sugar
1 teaspoon lemon juice
4 ounces white chocolate

2 tablespoons whipping cream
4 teaspoons cornstarch
4 teaspoons water

Serves 2–4

White chocolate gives this fondue a smooth, creamy texture. Feel free to use any combination of frozen berries.

1. If using frozen strawberries, break into pieces. Heat the berries on medium-low heat with the sugar, stirring, until they are mushy. Stir in the lemon juice. Process in a blender or food processor.
2. Break the chocolate into pieces. Combine the whipping cream and 2 ounces of chocolate in a metal bowl and place on top of a saucepan half-filled with simmering water. Melt the chocolate on low heat.
3. Add the strained berries and the remaining 2 ounces of white chocolate.
4. Dissolve the cornstarch in the water. When all of the white chocolate has melted, add the cornstarch-and-water mixture, stirring to thicken. Serve over vanilla ice cream.

Pumpkin Spice Fondue

Serves 6

You can substitute orange or tangerine for the pineapple slices. For an added treat, serve with pumpkin-flavored ice cream.

3 cups pineapple slices
2 cups chocolate chips
½ cup half-and-half or light cream
3 tablespoons honey

1 teaspoon cinnamon
½ teaspoon nutmeg
¼ teaspoon ground cloves, or to taste
15–20 small cookies

1. If using canned pineapple slices, pat dry on a paper towel. Refrigerate the slices.
2. Combine the chocolate chips and cream in a metal bowl and place on top of a saucepan half-filled with simmering water. Add the honey. Melt the chocolate on low to medium-low heat, making sure that it doesn't boil.
3. When the chocolate is melted, stir in the cinnamon, nutmeg, and ground cloves. Serve with the pineapple slices and cookies for dipping.

Spicy Pumpkin

Cooks disagree on the ideal spice combination for enhancing pumpkin's mildly sweet flavor. Most recipes include ground cinnamon, nutmeg, and cloves, but ground ginger and allspice are frequently added. Furthermore, the ratio of ingredients can vary. If you have your own favorite pumpkin spice recipe, feel free to use 1¾ teaspoons of it in place of the spices in Pumpkin Spice Fondue.

Caramel Fondue for Kids

40 caramel candies
¼ cup whipping cream
½ teaspoon vanilla extract
½ teaspoon ground cinnamon
8 medium bananas

1. Unwrap the caramel candies. Combine the whipping cream and caramels in a small saucepan and melt on low heat, stirring constantly. When the caramel is melted, stir in the vanilla extract and ground cinnamon.
2. Peel the bananas and cut in half lengthwise. Pour the sauce over the bananas.

Serves 6–8

Young children will enjoy making this simple dessert and can help unwrap all the caramel candies!

Creamy Caramel Fondue for Adults

2 cups white sugar
1 cup evaporated milk
4 tablespoons corn syrup
4 tablespoons butter
6 cups any combination of marshmallows, sliced fruit, and/or popcorn

1. Combine the sugar, evaporated milk, corn syrup, and butter in a saucepan and bring to a boil over medium heat, stirring to dissolve the sugar. Boil for approximately 5 minutes, until the mixture thickens.
2. Transfer the fondue mixture to the fondue pot and set on the burner. Keep the fondue warm on low heat. Serve with the marshmallows, fruit, and/or popcorn for dipping.

Serves 6

Apple slices, pineapple slices, and snacks made with crispy rice go particularly well with this recipe.

Light and Dark Fondue

Don't have any mini marshmallows on hand? Substitute 4 regular marshmallows and add them while melting the chocolate.

6 large bananas
50 miniature white and dark chocolate Hugs

½ cup whipping cream
20 mini marshmallows

1. Peel and slice the bananas.
2. Combine the chocolate Hugs and whipping cream in a metal bowl and place on top of a saucepan half-filled with simmering water. Melt the chocolate on low to medium-low heat, making sure that it doesn't boil.
3. When the chocolate has melted, stir in the mini marshmallows. Transfer the fondue mixture to the fondue pot and set on the burner. Keep the fondue warm on low heat. Serve with the bananas for dipping. Draw each banana slice through the fondue so that only one side is coated in chocolate.

Marshmallow Fondue

Serves 4–6

To transform this into an adult dessert fondue, simply add 2 tablespoons of either kirsch or peppermint liqueur, and replace the marshmallows with fruit for dipping.

10 caramel candies
½ cup evaporated milk
1⅓ cups semisweet chocolate chips

1 cup peppermint chips
60–80 mini marshmallows

1. Unwrap the caramel candies. Combine the evaporated milk and caramels in a metal bowl and place on top of a saucepan half-filled with simmering water. When the caramels are approximately half-melted, add the chocolate and peppermint chips. Melt on low to medium-low heat, stirring frequently and making sure the chocolate doesn't boil.
2. Transfer the fondue mixture to the fondue pot and set on the burner. Keep the fondue warm on low heat. Take two mini marshmallows and stick one on each prong of the dipping fork. Draw through the chocolate.

Toblerone Fondue

3 oranges
4 3.5-ounce (100 gram)
   Toblerone bars

⅔ cup light cream
15–20 peanut butter cookies

Serves 4

Toblerone's rich flavor means this recipe doesn't need extra spices or sea-sonings. Use any type of Toblerone bar.

1. Peel the oranges and separate into segments. Dry the orange segments on paper towels.
2. Break the Toblerone bars into pieces. Combine the cream and Toblerone pieces in a metal bowl and place on top of a saucepan half-filled with simmering water. Melt the mixture on low to medium-low heat, stirring frequently. Make sure that it doesn't boil.
3. Transfer the chocolate mixture to the fondue pot and set on the burner. Keep the fondue warm on low heat. Use dipping forks to spear the orange segments and draw them through the chocolate. Dip the cookies into the fondue.

Cheesy Tomato Fondue

40 wieners
¾ cup milk
3 10¾-ounce cans Campbell's
   cheddar cheese soup

⅓ cup tomato paste
½ teaspoon dried oregano

Serves 8

For an adult version of this easy-to-make fondue, feel free to add kirsch or another type of brandy.

1. Cook the wieners in boiling water. Remove and cut each wiener into 4 equal pieces.
2. Heat the milk and cheddar cheese soup in a saucepan on medium-low heat. Stir in the tomato paste. Stir the mixture frequently.
3. When the soup mixture is heated through, stir in the oregano. Transfer to a fondue pot and set on the burner. Serve with the sliced wieners for dipping.

Pizza Fondue

Serves 4–6

For an added touch, sprinkle the fondue with shredded mozzarella cheese or finely sliced ham and mushrooms.

⅓ pound ground beef
2 tablespoons olive oil
1 medium yellow onion, peeled and chopped
¾ cup milk
1½ pounds Monterey Jack Cheese, shredded
1 cup tomato sauce
¼ teaspoon dried basil
¼ teaspoon dried oregano
½ pound Italian salami, sliced
20 black olives, or as desired
Pickles, as needed
Soft Italian breadsticks, for dipping

1. Brown the ground beef in a frying pan. Drain and set aside.
2. In a medium saucepan, heat the olive oil. Add the onion and sauté until it is tender. Add the milk and warm on medium-low heat.
3. Add the cheese, a handful at a time. Stir the cheese continually in a sideways figure eight pattern. Wait until the cheese is completely melted before adding more. Don't allow the fondue mixture to boil.
4. When the cheese is nearly melted, add the tomato sauce and ground beef and heat through. Turn up the heat until the fondue is just bubbling and starting to thicken. Add the basil and oregano. Transfer to a fondue pot and set on the burner. Serve with the salami, olives, pickles, and breadsticks for dipping.

Pizza Origins

Contrary to popular belief, pizza is not an Italian invention. Egyptians, Romans, and even Babylonians feasted on flat discs of unleavened bread topped with olive oil and spices. However, Naples, Italy, was the birthplace of pizza as we know it. Today, different areas of Italy have their own regional specialties, but the Neapolitan pizza remains most popular.

Cheesy Tomato "Soup"

1 can condensed tomato soup
1 teaspoon celery salt
2 cups Parmesan cheese,
  shredded
1 cup mozzarella cheese,
  shredded
1½ tablespoons flour

½ teaspoon dried basil
1¼ cups milk
1 tablespoon lemon juice
Toasted Bread Cubes
  (page 245)

Serves 4–6

For extra
flavor, gar-
nish with
parsley
sprigs and a
few pieces of
cooked
bacon.

1. In a small saucepan, combine the tomato soup with 1 can of water. Stir in the celery salt. Keep warm on low heat.
2. Toss the shredded Parmesan and mozzarella cheese with the flour and dried basil.
3. In a medium saucepan, warm the milk on low to medium-low heat. Don't allow the milk to boil.
4. When the milk is warm, stir in the lemon juice. Add the cheese, a handful at a time. Stir the cheese continually in a sideways figure eight pattern. Wait until the cheese is completely melted before adding more. Don't allow the fondue mixture to boil.
5. When the cheese is melted, add the tomato soup mixture and heat through. Turn up the heat until the mixture is just bubbling and starting to thicken. Transfer to a fondue pot and set on the burner. Serve with the bread cubes for dipping.

Sour Cream Fish Balls

1½ pounds packaged frozen
   fish balls
1 green onion
2 lemons
2 cups sour cream

5 tablespoons Dijon mustard
2 teaspoons lemon juice
2 teaspoons fresh parsley,
   chopped
Salt and pepper to taste

1. Bake the fish balls according to the directions on the package.
2. Finely chop the green onion. Cut the lemons into wedges.
3. In a fondue pot, combine the sour cream, Dijon mustard, lemon juice, parsley, green onion, and salt and pepper. Serve the fish balls on a plate, garnished with the lemon wedges. Use dipping forks to dip the fish balls into the sour cream.

Fish Stick Dinner

Serves 6

Regular-sized frozen fish fillets can replace the smaller-sized fish sticks used in this recipe. Cut the fish fillets into bite-sized pieces.

1 cup button mushrooms
4½ cups oil, or as needed
1½ pounds frozen fish sticks

Quick and Easy Tartar Sauce
   (page 57)
Seafood Cocktail Sauce (page 46)

1. Clean the mushrooms with a damp cloth and wipe dry. Cut each mushroom in half.
2. Add the oil to the fondue pot, making sure it is not more than half full. Heat the pot on a stove element over medium-high heat. When the oil is hot, move the fondue pot to the table and set up the burner.
3. Use dipping forks to spear the fish sticks and the mushrooms. Cook the fish sticks until they are browned on the outside and cooked through. Drain on paper towels if desired. Cook the mushrooms until golden. Serve with the sauces for dipping.

Instant "Tiramisu"

1 package vanilla pudding
2 cups milk
¼ cup semisweet chocolate,
   grated

12–15 chocolate chip cookies
   for dipping

Serves 4

Rich vanilla
enhances the
flavor of
sweet choco-
late in this
easy-to-make
dessert. Serve
with canned
or seasonal
fresh fruit.

Combine the pudding with the milk and prepare according to the directions on the package. Place in a cheese or dessert fondue dish in the middle of the table. Sprinkle with the grated chocolate. Serve with the cookies for dipping.

Beans 'n' Franks

¼ pound Cheddar cheese
1 teaspoon cornstarch
12 wieners
2 slices raw bacon

2 teaspoons sugar
2 cans pork and beans
1 tablespoon prepared mustard
Toasted Flatbread (page 245)

Serves 4

Dijon,
American, or
another type
of mustard
can be used in
this recipe,
according to
your prefer-
ence.

1. Finely dice the Cheddar cheese. Toss with the cornstarch and set aside.
2. Cook the wieners in boiling water for 3 to 5 minutes. Drain thoroughly. Sauté the bacon until crisp, sprinkling the sugar over the bacon when it is nearly cooked. Cool and cut into 2-inch pieces.
3. Heat the pork and beans in a saucepan over medium-low heat. Add the cheese, a handful at a time. Stir the cheese constantly in a figure eight motion. Wait until the cheese is melted before adding more.
4. Stir in the mustard and sliced bacon. Transfer to a fondue pot and set the burner on low heat. Serve with the wieners for dipping. Eat with the Toasted Flatbread.

"Roman" Fondue

Serves 4

Feel free to substitute chopped almonds for the walnuts, and to add fresh fruit in season.

¾ *pound seedless green grapes*
½ *pound mascarpone*
½ *pound ricotta cheese*
¼ *cup apple juice*
¼ *cup chopped walnuts*
¾ *pound dates*

1. Wash the grapes, drain, and pat dry. In a cheese or dessert fondue dish, combine the mascarpone and ricotta cheeses. Stir in the apple juice. Sprinkle with the chopped walnuts.
2. To serve, stick 1 grape and 1 date on each prong of a 2-pronged dipping fork, or place 2 grapes and 2 dates on a metal skewer. Dip into the cheese fondue.

Creamy Breakfast Fondue

Serves 4

This sweet but nutritious breakfast could also make a light dessert. For breakfast, serve with fruit juice.

½ *loaf crusty whole wheat bread, sliced*
2 *tablespoons plus 2 teaspoons orange marmalade*
1⅓ *cups ricotta cheese*
5 *tablespoons raisins*

Cut each slice of bread into quarters. In a medium bowl, cream the orange marmalade into the ricotta cheese. Stir in the raisins. Transfer to a standard cheese fondue dish and serve with the bread quarters for dipping.

Wonton "Wings"

4½ cups oil, or as needed   2 teaspoons sugar
12 wonton wrappers

Serves 6

1. Add the oil to the fondue pot, making sure it is not more than half full. Heat the pot on a stove element over medium-high heat. When the oil is hot, move the fondue pot to the table and set up the burner.
2. Fold the wrapper in half so that it forms a triangle, and then fold in half one more time. Stick the dipping fork through the middle of the wrapper. Cook the wrapper briefly in the hot oil until it turns golden brown (about 30 seconds). Drain on paper towels. Cool and sprinkle lightly with the sugar.

It's impossible to eat just one of these! Feel free to use egg roll wrappers in place of wonton wrappers.

Wonton Wrappers

Made with flour and water, wonton wrappers are a smaller and thinner version of egg roll wrappers. Pork-filled wontons are the key ingredient in Chinese wonton soup. Wontons take their name from their resemblance to tiny clouds when floating in the soup: Wonton means "swallowing a cloud."

Fried Ice Cream Balls

Serves 6

Children
love this
sweet treat,
and they
can help
prepare this
easy version
made with
sliced bread.

½ cup cornflakes
1 pint vanilla ice cream
6 cups oil, or as needed

12 slices white bread
½ cup packed brown sugar

1. Cover a tray with foil, and place in the freezer. Crush the cornflakes.
2. Mold the ice cream into 6 balls each 2 inches in diameter (the size of a large golf ball). Roll in the crushed cornflakes. Wrap each ball in aluminum foil and freeze on the tray overnight.
3. Heat the oil in the fondue pot on a stove element. While the oil is heating, cut the crusts off each piece of bread. Wrap 2 pieces of bread around each ice cream ball, gently molding the bread so that the ice cream is completely covered. Return the ball to the freezer.
4. When the oil is hot, move the pot to a table and set on the burner. Remove an ice cream ball from the freezer. Briefly fry in the hot oil, just until the bread turns golden. Drain on paper towels. Roll in the brown sugar. Continue with the remainder of the ice cream balls.

CHAPTER 13
Bread Dippers

Toasted Pita Chips

6 pita breads

Serves 6–8

Use as a dipper with cheese fondues, or pair with yogurt to serve with meat or seafood fondues.

Cut each pita in half, and cut each half into 3 wedges. You should have 6 wedges per pita bread. Toast the chips in a toaster oven for about 6 minutes until cooked through. Cool and serve.

Hot Pita Toast

Serves 6–8

These spicy chips can be prepared ahead of time and stored in a sealed container until ready to serve with the fondue.

6 pita breads
9 tablespoons olive oil

3 teaspoons garlic salt
3 teaspoons pepper

1. Preheat oven to 350°F.
2. Cut each pita in half, and cut each half into 3 wedges. You should have 6 wedges per pita bread. Brush one side of each wedge with olive oil and sprinkle lightly with the garlic salt and pepper. Turn and brush the other side.
3. Bake the pita wedges for 6 to 7 minutes, turning over once halfway through. Serve hot, or cool before serving.

Toasted Flatbread

6 pieces flatbread

¾ teaspoon freshly ground
   black pepper

9 tablespoons olive oil

Serves 8

1. Preheat oven to 350°F.
2. Cut each piece of flatbread in half, and then each half into 4 equal
   wedges. Combine the pepper with the olive oil and lightly brush over
   both sides of each wedge.
3. Bake the flatbread for 6 to 7 minutes, turning over once. Serve warm
   or cool.

Try experimenting with different types of flatbread and seasonings, such as sun-dried tomato flatbread brushed with olive oil and dried basil.

Toasted Bread Cubes

1 loaf whole wheat bread,
   sliced

½ cup melted butter or olive oil

¼ cup caraway seeds

Serves 4–6

Brush 1 side of each bread slice with 1 teaspoon of the melted butter
and sprinkle with ½ teaspoon of the caraway seeds. Broil the bread
on that side. Repeat with the remaining butter and caraway seeds on
the other side; broil. Cut the toasted bread into rectangular cubes
approximately 2 inches long and 1 inch wide.

Use these flavorful bread cubes in place of regular bread cubes when you want to add a bit of extra flavor to a cheese fondue.

Basic Bruschetta

Serves 4–6

Bruschetta is the perfect accompaniment to many cheese-based fondues. For best results, use extra-virgin olive oil.

1 French baguette
2 garlic cloves

½ cup extra-virgin olive oil

Cut the baguette into ½-inch slices. Broil in the oven on both sides. Smash the garlic cloves, peel, and cut in half. Rub the garlic over both sides of the toasted baguette slices. Brush with the olive oil.

Bruschetta with Roma Tomatoes

Serves 4–6

For extra flavor, add 3 or 4 chopped capers to the tomato mixture before broiling the second time.

1 garlic clove
1 Roma tomato

1 baguette
¼ cup olive oil

1. Smash the garlic clove, peel, and cut in half. Wash the tomato, remove the stem, and finely dice.
2. Cut the baguette into ½-inch slices. Broil one side of each of the slices. Rub the garlic over the toasted side. Spread the diced tomato over the other side and drizzle with a bit of olive oil. Return to the oven and broil the untoasted side.

Bruschetta Fondue Cubes with Vegetables

1 small yellow onion
1 tomato
½ cup olive oil

1 baguette
2 garlic cloves

Serves 4–6

1. Peel and dice the onion. Wash the tomato, remove the stem, and finely dice. Heat 1 tablespoon olive oil in a frying pan. Sauté the tomato and onion until the onion is tender.
2. Cut the baguette into ½-inch slices. Broil in the oven on both sides. Smash the garlic cloves, peel, and cut in half. Rub the garlic over both sides of the bread. Brush the toasted baguette slices with the remaining olive oil. Cut the bruschetta into bite-sized cubes, about the size of croutons.
3. Place the sautéed tomato and onion into small individual serving bowls. Spear the bruschetta cubes with a dipping fork. Dip into the cheese fondue, and then into the tomato mixture.

Bruschetta or Crostini?

The main difference between these two Italian classics is the size of the bread and the toppings used. Bruschetta consists of grilled baguette slices, while crostini are really tiny round pieces of toast. While other toppings may be added, the standard bruschetta recipe calls for the grilled bread to be rubbed with garlic and lightly brushed with olive oil. By contrast, popular crostini toppings include everything from chicken livers to fish. Both bruschetta and crostini make excellent appetizers.

Serve with Classic Swiss Cheese Fondue (page 16), Plowman's Lunch Fondue (page 19), Garlic Fondue (page 36), or Italian Cheese Fiesta (page 37).

Appendices

Appendix A
Menu Suggestions

Appendix B
Online Shopping

Menu Suggestions

Weekday Meals

Breakfast Fondues
Welsh Rarebit (page 178)
Ham and Cheese Fondue (page 28)
Breakfast Fondue (page 30)

Lunch Fondues
Plowman's Lunch Fondue (page 19)
Cream of Celery Soup (page 156)
Tomato Soup Fondue (page 157)

Supper Fondues
Pizza Fondue (page 236)
Fish Stick Dinner (page 238)

Quick and Easy
Fish Stick Dinner (page 238)
Cool Yogurt Fondue (page 190)
Sour Cream Fondue (page 205)

Fondue Suggestions for Special Occasions

New Year's Eve
Classic Mongolian Hot Pot (page 167)
Japanese Sukiyaki (page 170)
Champagne Fondue (page 214)
Spicy Beef Bourguignonne (page 88)

Valentine's Day
Tiramisu for Two (page 215)
Mascarpone with Baked Pears (page 218)
Champagne Fondue (page 214)
Blushing Fondue (page 213)
Macaroons Dipped in White Chocolate
(page 209)

Independence Day
Red, White, and Blue Fondue (page 199)

Cocktail Party Starters
Marinated Cheese Cubes (page 73)
Deep-Fried Cheese (page 42)
Chicken Egg Rolls (page 99)
Pork Balls in Coconut and Lime (page 119)
Vegetable Spring Rolls (page 158)

Special Occasion Dessert Fondues
Toblerone Fondue with Orange Liqueur
(page 186)
Elegant Chocolate Fondue (page 189)
Decadent Chocolate Berry Sauce (page 196)
Doughnut Fondue (page 200)
Sweet, Sour, and Spicy Apple (page 198)
Instant Mocha (page 188)

Special Occasion Cheese Fondues

Classic Swiss Cheese Fondue (page 16)
Sweet Goat Cheese with Roasted Red
Peppers (page 23)
Raspberry Swirl (page 35)
Blue Cheese Fondue (page 22)

Party Menus

Chicken Egg Rolls (page 99)
Mixed Meat Hot Pot (page 168)
Hot chili oil, soy sauce, and sesame paste
for extra dipping sauces
Beer

Fried Three Mushrooms (page 161)
Spicy Beef Bourguignonne (page 88)
Classic Beef Bourguignonne (page 88)
Roasted Red Peppers (page 150)
Fried Asparagus and Zucchini (page 157)
Pickles, relish, and pickled onions for garnishes
French Bread
Burgundy

Vegetable Spring Rolls (page 158)
Butterfly Prawns Dipped in Lemon Pepper
(page 142)
Tempura Shrimp (page 131)
Marinated Tomatoes (page 147)
Marvelous Mango Chutney (page 50)
White wine

Mexican Fondue with Guacamole Dip
(page 164)
Extra Tortilla Chips
Mexican Chocolate Fondue with Kahlua
and Strawberries (page 194)
Beer

Vegetable Spring Rolls (page 158)
Japanese Sukiyaki (page 170)
Soy sauce, Soy and Wasabi Sauce (page
59), and sesame paste
for extra dipping sauces
Oriental Vegetable Salad with Mediterranean
Dressing (page 147)
Sake

Classic Bacchus Fondue (page 94)
French Pistou with Cheese (page 66)
Fried Three Mushrooms (page 161)
Red wine

Tandoori-Style Chicken Wings (page 98)
Lamb Kebabs with Sun-Dried Tomatoes
(page 123)
Indian Curried Lamb (page 124)
Sweet Banana Chutney (page 47)
Beer

Online Shopping

Fondue Ingredients

DEAN & DELUCA

www.deananddeluca.com
Based in the United States, they have an excellent supply of cheese from around the world, including several varieties of Italian cheese.

THE EPICUREAN CHEESE SHOP

www.fromages.com
Based in France, they have a large selection of quality French and Italian cheeses, including several varieties of goat's milk cheese. A separate Web site for customers in the United States can be found at *www.cheese-online.com*. While more limited than the main site, the selection is still extensive. The Web site includes a comprehensive library covering different types of French cheese.

GHIRARDELLI CHOCOLATE

www.ghirardelli.com
Famous throughout the world, Ghirardelli sells a number of chocolate gift baskets online. Ghirardelli chocolate bars provide an interesting alternative to Toblerone in chocolate dessert fondue recipes.

WILLIAMS-SONOMA

www.williams-sonoma.com
They carry high-quality chocolate chips specifically designed for fondue, including peppermint-flavored chips.

Fondue Equipment and Accessories

FANTE'S KITCHEN WARES SHOP

www.fantes.com

In addition to standard fondue pots, they have an excellent selection of Mongolian hot pots. They also carry replacement alcohol burners and fuel. Fondue accessories include plates and dipping forks.

THE FONDUE FACTORY

www.fonduefactory.com

They carry both stainless steel and enamel fondue pots, serving plates, and individual serving bowls.

GOLDA'S KITCHEN—KITCHENWARE FOR CANADIANS

www.goldaskitchen.com

They carry several stainless steel fondue pot sets, plus warming dishes for keeping vegetables and other side dishes warm while preparing and cooking the main fondue. They also carry specialty dipping forks with up to four prongs for chocolate and cheese fondues.

Index